MANAGERIAL ECONOMICS

MANAGERIAL ECONOMICS

Arvind Sahani

CYBER TECH PUBLICATIONS
4264/3, Ansari Road, Daryaganj, New Delhi-110002 (India)
Ph.: 011-23244078. Fax: 011-23280028
E-Mail: cyberpublicationsdelhi@yahoo.com

MANAGERIAL ECONOMICS

Arvind Sahani

First Edition 2009

Published by :

G.S. Rawat for **Cyber Tech Publications**
4264/3, Ansari Road, Daryaganj, New Delhi-110002 (India)
Ph.: 011-23244078. Fax: 011-23280028
E-Mail: cyberpublicationsdelhi@yahoo.com

Printed at : **Amit Enterprises**, Maujpur, Delhi, (9810878184)

PREFACE

Over the past dozen or so years, business school curriculum committees have taken steps to strengthen the analytical and critical thinking skills of business students. Employers of business school graduates are demanding better thinkers. Many of us who teach economics to business students believe that training in economics not only helps business students better understand and predict the economic forces shaping real-world business decisions, but also serves to develop and strengthen overall analytical skills of students of all majors.

Managerial economics brings together topics in microeconomics that can be applied to business decision making to create a valuable way of thinking about markets and business decisions. The objective of this book is to help business students become architects of business strategy rather than simply middle managers plodding along the beaten path of others.

The primary goal of this book has always been, and continues to be, to teach students the economic way of thinking about business decisions. Managerial Economics develops critical thinking skills and provides students with a logical way of analyzing business decisions.

Managerial Economics has always been a self-contained book that requires no previous training in microeconomics. While maintaining a rigorous style, this book is designed to be one of the easiest books in managerial economics from which to teach and learn. Managerial Economics carefully develops and applies the most useful concepts for business decision making.

— *Author*

CONTENTS

1

INTRODUCTION

This chapter provides an introductory overview to the Strategic Leadership and Decision Making (SLDM) Course, discusses the unique nature of strategic decisions, reviews the literature on executive-level leadership, and analyzes how leader performance requirements change as a function of organizational level. What you should come away with is a framework for understanding strategic leadership and decision making. As we move through SLDM, you will "flesh out" the framework in increasing detail.

What is a strategic decision, and how is it different from other types of decisions?

The Character of Strategic Decisions

Strategic decisions are far reaching and consequential for the organization and typically involve the commitment of vast resources. They play out over long time frames and have significant opportunity costs. Strategic decisions should be made within the context of a long-term view or vision, of both the desired end-state and potentially undesired end-states brought about by the contemplated course of action. The desired end-state and potentially undesired end-state can be differentiated by the intended and unintended second- and third-order effects of a strategic decision.

Strategic decisions often must be made under conditions of substantial uncertainty, particularly when complex policy objectives must be reformulated in the face of a dynamic, sometimes volatile strategic environment. Initial assumptions about the environment and other players may be incorrect or incomplete. The complexity of policy decision making within large, bureaucratic systems is evident in national policy debates about taxes, entitlements, and budget deficits. While most wish for a balanced budget, there is-in an era of increasing competition for resources- strident position-taking with regard to how to do it. Drug war and trade agreements such as NAFTA are other examples of complex issues. The range of factors relevant to these decisions is seldom fully known, at least to any one player in the decision process. And the total range of possible effects-direct, second-, and third-order-of a given policy decision may be so complex that even the most exacting search misses something.

VUCA

V VOLATILITY

U UNCERTAINTY

C COMPLEXITY

A AMBIGUITY

Added to the problems of volatility, uncertainty, and complexity is the difficulty of determining the validity of inputs to the decision process. Many key events are ambiguous, especially when dealing cross-culturally, leading to differences in interpretation and contextual meaning. Such conditions foster ideological biases, special interests, and tensions between organizational subcultures. Thus, a strategic leader must know how to identify sound inputs embedded in a swamp of biased arguments. This task is made more difficult when inputs come from a wide variety of disciplines beyond the scope of any single executive. And, many strategic decisions must be made in crisis situations or under other stressful conditions.

Strategic decisions often emerge from arenas of strong partisan competition for resources. The national political arena is intended to foster debate about the allocation of resources for the national good. Partisan competition for resources reflects the advocacy positions of the major parties as they represent their constituencies, and their positions are represented in an adversarial manner. The hard bargaining often takes the form of positional negotiating, rather than in a process searching for common goals and pathways acceptable to all constituencies.

The decision making process must ensure that all competing views are heard and that priorities among them are sorted out. More importantly, the process must ensure some reasonable level of agreement or consensus about the intended end-state and a commitment to the course of action. Without agreement on goals, there can be little hope of collective effort.

There also is the dilemma of assumptions. Some assumptions taken as incontrovertible may in fact be questionable. In the decision making process, these assumptions are often not questioned, to the chagrin of the decision maker. A good example is the "Domino Theory" that guided many policy decisions in the 1960s and 1970s. It was assumed that containment of communism required a band of non-Communist states encircling the Communist powers be maintained. The insurgent challenge to the Republic of Viet Nam thus was construed as a challenge to global security and to U.S. objectives. McNamara (1995) asserts this assumption was fundamentally flawed because it ignored a thousand years of history in Indo-China and intense Vietnamese nationalism. An unbiased study of that history would have revealed the flawed assumptions.

Direct/Indirect Effects

Some decision effects are indirect, often unforeseen, and therefore unintended. A given policy decision may set into motion a string of cause-and-effect events that play out over a number of years. Some of these second- and third- and even fourth-order effects may be unanticipated, and undesired. Effective strategic decision making requires planned responses to second- and third-order effects; it is more like chess than checkers. There are more options, the game is not linear, and the plethora of potential outcome often is unanticipated.

The contrast between the peace agreements of the two World Wars is illustrative. Following World War I, peace agreements were traditional within the context of a thousand years of European existence. The agreements severely punished the aggressor. By contrast, the strategic vision of Marshall and other Western political leaders after World War II established the necessary conditions for re-emergence of former aggressor nations as respectable members of the world community. The narrow and foreshortened vision of the 1917 decision makers reflected a lack of understanding of the indirect effects of their policies, and of the complex, dynamic system of cause and effect associated with their decisions.

Other effects are hard to gauge and may be badly estimated. This is particularly true when the system involved is complex, incompletely understood, or when the policy impacts across cultural boundaries.

The economy is an example of a system that is incompletely understood. In balancing the budget, some argue for cutting capital gains taxes, citing higher total revenues obtained when lower capital gains tax rates have been applied. Others ask the question, "How can that be?" The answer lies in the dynamics of the system and the assumptions one makes about how the capitalist system works.

Assumptions about direct and indirect effects of different monetary policies are also different, reflecting incomplete understanding of the economic system, including its dynamic interrelationships with other systems. (For example, the emphasis on education, on the one hand, and tax reduction, on the other hand, reflect different assumptions not only about direct and indirect effects, but also about the interrelations between economic and non-economic factors important to the nation's global competitiveness.)

Finally, the two opposing U.S. political parties reflect two different subcultures. Culture, broadly speaking, is the collection of beliefs, values, assumptions, and expectations held by members enabling them to understand the actions of others. This understanding gives meaning to their work, and tells them how to behave in harmony with others. To the extent major differences between the parties remain unresolved, so will the debates remain unresolved and a unifying vision of shared national goals and objectives will remain obscured.

Strategic Decision

- CONSEQUENTIAL, NOT UNIMPORTANT
- LONG-TERM, NOT SHORT-SIGHTED
- SYSTEM-WIDE, NOT STOVE-PIPED
- CONTEXTUAL, NOT STRUCTURAL
- RARELY FINAL.

The decision making process at the national level is similar to that at lower levels, but there are important differences. First, most decisions are shaped and made by small groups involving diverse personalities, ideologies, and organizations. Second, because of the small-group process, negotiation and compromise are the norm. Third, decisions are rarely final; rather, the dynamic environment requires continuous reassessment. Fourth, the large amount of relevant data from diverse disciplines at the national level necessitates the use of sophisticated techniques to integrate quantitative and qualitative factors in a manner not found in lower levels of decision making.

OBSTACLES TO EFFECTIVE

Strategic Decision Making

- FORE-SHORTENED VISION OF POLICY MAKERS.
- DISAGREEMENT ON DESIRED END-STATE.
- INCORRECT OR INCOMPLETE ASSUMPTIONS.
- INCOMPLETE KNOWLEDGE OF RELEVANT FACTORS.
- MIS-ESTIMATION OF POLICY EFFECTS.
- MIS-CALCULATION OF INDIRECT EFFECTS.
- INCOMPLETE UNDERSTANDING OF SYSTEM DYNAMICS.
- INCOMPLETE UNDERSTANDING OF CROSS-CULTURE EFFECTS.
- PARTISAN RESOURCES COMPETITION.
- MISMANAGEMENT OF THE DECISION MAKING PROCESS

The decision making process just described has inherent problems. It often is slow and frustrating to executives accustomed to making firm decisions based on professional judgment. Negotiation and compromise can lead to the least common-denominator solution, especially if the decision making process is poorly managed. Groups and organizations tend to develop official "definitions of situations" that discourage diverse views and can fall into a malaise described as "groupthink" (Janis 1983). And, bureaucratic ploys and strategies lead to power struggles, confrontation, and adversarial relationships. These contaminating variables distort the process, and lead to less than rational decisions.

Strategic decision making is the ability to think insightfully about consequential events over time, to understand what causes long-range effects in and on complex and dynamic systems, and to bring partisan, competing interests together under shared goals. Within the context of decision making, "strategic" implies consequential, long-term, complex, system-wide and, at times, poorly understood, ambiguous, and uncertain characteristics. Increasingly, the worldwide environmental context of strategic decision making is also fast-changing and volatile.

Some of the skills effective for decision making at the operational level are, of course, appropriate at strategic policy-making levels. Sound judgement, analytical abilities, and a systematic approach to problem solving are critical skills at all levels. Other skills may, however, not be transferrable, and can even be obstacles to problem solving at more senior levels. Thus, the transition from operational decision making and problem solving at lower levels to performance at the strategic level is essential.

Foundations for Strategic Leadership and Decision Making

This leaves open the nagging question of how best to prepare for effective performance in the arena of national security decision making. The complexity of the strategic process argues against standardized formats. Rather, it is more appropriate to develop an executive skill referred to as perspective-taking. This skill- one not always easily or equally well-provides a base for national security decision making.

The existing literature on executive leadership has been categorized into four bodies of major theories: conceptual complexity, behavioral complexity, strategic management, and visionary/inspirational leadership (Zaccaro 1996). While the four bodies are distinct in many aspects, there are some common views about what it takes for executives to be successful.

Conceptual Complexity Theories. The basic premise of conceptual complexity theories and models is that executives operate within increasingly complex environments, characterized by greater information processing demands, and by the need to solve more ill-defined, novel, and complex organizational problems. To survive and thrive, executives require significant conceptual abilities to make sense of, and successfully navigate within, these complex environments (Zaccaro 1994).

Stratified Systems Theory (SST) posits seven naturally occurring levels in large organizations. Each level has an associated level of complexity. The key personality variable in Stratified Systems Theory is conceptual capacity, defined as the generalized set of abilities that help an individual to cope in task environments characterized by volatility, complexity, ambiguity, and uncertainty (McGee, Jacobs, Kilcullen, & Barber 1996; McGee 1997). As an individual rises through the hierarchy of an organization, higher levels of conceptual capacity convey competitive advantage to that individual and to the individual's organization.

*QUINN'S COMPETING VALUES MODEL**

FLEXIBILITY	PREDICTABILITY
INTERNAL	
MENTOR	COORDINATOR
FACILITATOR	MONITOR
EXTERNAL	
INNOVATOR	DIRECTOR
BROKER	PRODUCER

*Adapted from Zaccaro 1996

Behavioral Complexity Theories. Emphasis in behavioral complexity theories and models is on multiple roles and behavioral patterns required of executive leaders (Zaccaro 1996). Major theories include Mintzberg's (1973, 1975) classification of managerial roles, Tsui's (1984) multiple constituency framework, and Quinn's (1988) competing values framework.

Executives deal with multiple constituencies that make differing demands. These constituencies can be internal to the organization (e.g., superiors, peers, subordinates) or external to the organization (e.g., competitors, investors, the media). Executives must display differing behaviors to be effective because these constituencies have differing values. What the media values is very different from what Congress values.

*MINTZBERG'S MANAGERIAL ROLES**

INTERPERSONAL ROLES

FIGUREHEAD

LEADER

LIAISON

INFORMATION ROLES

MONITOR

DISSEMINATOR

SPOKESMAN

DECISIONAL ROLES

ENTREPRENEUR

DISTURBANCE HANDLER

RESOURCE ALLOCATOR

NEGOTIATOR

*Adapted from Mintzberg, 1975, reported in Zaccaro, 1996.

Strategic Management Theories. Strategic management theories and models argue that executive effectiveness emerges from an appropriate fit between the organization and its environment. The role of the executive is analysis, creation, and management of this fit. Executives scan and analyze the environment, formulate appropriate coping policies and strategies, implement these policies and strategies, and evaluate consequences given subsequent organizational conditions.

Empirical support for strategic management theories and models focuses on executive characteristics of strategic leadership and decision making, with demographic and personality variables receiving the most empirical support (Zaccaro 1996).

Visionary/Inspirational Leadership Theories. Visionary/ inspirational leadership theories and models include theories of charismatic and transformational leadership. The common theme is that leaders develop and use their vision to structure and to motivate collective action. Considerable emphasis is placed on empowerment and development of human resources, especially subordinates. These models of leadership offer a number of characteristics that enhance a leader's ability to lead, including cognitive abilities (e.g., creativity, reasoning skills, intelligence, verbal ability, cognitive complexity), self-confidence, motivation, propensity for risk, and social skills.

Stratified Systems Theory (SST). A key notion in the development of executive-level leaders is the changing nature of performance requirements as a function of organizational level. What we need is a tool for understanding the nature of those differing performance requirements.

Stratified Systems Theory is a body of theory that asserts leadership tasks at the top of large-scale organizations are quite different from those at the lower levels. This is because the nature of work changes as an individual moves up through the hierarchy of an organization.

*Levels of Organizational Stratification Proposed by Stratified Systems Theory**

There are three broadly defined strata to most large-scale organizations: the top levels (strategic), the midlevels (organizational), and the bottom levels (production or action-oriented). Relatively inexperienced leaders-ensigns, lieutenants, and captains-at the lower levels are responsible for getting things done, so they are action-oriented. They have little latitude in the decisions they make, procedures they use, and the degree of innovation they can employ. They may improvise but rarely can they innovate because, at their level of leadership, consistency of action is important. The midlevels are responsible for setting midterm goals and directions and developing the plans, procedures, and processes used by the lower levels. Plans, procedures, and specified processes are major tools for coordinating effort, particularly in large-scale organizations with many independent parts that must act in a coordinated way. The mid-levels are also responsible for prioritizing missions and allocating resources to tailor capability at the lower levels. This includes supervising resource allocation plans that implement concepts developed at higher levels, as in the Department of Defense's Planning, Programming, Budgeting, and Execution Systems.

Top-level leaders-three and four stars-are responsible for the strategic direction of their total organization within the broad context of the strategic environment-increasingly global. By its very nature, the term "strategic" implies broad scale and scope, a mode of forward vision extending over very long time spans-in some cases out to fifty years or more. So, strategic leadership and decision making is a process by which those responsible for large scale organizations set long-term directions and obtain, through consensus building, the support of constituencies necessary for the commitment of resources.

The ICAF Experience

Your ICAF year marks a transition from duties you have had to responsibilities of an increasingly strategic nature with far-reaching influence. To be effective, you will need to be more proactive, rely less on established ways of doing things, and depend more on analytic, integrative, and evaluative thinking skills.

The national security decision making system includes the federal bureaucracy, the statutory functions of the major components, and the interrelationships among them. For example, in the defense budget, we need to understand the Planning Programming Budget Execution System (PPBES), the role each organization/agency/office plays in the process, and the influence of strategic constituencies, including foreign and domestic. In the formulation of foreign policy, we follow a similar procedure and need to understand, the National Security Council (NSC), the Congress, relevant governmental departments, and strategic constituencies outside of our government, including foreign nations.

However, the formal part of a social system is only the tip of an iceberg. The essence of the larger system is the informal subsystems within which personal-bureaucratic-political proposals and policies emerge. Formal systems are described in rational, logical terms that are comfortable to deal with. Informal systems are described in nonrational (not irrational) psychological terms. There is a world of difference.

The ICAF curriculum addresses both the content and the process of national security decision making, to include both formal and informal aspects. The Strategic Leadership and Decision Making course examines the human element of the process.

THE STRATEGIC ENVIRONMENT

> *You are living in the period of time that will produce more change for humanity than any previous era in history. It is a time of extraordinary importance that will fundamentally reshape almost every aspect of your life during the next two decades. Wholesale change is taking place in almost every segment of your reality-and the pace will only increase in the coming years.*

The process of strategic leadership and decision making begins with an assessment of the environment within which it occurs. Strategy can be compared to a plan, except it is broader in scale, long term in nature, and surrounded by more uncertainties. The strategic choices of organizations-and nations-also may be limited by constraints imposed by their environments, e.g., the state of near-famine in North Korea. Both North and South Korea desire integration of the peninsula. However, the two concepts of how this would happen, and which political system would become dominant, are radically different. Thus, environmental factors are influencing capabilities for strategic choices that may not be fully played out for many years. Perhaps previous strategic choices by each of these nations, dating back as far as three or four decades, may well have shaped the constraints and opportunities in the present environment.

This concept of shaping the future is important for decision makers. Successful strategic decisions will, either by design or accident, shape both future conditions and the competitive *advantage* enjoyed by the organization or nation at that time.

A GENERAL MODEL OF HOW ENVIRONMENT PROMPTS STRATEGIC DECISIONS

The significance of competitive advantage stems from the competitive nature of open systems. Organizations—and nations— are open, or only partially bounded, systems, that are dependent on their environment for resources. When resources are in short supply, organizations-and nations-must compete for them. They do so by scanning forward, creating estimates that enable them to identify long-range goals, and put into motion courses of action designed gain competitive advantage.

COMPETITIVE ADVANTAGE

AN ATTRIBUTE OF AN ORGANIZATION OR INSTITUTION- OR NATION- THAT ENABLES IT TO COMPETE MORE EFFECTIVELY FOR RESOURCES, AND THUS TO SURVIVE.

THE STRATEGIC SCAN

The purpose of national security strategy is to set and achieve objectives that, in the long term, will provide a high level of security for the nation and its citizens. This purpose is expressed in a process that scans the strategic environment, forms an assessment, conceives long-range objectives, and formulates long-range plans to achieve them.

KEY QUESTIONS ABOUT THE STRATEGIC ENVIRONMENT

- WHO ARE YOUR MAJOR COMPETITORS?
- HOW COMPETITIVE IS YOUR ORGANIZATIONS FOR THE LONG TERM? wHY?

- WHAT ENHANCES/DETRACTS FROM YOUR LONG-TERM COMPETITIVENESS?
- WHAT CAN YOU DO/ARE DOING FOR YOUR STRATEGIC PLANNING TO REMOVE LONG-TERM OBSTACLES AND EXPLOIT ADVANTAGES?
- DO YOU ANTICIPATE MAJOR RESOURCES PROBLEMS FOR THE FUTURE? iF SO, HOW DO YOU PLAN TO DEAL WITH THEM?
- DO YOU SEE ANY THREATS TO YOUR LONG-TERM SURVIVAL?

This strategic scan is extraordinarily difficult, and examples of inaccurate scans abound. Some of these can be attributed to the fundamental difficulties involved in "seeing the future." It seems paradoxical to speak of an environmental scan reaching out 20+ years, and, in fact, this is possible only in the broadest terms.

Strategic decision makers must gain a sense of dynamic forces in their environment to create good strategy. One building block is to obtain a sense of history, coupled with the reflection needed to examine the flow of events over time in order to understand the cause and effect linkages that have been operational. A frame of reference must be built.

A second critical building block is the conceptual skill and openness needed to test the historical frame of reference over time, to ensure it is still representative of the real world. This obviously speaks to the use of feedback loops.

Barriers to accurate strategic scans exist in both the environment, and in the decision maker. George (1980) describes many of the barriers internal to the decision maker. They include his/her personal view or stake in the outcome, which may make objective considerations difficult.

Other barriers are the personal values of the decision maker that might lead to evaluations not shared by other players; the risk that a course of action might fail and threaten self-esteem; the risk that a course of action might hurt career prospects; and the risk that advancing a course of action might lose the support of key constituencies.

The strategic decision making process must deal with the four barriers described in the previous chapter: rate of environmental change (volatility), unpredictability of change (uncertainty), the intricacy of key decision factors (complexity), and vagueness about the current situation and potential outcomes (ambiguity).

Rate of Change: Volatility

Peter Vaill coined the phrase "permanent white water" to describe the rate of environmental change in the world as we know it. Futurist John Peterson estimates that the total amount of information in the world is doubling every 18 months or less. And new technology is making it possible to generate even newer technology faster; microchips now being produced are themselves being drawn by computers, because they are too complex for humans to construct by hand.

A ROBUST SYSTEM

CAPACITY FOR TIMELY SYSTEM CHANGE. EITHER ANTICIPATE OR ADAPT TO ENVIRONMENTAL CHANGE TO MAINTAIN COMPETITIVE ADVANTAGE.

- ACCURATE, COMPREHENSIVE ENVIRONMENTAL SCAN
- ACCURATE ARTICULATION OF KEY VALUES, BELIEFS, AND ASSUMPTIONS
- FREEDOM TO QUESTION VALUES, BELIEFS, AND ASSUMPTIONS
- CREATIVITY TO FORMULATE NEW OPTIONS
- TOLERANCE OF RISK INVOLVED IN NEW COURSE

This relevance of volatility to strategic leadership and decision making stems from the competitive nature of the world. Nations, states, organizations, societies- systems and subsystems- all seek increased wealth or power, or both. But power and wealth are finite commodities, so the stage is set for competition. Even when great strategic alliances such as NATO are formed, it is with a view toward attaining a competitive advantage in relation to another strategic alliance.

However, the character of competition is also changing. For example, a competitor can be hurt by rapid obsolescence of its capital-intensive weapon system, so it might make sense to pursue new development with just that aim in mind-not the destruction of that system on the battlefield, but rather by superiority on the balance sheet. Just such a strategy was a factor in the planning of weapons systems development in this country from the late 1970s until the collapse of the Soviet state in 1989. That world-changing collapse came when the Soviets could no longer compete economically.

Finally, much of the incredible success of coalition forces in the Persian Gulf War grew from two technology advances: imaging technology that enabled (primarily) U.S. armor to see and engage Iraqi armor outside the target acquisition range of the Iraqis; and precision guidance technology that enabled aircraft to engage Iraqi forces outside the effective range of Iraqi armor. The critical lesson is that both technology advantages were outcomes of U.S. decisions made years earlier directing capital investment into research and development, in contrast to Iraqi decisions to continue capital investment in amassing products of old technology.

It would be simplistic to leave this example just at the level of decisions about research and development. Both sets of decisions also reflected underlying assumptions by strategic leaders about the nature and rate of change in the world environment. One set of assumptions was accurate; one was not. Environmental change often determines where the point is reached when a change in policy should be initiated. There may be only a thin line between success through persistent advocacy for change, and failure because of inability to change.

History is littered with examples of strategic decision makers who did not see change in time. The advent of air power is an example. In the 1920s and 1930s, promising careers were terminated because of air power advocacy. Yet, World War II saw the first decisive naval engagement where no surface ship fired at an enemy surface ship- the Battle of the Coral Sea. Only the advent of World War II's armored formations quelled the remaining horse cavalry champions. And just a few years later, only the influence of the Congress kept a nuclear submarine advocate on active duty.

The lesson is clear. Without visionary leaders who can guide reformulation of strategic policies and objectives, the nations, organizations and societies they lead are placed at competitive disadvantage. And change is volatile, driven on the "hard" side by technology and on the "soft" side by advancing communication's capabilities. The challenge to strategic leaders, to their leadership and decision making processes is increasing at a critical pace.

Uncertainty About the Present Situation and Future Outcomes

Strategic leadership is complicated not only by the rate of change in the global environment, but by uncertainty about what the effects of even known changes are likely to be. This uncertainty results from both the complexity of systems and subsystems at the strategic level and from incomplete knowledge about the current situation.

Uncertainty also arises from the competitive nature of leaders on the world stage who understand that significant competitive advantage often is gained through surprise. Therefore, strategic actors seek to conceal their strategic directions, particularly their means for achieving their directions, from their competitors.

The deception planning integral to achieve surprise for Operation *Overlord*-the Allied invasion of northern France in 1944-is an excellent example. Through a complex set of channels, information was fed to the German High Command that led to a devastatingly incorrect estimate of the situation and Allied intentions.

These channels included the "turning" of the entire Axis spy network in Britain, the fortunate presence of dedicated double agents, and a huge electronic shell designed to show the presence of a powerful Allied force in England opposite the port of Calais. So, strategic leadership and decision making sometimes must resolve uncertainty by penetrating an enemy's carefully laid screen designed to confuse.

Multiplicity of Key Decision Factors: Complexity

On a global scale, the demise of the U.S.S.R. as a superpower, because of its inability to compete economically, should have been predictable. In fact, this outcome was the objective of U.S. resources allocation strategy during the Reagan era. Perhaps today's strategic policy makers do not fully understand the complexity of the multipolar world that now follows the end of the U.S./USSR bipolar world, and have not yet developed an adequate philosophy to guide the formulation of national objectives for the 21st century. In consequence, much debate continues about future strategic courses of action.

The nation's long-term energy policy provides a good example. Faced with continuing depletion of global petroleum reserves-and with accumulating environmental damage as a result of burning fossil fuels-a long-range energy program would seem essential. Our society rests on the effective operation of many complex subsystems, three of which are agriculture, manufacturing, and transportation.

Distress in one means the others cannot function effectively. In particular, without the transportation system, large scale urban life as we know it would not be possible. Yet all these systems depend on fossil fuels, and the nation has not moved significantly toward decreased dependence on these fuels, particularly imported petroleum, in the face of known increased competition for petroleum as developing nations industrialize.

The significance of this lack of movement is apparent when the delicate balance of the monetary system and its sensitivity to inflationary pressures, are taken into account. The near-cataclysmic response of the national leadership to the blip in gasoline prices in the late spring and summer of 1996 suggests how delicate the balance is. A rise in prices of less than twenty cents per gallon triggered a sell-off from the strategic oil reserve and a call for temporary repeal of a part of the federal gasoline tax. Such a blip is certain to re-appear in much magnified form in the future if a valid, long-term strategic policy is not developed and implemented. Another example is the debate about capital gains taxes. The data seem to show that a high capital gains tax suppresses federal tax income from capital gains. A high tax rate inhibits investor sale of capital investments in order to realize gain. So, a lower tax is better for deficit reduction, an apparent contradiction. But the question remains whether this is good or bad, even if it is true. It seems likely that a decrease in capital gains taxes would also tend to depress the stock market, as investors sell stock to realize gains. Is that right? If so, is it good or bad? And, for whom?

System complexity impacts hugely on the capacity of leaders as strategic decision makers to formulate and execute effective policy. Cause and effect relationships are difficult to see, much less assess, when there are many causes, and when many divergent effects exist.

Determination of cause and effect relationships is made more difficult by uncertainty about the time lag of effects in complex systems. In addition, there may be many-linked cause and effect chains. A given initial cause may produce an effect that gives rise to a second-order effect which may, in turn, give rise to a third-order effect.

The challenge to strategic leadership is twofold: a frame of reference, or perspective, that is dynamic enough for the decision maker to recognize, understand, and explain to others; and a leader's mastery of decision tools and processes that enable him or her to bring a broader set of perspectives than just his/her own into the decision making process.

Lack of Clarity About the Meaning of an Event: Ambiguity

Ambiguity exists when a given event or situation can be interpreted in more than one way. System complexity contributes ambiguous meaning, as does uncertainty about the full range of factors operating in a situation. Ambiguity may also exist because the intentions of significant actors in the strategic situation may either not be known or may be misinferred.

In intelligence work, for example, it is easier to provide an accurate estimate of capabilities than of intentions, because intentions often are cloaked inside the shell of a complex and effective deception plan.

The operations plan that was executed during the Gulf War seemingly was invisible to the Iraqis for at least two reasons. First, there was a deception plan, one that worked as well as the D-Day deception plan in World War II.

In the Persian Gulf, the Marine forces may well have been frustrated by their limited participation, but in all likelihood they saved many lives on both sides by tying down Iraqi forces on the coast. Second, control of the skies took the "eyes" away from the Iraqis, so that they could not see the massive maneuver to the west across the Saudi high desert. They misinterpreted what they could see, and were vulnerable to the end sweep by highly mobile coalition forces.

Leaders must expect to encounter ambiguity as they transition to more complex situations in their organizations. Strategic leaders also must do a great deal of consensus building, as a normal part of their leadership roles.

The consensus decision making process is designed to uncover information not previously held, perspectives not previously understood, and knowledge not previously applied to the solution-generating task.

The challenge to strategic leadership is recognizing that the decision maker cannot have a "stand-alone" perspective, and that effective strategic decisions must flow from a managed process that produces a perspective through consensus that is broader than any single person probably possesses.

National Security Strategy

Volatility, uncertainty, complexity, and ambiguity (VUCA) are not independent concepts. While each may describe certain aspects of a decision task. Each feeds the other. Strategic policy objectives are formulated within the context of this VUCA world.

To say that there is a new world order, and that the United States is the single remaining super-power somehow gifted with the responsibility for global leadership, is to do no more than open the door on the process of strategic policy formulation. The hard work is in formulating policy objectives that are compatible with the world that will emerge over the next three or four decades. These are the policy decisions that will have added value to the world community as well as to the nation itself. This "new world" is now being shaped both by environmental forces and by the actions of key players on the world scene.

In 1980, the Tofflers wrote about a sea change-a contextual change of such mammoth proportions that old paradigms would no longer suffice. The Tofflers described two major revolutions that have transformed the course of human history, and asserted that we are now in the midst of a third revolution. The agricultural revolution began some 10,000 years ago, and the industrial revolution some 300 years ago. Each produced sweeping changes in how human effort was organized.

Now we have a third revolution-a third wave, a third age-the Information Age. With it comes an inundating wave of writings about what the information age is all about and what it will do either to or for us. The "third wave" is thought by many to be a dominant force transforming nations and societies, leading to a qualitatively different paradigm by which to interpret world events.

Just as the economic superstructure in the advanced industrial nations rests on food production, so the technology of the Information Age rests on the productive capacity of the Industrial Age. But the vast societal and cultural changes that are likely to occur later are unclear. The only certain things are that the world will get more complex, and will change in ways not clearly seen now.

The challenge for strategic leadership is to understand the dynamics of change that are now occurring, and develop the clearest possible visualization of the end results of change, with enough lead time to ensure a competitively advantageous position can be achieved.

VUCA as a Base

Coping with VUCA is the essence of strategic leadership. And, if the United States is to aspire to permanent global leadership, VUCA requires understanding different cultures, different kinds of national objectives, and different means other nations employ to achieve their objectives. And the logic for working effectively with nations around the globe must include not only competitive advantage for the United States, but "value added" for other nations.

We know what our existing knowledge lets us know and we see from our own perspectives, sometimes dimly. We make assumptions about other cultures, often mistakenly, based on what is reasonable in our own culture. We infer intentions based on what our intentions would be in that situation, "if we were they." Strategic leadership must, of necessity, be based on a broader frame of reference. Using a VUCA Time Horizon will help provide that reference.

2

INFORMATION AGE AND STRATEGIC DECISION MAKING

The one thing we can be sure of is that the world that will emerge from the present rearrangement of values, beliefs, social and economic structures, of political concepts and systems, indeed, of world views, will be different from anything today imagines. —Peter Drucker "Post Capitalist Society"

As the future is uncertain, the only thing relatively clear is that much of what we will experience in the future will be different from the past. We must understand it is not information or even technology that will produce this unprecedented change, but the impact of technology on all aspects of human life; not computers or even bits and bytes, but the ability to apply and integrate rapid technological change. The focus must not be on the World Wide Web, but instead on how the Web influences values, beliefs, social and economic structures, politics, our view of the world and the way we think and behave.

Futurist John L. Peterson forewarns that, "We are living in a period of time that will produce more change for humanity than any previous era in history." Peterson and many others believe that wholesale change is and will continue to take place in every segment of the world and that the pace of that change will continue at an unprecedented rate, gaining momentum with time. If this futurist is correct, the coming decades will have staggering implications for the environment and present both hazard and opportunity for the strategic leader. In fact, Moore's law suggests that memory capacity will continue to double every 18 months. If senior leaders want to take advantage of this fast paced, changing world and avoid the pitfalls associated with it, Peterson believes they must understand at least three things.

- Have a broad understanding of what this new environment is all about.
- Understand the major forces that are driving this monumental change.
- Understand how they can think and see the world differently than they have before.

IN THIS NEW WORLD: Will leaders focus on shaping a fast changing environment to their organization or will they focus on creating an adaptive organization that will adjust to meet the fast changing environment?

- What will be the new demands and pressures placed on senior leaders of the future?
- How can leaders hope to cope with this "permanent white water" environment?
- How can leaders absorb and use the vast amounts of information needed for the complex, fast moving, decision making environment?
- Can leaders be found that already have the requisite cognitive skills required to process massive amounts of information quickly and efficiently for competent decision making in the strategic environment?

Crucial question: "Is the leader of the future going to control technology or is the technology going to control the leader"?

Alvin and Heidi Toffler have been writing about the emergence of a "new civilization" where humanity advances a quantum leap forward to a future fraught with deep social upheaval and massive restructuring. The Tofflers call this new civilization the "Third Wave."

Think about a wave in a large body of water and you will begin to see Toffler's model of change. Multiple waves may exist at the same time, one following another, building momentum and crashing into the shore across many fronts. Often one wave will crash into others creating a violent and chaotic milieu. The global environment also can be turbulent, full of currents, eddies, and maelstroms which conceal deeper, historic waves.

Conversely, a wave may cancel out another. In the real world, crests and crosscurrents created by waves of change exist in work, family life, attitudes and even morality. The human race has already undergone two great waves of change, the Agricultural and Industrial Ages. The third, Information Age, wave suggests a new civilization, new ways of working, living, and competing. It will produce new economic structures, new politics, new security issues and new ways of thinking and decision making.

It is important to understand the impact of not only just information and technology on industry or the economy, but about change in all aspects of human life. This "New World" will have its own distinctive outlook, its own way of dealing with time, space, logic, and causality.

WAVE	**PERIOD**	**ACTIVITIES**	**TIME SPAN** (years)
****	Hunter/ Gatherer	Nut/berries/ game	Tens of Thousands
First Wave	Agriculture Age	Farming	Thousands
Second Wave	Industrial Age	Mass production	Hundreds
Third Wave	Information Age	Specification/info	Decades

Alvin and Heidi Toffler see this as a revolutionary period of change. Moreover, they assume that the coming decades will be filled with turbulence, upheaval, and violence. They also believe that the third wave world will not destroy itself but instead transform the way people all over the globe live, work, play, and think. The old ways of doing things simply will not work any longer in this new environment.

The information age is upon us! None of the items in the list below existed just three decades ago.

THE LAST THREE DECADES HAVE PRODUCED:

Cellular phones

Cable TV

Home Computers

Compact Discs

VCRs

Fiber optics

Broadcast satellites

CNN@

Automatic tellers (ATM)

Super Bowl

Microsoft@

Federal Express@

TV@

Internet or the WWW

Laser guided Munitions

Stealth

GPS

M1, F15/16/117, B1/2

If we look at John Petersen's discussions of the future, they begin much like the Toffler's. He also describes humankind as hunter-gatherers for the first 35,000 years, but opens his first period with the agriculture era about 5,000 years ago. Petersen identified this era with the beginning of formal written communications and the first movement of people into towns and cities.

Only 500 years have passed since the beginning of the third era, "the industrial revolution," an era much like the second wave of Toffler's wave theory but marked primarily by the invention of the printing press. Peterson, like many others, calls the current era the "information age". He marks the beginning of this era with the arrival of the microcomputer about 25 years ago.

PETERSON'S PARADIGM SHIFTS

25,000	First notational	Hunter-gatherer
5,000	Writing system	Agriculture
540	Printing press	Industrial
27	Microprocessor	Information

The 15th and 16th centuries characterized a renaissance, an age of enlightenment. The changes the world had a profound effect. According to John Peterson, the information age will characterize the "super renaissance." Much like the renaissance of the 15th and 16th centuries, the "super renaissance" will have long-term implications:

15th and 16th Centuries	**1980 - 2020**
Newtonian Physics	Quantum Mechanics
Renaissance/enlightenment	- Microprocessor
Printing Press	-Super Renaissance
	Ecological Threats

One of the most interesting aspects of the Peterson's model concerns the length of each succeeding era. A review Peterson's time pattern implies that the information age might only be 40-50 years long. We may already be half way through the shortest and most explosive era of human history.

TECHNOLOGY AND THE STRATEGIC LEADER

One of the most important functions of any strategic leader is to think and communicate ideas effectively. A leader must understand the basis of today's information systems and the relevance of technology to today's strategic environment.

The basic nature of most organizations is to resist change. Many have not yet recognized that the explosion of technology is forcing a tidal wave of change that is profoundly affecting both organizations and leaders. The national security environment is no exception, and may be feeling the effects of this change sooner than the rest of society as a whole.

Looking at the strategic environment in the information age, we recognize the information age flood of technology has made it possible to provide more complete, accurate, and timely information to the decision maker. Information technologies are being used more frequently as the cost of processing information improves. Many tasks are enhanced by application of computers, communications, and information management systems; yet, random unskilled application of these tools can lead to disaster for leaders and their organizations. Many senior leaders have not yet realized the full implication, both positive and negative, of the evolving technology in the global information age:

- "Computers are too complex and I'm too old to learn about them now."
- "I tried it once and computers don't like me!"
- "Dont fix it if it ain't broken and besides I've gotten along without a computer for years."

Even though some senior leaders initially feel this way, experience shows that when new information technologies are introduced, executives realize the systems indeed help with even the most difficult decision making tasks and issues. Today, computers and information systems are necessary to all aspects of the strategic environment and senior leader work.

INFORMATION PROCESSING

As the Army moved into the late1980s, a major technical report was released to the Chief of Staff of the Army. It was a long-term research program that studied information, and systems theory in large organizations. If you are interested in the detailed research results of the study, you can obtain the complete report (X=H 1979).

Like most leaders then and now the Army was searching for factors or sets of factors that make up the elusive shortfall between "what is" (where we actually are) and "what could be" (the potential of the organization, "Be all you can be").

But what was the factor or factors? They knew it had something to do with "organizational performance." They knew it was also based on how an organization was run, and how its processes were coordinated, integrated, and controlled. It was not just management, leadership, and organizational development. It was all of these factors and more.

They also knew X had to be related to the fact that the organization must work through people. X was the conceptual binder, the thing that provided the synergy, the thing that brought powerful notions together.

WHAT COULD BE (POTENTIAL)

|

X=?

|

WHAT IS! (ACTUAL)

The end result of all of their research and work was that the unknown factor was "H," and H was INFORMATION!! Information made the difference. It was nothing more than the concept of MATTER and ENERGY, ORGANIZED BY INFORMATION. The task is to increase the efficiency and effectiveness of how we use information in our organizations.

The X=H research was conducted by HUMRO over a five year period. It compared over 150 organizational events that clearly demonstrated a direct link between efficiency of information flow and the effectiveness of the organization. Some argued that differenceof information flow is no more than good leadership and that good leadership is nothing more than turning information into action.

If this is true, then information management should answer the common sense notions of how to run an organization, as it is the conceptual binder pulling all of these ideas of leadership, organizational development, resource management, command and control and communications together.

However, information as we have described it so far seems to be a specific thing. Bits and bytes. Measure this and measure that. If the clear, precise, and factual cognitive dimension was the only one, then putting H to work to solve for X would be simple and we could use information management alone to get the job done. Consider the phrase:

"SON OF A BITCH"

There are two dimensions at work here. One dimension of this declaration is cognitive and one affective. This phrase used strictly from a cognitive dimension is a clear statement of fact about a hound dog. However, it probably triggered an affective dimension in you giving it a different meaning. The affective dimension is the one that carries feelings, sentiment, and emotion. It is this function of context, culture, and values; group norms, gestures, and expressions; as well as modulations of volume, rate and lag time that gives it meaning. Information is a function of both cognitive and affective dimensions.

How important is the affective dimension in the transfer of information? Research suggests that only about 7% of total meaning comes from words, inflection 38%, gesture and expression about 55%. Since information must flow through people there is always an affective dimension. If we choose to ignore the affective dimension and look at only the cognitive flow of information, solving for X answer is easy. However, one of the most important findings of the research was that the "greatest" breakdown of organization performance was not the cognitive or technical dimension but rather the social and human (the affective dimension). The human dimension is certainly important to the leader for planning and transferring information in the organization. This approach to understanding information processing begins to clarify the important differences between just employing data and information, versus skillful information management.

Amid an ever-expanding availability of information at every level of management, the leader is faced with the responsibility of managing information while providing valuable data to the organization. General Colin Powell, while Chairman of the Joint Chiefs of Staff, shared his thoughts about the important role of information management for strategic decision making.

At the height of the Persian Gulf Conflict, the automated message-processing network passed nearly two million packets of information per day through the gateways in Southwest Asian. Theater of Operation. Efficient management of information increased the pace of combat operations, improved the decision making process, and synchronized various combat capabilities. The technology developed to support these networks proved to be a vital margin that saved lives and helped to achieve victory. (Joint Training for Information Managers, 1996)

Col Paul T. Haig discussed the transformation both minds and culture in his article in *Parameters* (1996). He believes that as technology transforms culture it will also transform the way people think. Information management and manipulation are replacing knowledge acquisition and inference. Experts are defined by their ability to recognize underlying patterns so that more accurate facts can be acquired. It is becoming more important to know what to ask for to avoid being overrun by a variety of answers.

Second, the basis for learning is changing. The battle began over "real world learning" versus the information age "virtual reality." The ability to "what if " learn from mistakes, and repeat the task by computer analysis over and over, has changed the way we learn.

Third, systemic decision making is taking over the use of intuition. If we are not careful technology also can cause paralysis through analysis and incline leaders to neglect intuitive skill commanders use as an important advantage in the often uncertain and ambiguous environment of the strategic leader. Possible over-reliance on automated and structured systems can stunt intellectual growth and limit executive effectiveness in unfamiliar environments.

NATIONAL SECURITY ENVIRONMENT

Admiral William A. Owens, former vice chairman of the Joint Chief of Staff, suggests that three simultaneous revolutions have pushed the national security community and, more specifically the military, toward major change. The first came from the revolution in world affairs brought about by the implosion of the Soviet Union and the end of the cold war. The second, a related revolution, was the reduction of the defense budget, accelerated because of the Soviet demise. The third, called the "revolution in military affairs" or the "revolution in security affairs" at the strategic level, happened in part because of the early investment in technology by the military. That investment has accounted for leveraging improvements in using military force more effectively. Owens suggests that the U.S. military will be the first to pass through the revolution in military affairs, and will emerge with great technological strengths. These strengths will provide an edge across the entire spectrum of contingencies against which the U.S. may need to commit its military forces. This U.S. technical revolution in military affairs is based on a "system of systems" approach and is broken into three major categories:

- Intelligence
- Command and Control
- Precision force (*Dominant Battlespace Knowledge*, 1996)

ALONG CAME THE INFORMATION AGE

What is it about the information environment that makes such an impact on the senior leader/executive environment? In order to better understand the implications of information age and where it may be going, we need to understand how it got here.

It seems that in the evolution process only occasionally has human thinking and intellect developed in historical proportions and quantum leaps. The links between various tools and human thought account for much of it. Dr. Douglas C. Engelbart, at the Stanford Research Institute, Augmenting Human Intellect Research Center, examines these relationships::

More than 20,000 years ago, humans developed spoken language abilities. This allowed them to pass knowledge along from generation to generation. Therefore, people were able to accumulate more knowledge than any one person could learn in a lifetime and allowed people to deal better with more complexity. But the amount of information that could be accumulated was bounded by the memory capacity of any given individual. The use of myths and ballads made memorization easier, but the limits of memory restricted the evolution of intellect. About 6,000 years ago, humans developed the ability to write- not only pictures that represent whole ideas, but also pictures that represented part of ideas. The next jump was in about 3100 BC, when the Sumerians began combining these pictures with phonetics to look like abstract ideas. These written sounds, represented a massive leap in human ability to express complex thoughts in writing. As a result, we were able to be more and more specific communicating complex, abstract ideas.

Writing continued to develop and soon began to match spoken language in its richness. This allowed us to save significantly more information than could be remembered in stories and songs, and in turn expanded our ability to deal with a complex world.

We all know that just over 500 years ago, Gutenberg developed the movable-type printing press, and widespread dissemination of information became possible. In combination with improved communications and trade, the printing press led to the spread of knowledge across social and political boundaries and put books in the hands of the masses. The general education level of the population increased, society could now focus studies on more advanced subjects.

Although technology continued to advance during the second wave industrial world, the birth of the computer and the computer chip has signaled the beginning of the "information age" and the quest for a new era of data, information and knowledge collection.

TOOLS FOR THINKING

The information age has recently begun to develop tools for leveraging, thinking, and decision making. Even though most information systems professionals are concentrating on automating routine transactions, a small group of information systems experts have pursued a different course.

Dr. Douglas Engelbart at Standford's center for Augmenting Human Intellect has begun to develop tools that were not designed to capture more keystrokes or process data into reports, but to help people think. His research led to the invention of many of the devices and tools now considered the leading edge of computing, including the mouse, windows, hypertext, and electronic publishing: all tools designed to leverage the individual's ability to think.

In the 1970s, the idea of enhancing human thought through computers wasn't a popular notion. People saw the computing world through an administrative lens. The environment changed some in the 1980s with the infusion of the PC into the home and business but it was still very much a word processor, or database tool understanding of technology. The view has changed some since the 80s but not dramatically. Many still connect computing with office administration. However, those who truly understand the potential of computers for thinking and communications are doing business differently. These visionaries are proving that improvements in our ability to work with information can lead to significant leaps in intellectual abilities and organizational productivity. Much like the findings of the X=H research, government and industry are leveraging their leaders and organizations with management techniques.

The information age has arrived globally. The Internet is growing by leaps and bounds, and President Clinton's current budget includes a $2 billion dollar technology initiative to connect every classroom, library, and hospital in the United States to the Internet by 2000.

INFORMATION PROCESSING, COGNITION, AND DECISION MAKING

Since senior leader and executive worth is measured by what they know and the success of the decisions they make, a look at how information technology can enhance cognitive capacity and decision making is imperative.

Using systems theory, we'll relate this process to a systems model you will learn in SLDM. (INPUT - PROCESS - OUTPUT) Thinking or cognition can be described as a process of gathering data and information (Input), sorting and relating it (Process), and creatively and critically viewing it to induce or deduce new ideas (Output). Don't forget feedback is an essential part of any system to grow and learn.

Computer and information systems work the same way. They are systems. Input devices bring information into the computer system. The input devices would be the keyboard, the scanner, or various types of drives. The processor (CPU - computer-processing unit) is the computer itself. The output (devices like the monitor/screen or printer) rounds out the system. All computer systems must have these components (like the human decision process) It is the speed and accuracy of the computer executing this process that has promoted its success.

INPUT ———> PROCESS ———> OUTPUT
<——— FEEDBACK <———

Like the computer, human processing of information is limited by the capacity of the machine. Human processing is biologically limited by two major factors: First, the capacity of long-term memory (a constraint of how much information we can accumulate without the help of aids such as writing), and second, short-term memory (how long we retain information). The mind is like a mental "scratch pad" that can hold only a limited number (usually 7 to 12 clusters) of thoughts at a time. (And you thought the "chunking" of telephone numbers or the clustering of the SSNs was just an accident.) These constraints of our memory can limit our ability to distill, relate, and view ideas. As we improve our ability to structure and organize symbols (such as language) outside our heads, we expand our ability to think. This ability to manipulate information has far reaching implications for advances in human cognition and decision making. With the help of information technology as a lever we are preparing for the next leap in the evolution of human cognition.

What can computing and information management offer the strategic leader?

- It gives immediate, direct and focused access to millions of ideas, publications, and documents from around the world. (WWW has >160,000 servers or networks around the world).
- It allows almost unlimited capacity to store everything known and access it at will. Storage capacity has grown at an unbelievable rate.

- It allows communication with local, organization-wide, and global networks.
- It allows exploration of ideas in a variety of forms and the free manipulation of those ideas. (E-mail forums, chatrooms, bulletin boards, and powerful search engines on the web freely expose ideas from all around the globe.)
- With the advent of expert systems, the computer can now interact as a peer or instructor would, distributing more creative, effective, efficient, and thoughtful ideas and solutions to problems. ("Wizards" and decision support systems influence all aspects of our lives.)

As computers began to do more resource intensive processing of data, they allow time for people to process more complex issues and thoughts. And, as computers provide a higher knowledge and comprehension level of information, there also is more time for leaders to concentrate on senior level tasks requiring social interaction and complex information processing.

Computers have dramatically extended our memory capability, and memory and cognitive capacity are the two elements that form the basis of our thinking process. Computers are supplements to this process and, although they will not take the place of strategic leaders, they can become a powerful tool to help senior leaders become more efficient and effective. The correct use of information tools can certainly leverage strategic leadership and decision making when properly applied.

The only hope for successfully dealing with the complex "third wave" global environment is to outsmart it. Intelligence is the best bet for surviving in the complex strategic environment, therefore, leveraging intellect with technology is a must. Similarly, the organizations we construct can no longer depend on size to be successful. Today, small organizations tend to be as efficient and productive as large ones. Small organizations are inherently more flexible and better able to respond to the complex environment. Companies are quickly moving away from mass production toward specialty products, and custom military units like special operations units and cross-attached units for specific purposes are all part of the fast moving "third wave" world. Strategic leaders will encounter an environment that has less bureaucracy, smaller staffs and a faster moving and changing world to operate in.

In the information age, organizations must find ways of increasing intelligence and learning and use various systems of feedback loops to adjust the decision process of the organization. Computer information systems are ideally suited to assist with all phases of the decision making process: input, processing, output and enhancing the feedback of the system.

A primary question a leader must ask is: How do we make our organizations "smarter"? Part of that answer has to be: How do we make our leaders smarter? How do we build on the "Human Capital" that our leaders and experts in our organizations possess? Senior leaders' knowledge depends not only on the power of the leaders' mind, but on their ability to leverage that knowledge with proven tools and methods during the decision making process.

In this post-industrial era, the success of organizations seems to lie in human capital (HC) and systems capabilities of the organization rather than in actual physical assets. The capacity to manage human knowledge-and to convert it into useful products and services-is fast becoming the "critical" leader skill of the age. Despite the growing importance of expertise, few systematic answers to even basic questions are available:

- What is senior executive knowledge?
- How can it be developed?
- How can we better leverage it?
- What role do computer and information systems have to play in this leveraging process? What tools are available to leverage these valuable assets?

ALTERNATIVE FUTURES?

The Air University's 2025 research team created a number of possible separate worlds for the future. The four most challenging, interesting, and difficult for the United States served as guides for their research. Two additional worlds—an intermediary world with selected characteristics of other worlds and a world that was a partial evolution to the future of 2025, Crossroads 2015—served as baselines for the 2025 analysis. The worlds that emerged follow. That a look at the proposed environments of the future, the unique opportunities and challenges in each world for the strategic leader.

Gulliver's Travels. This is a world of rampant nationalism, state and nonstate sponsored terrorism, and fluid coalitions. Territorialism, national sentiments, the proliferation of refugees, and authoritarian means flourish.

The United States is overwhelmed and preoccupied with such worldwide commitments as counterterrorism and counterproliferation efforts, humanitarian assistance, and peacekeeping operations. The United States is attempting to be the world's policeman, fireman, physician, social worker, financier, and mailman.

This situation forces the U.S. military to devise concepts of operation for meeting expanding requirements while maintaining a high operational tempo during a period of constrained budgets. The U.S. world view is global, the difference in rate of growth and proliferation of technology (TeK) is constrained-evolutionary, not revolutionary-and the world power grid is dispersed. Zaibatsu. In Zaibatsu, multinational corporations dominate international affairs and loosely cooperate in a syndicate to create a superficially benign world. Economic growth and profits are the dominant concerns.

While conflict occurs, it is usually through proxies and is short lived. Military forces serve more as "security guards" for multinational interests and property rights. Technology has grown exponentially and proliferated widely. Global power is concentrated in a few coalitions of multinational corporations.

The main challenge to the U.S. military in this world, which is becoming unstable due to rising income disparities, is to maintain relevance and competence in a relatively benign world where the United States is no longer dominant. The U.S. world view is limited as domestic concerns take precedence.

Digital Cacophony. This is the most technologically advanced world resulting in increased individual power but decreasing order and authority in a world characterized by fear and anxiety. Advances in computing power and sophistication, global databases, biotechnology and artificial organs, and virtual reality entertainment exist.

Electronic referenda have created pseudo-democracies, but nations and political allegiances have given way to a scramble for wealth amid explosive economic growth. Rapid proliferation of high technology and weapons of mass destruction provide individual independence but social isolation. The U.S. military must cope with a multitude of high technology threats, particularly in cyberspace. The U.S. worldview is global, technological change exponential, and the world power grid dispersed.

King Khan. This world contains a strategic surprise in the form of the creation of a Sino-colossus incorporating China, Taiwan, Malaysia, Singapore, and Hong Kong. U.S. dominance in this world has waned as it has been surpassed economically by this entity and suffered an economic depression. This has led to a rapidly falling defense budget and hard choices about which national priorities (core competencies) to maintain in a period of severe austerity.

The American Century has given way to the Asian Millennium and the power, prestige, and capability that were once American now reside on the other side of the Pacific Rim. The U.S. world view is decidedly domestic as it copes with problems at home, the growth in technology is constrained and world power is concentrated in a Chinese monolith whose economy, military, and political influence dwarfs those of the United States. The United States has come to resemble the United Kingdom after World War II-a superpower has-been.

Halves And Half Naughts. This is a world in which there are both changing social structures and changing security conditions. The main challenge to the military is to prepare for a multitude of threats in a world dominated by conflict between haves and have-nots. The world has split into two unequal camps: a small, wealthy, technologically advanced, politically stable minority of the states and peoples of the world (roughly 15%) and the poor, backward, sick, angry, unstable vast majority of the world's states with people who have little, and therefore have little to lose, in seeking redress of their grievances.

The U.S. world view is global but only because of the threats to its security represented by these masses. Technology and power are bifurcated exhibiting trends in both directions in the divided world.

Crossroads 2015. In Kurdish areas of Eurasia, the US uses programmed forces from 1996-2001 to fight a major conflict. The choices and outcomes made at this juncture have much to do with determining which of the worlds of 2025 will emerge a decade later. The American world view is global, TeK is constrained, and the world power grid is seen as concentrated but beginning to become dispersed. Potential future conflict centers on events involving disputes between the Ukraine and a resurgent Russia and the reaction of the rest of the world to such a conflict.

The United States in 2015 still has global commitments and concerns, but a constrained rate of economic and technological growth. Whether the US chooses a more isolationist path because of these pressures, or chooses a more activist role with the sacrifices that would require, is the major question to answer in shaping the world of 2025.

CONCLUSION

No one can predict where the information age will lead us. No one can reliably predict whether technology will ultimately enhance or impair the human dimension of senior leadership but one thing is sure-technology is here to stay. Either we master technology or technology will master us.

SYSTEMS THINKING AND LEARNING ORGANIZATIONS

The systems paradigm is a way of thinking about the strategic environment, and how to develop processes in organizations that achieve strategic goals. The systems paradigm should be viewed as a tool that leaders can use to design their organization's capability to: (1) analyze tactical and strategic environments; (2) develop and enact strategies in response to environmental demands; and, (3) sustain an adaptive and productive organizational culture. These three types of organizational processes are important in determining whether an organization can achieve strategic objectives in competitive environments.

A Leader's Strategic Analysis of the Environment

In 1997, Monsanto's CEO Robert Shapiro's analysis of Monsanto's strategic environment surfaced the future need for the company to create low cost, environmentally friendly products. He announced that Monsanto would begin its transformation from the chemicals company (ranked 4th in Fortune's 1996 domestic industry ranking and 18th in Fortune's global industry ranking) into a life sciences enterprise devoted to improving human health by seeking synergies in biotech, pharmaceutical research, and food products.

Developing and Enacting Strategies in Response To Environmental Demands

The Zoltek Company, in St. Louis, Missouri, manufactures carbon fiber, a versatile, light and strong material with wide uses ranging from golf club shafts to the tail section of the Boeing 777 jet liner. Its chairman, Zsolt Rumy has the strategic goal of being the leader in the commercialization of low cost carbon fibers for non-aerospace applications. To achieve this objective, the firm is enacting its strategy in two ways. First it has developed manufacturing process to drive down production costs. Second, it has established a series of strategic partnerships with companies such as B.F. Goodrich, General Motors, and Owens Corning for strategic positioning and growth in the marketplace.

An Adaptive and Productive Organizational Culture

Harvard Professor Rosabeth Moss Kanter concluded from her study of large U.S. corporations that successful organizations have cultures that encourage multiple sensing mechanisms to the environment and enable quick reactions to changing environments by generating the best combinations of people for the job. These examples illustrate one of the key principles in the systems paradigm: an organization's survival is based on sensing, analysis, and interaction with its environment. It is important to establish a set of definitions of terms that are highly relevant to the systems paradigm in strategic decision making.

Terms such as *strategic, decision making processes,* and *systems* are used in both every day conversation and in professional settings. Consequently, each of these terms are subject to misinterpretation when used within specific discussions in this chapter.

WHAT IS STRATEGIC?

The term strategic has three components. The first refers to the top level of the organization and the principal or principals who are ultimately responsible for the organization's actions and consequences of those actions.

The second and third components add temporal and risk dimensions to the decisions these principals are responsible for. Strategic outcomes are long term in nature and may not materialize for at least 10 years. Moreover, strategic outcomes contribute directly to the survivability of the organization.

DECISION MAKING PROCESSES

Decision making is associated with an individual, the leader; or, to small groups, such as a management team. Decision making also refers to the strategic decisions made by the principal or principals in an organization, as well as the collective information processes within organizations that precede, support, or follow those decisions. These processes include, but are not limited to: interpretation of issues, deliberations conceiving data and information, problem definition, development of decision options, and the selection of a course of action.

WHAT IS A SYSTEM?

Systems are composed of interrelated components such that the properties of both the system and its components are changed if the system is disassembled in any way (Ashmos and Huber 1987). There are different levels of systems, ranging from the simple mechanical systems with predetermined, motions of levers and pulleys (e.g., an automobile engine) to complex social organizations acting to accomplish objectives. The systems paradigm focuses on these processes that exist among system components, and between system components and the environment.

SYSTEMS THINKING

It is safe to say that all of you have been acquainted with the cybernetic or control systems of inputs, transformation processes, outputs, and feedback loops that maintain equilibrium. These system components operate within an environment as shown on the next page (figure). The cybernetic system has been used in a variety of disciplines as the general model of the systems paradigm. Cybernetic systems are closed systems, largely unaffected by the environment where they reside. By its definition, a cybernetic system is an inappropriate representation of the complex processes that occur in organizations, and particularly the strategic decision making processes in organizations.

ORGANIZATIONS ARE OPEN SYSTEMS

Today, organizations exist in competitive global environments where there is strong competition for resources, markets, skilled employees, and innovations. At the same time, many organizations confront environments that are unpredictable and complex. Organizational environments are multifaceted and can be categorized in the following way:

- The Competition: The competitive tactics between firms in an industry or business.
- Customers: Includes direct sales or companies that acquire another firm's customers through outputs for resale.
- The Technological Sector: The development of new production techniques and methods, innovation in materials and products, and general trends in research and science relevant to the organization

- The Regulatory Sector: Federal and state legislation and regulations, city or community policies, and political developments at all levels of government
- The Economic Sector: Factors such as stock markets, rate of inflation, foreign trade balance, federal and state budgets, interest rates, unemployment and economic growth rate
- The Sociocultural Sector: The social values of the general population, the work ethic, and demographic trends. (Daft, Sormunen, and Parks 1988)

First, as open systems, organizations are highly engaged with their environments. Successful organizations develop characteristics and perform processes that allow them to adapt to constraints, threats, and opportunities. They import capability from the environment. This capability can be achieved by acquiring another organization through a joint venture; or by improving their human and physical capital; or by obtaining the information needed to transform that capability into desired outputs such as physical goods, services, or a focused set of monetary or operational actions. Next, organizations' transformation processes are cyclical in nature, that is to say they are a predictable, ordered set of processes that might be determined by a budget cycle, a sales cycle, or a growing season. These well-ordered processes create negative entropy, the resistance to disorganization. Negative entropy maintains the reliability of transformation processes in spite of changes in environmental conditions.

Open systems also have environmental scanning processes that might exist in the recruiting directorate, the market research department, or the complaint department to provide information about the systems performance and to adjust processes within the system.

Another feature of open systems is that they operate under conditions of dynamic homeostasis, the process of preserving the character of the system through its growth. Open systems use internal processes of review to modify their environmental scanning, input, transformation, and output processes to adapt to the changing VUCA factors of the environment, while still staying focused on their core competency. These modifications culminate in the quantitative and qualitative growth of an organization's capability to respond to future contingencies.

The systems paradigm is a useful model of the capabilities of government agencies, particularly the Department of Defense. Defense bureaucracies process tremendous quantities of information about the external environment to produce threat analyses, implement processes that transform information about manpower and resources into combat capability, and adjust internal processes for synthesizing information to support all levels of decision making. But there's a potential problem. The Defense Department, to achieve stability, uses sets of standards, to accomplish programmable outcomes. The sets DOD has been using may not be suited to respond to potential environmental challenges.

Change rather than stability has engulfed us. There are endless calls for the reinvention of government, acquisition reform, and defense realignment, as well as cautions about the revolution in global military affairs and the growing threat of terrorism. These changes in the environment have strategic implications beyond the realm of a single decision maker or even a top management team. But the systems paradigm prompts and demands that future leaders analyze their organization's capability to respond to these VUCA issues. Here are some points to consider:

- Each issue will have a unique set of environmental factors that have an impact on the organizational system. Which parts of the organization are designed to detect and analyze those factors?
- In light of these issues, can greater efficiencies be derived for obtaining inputs such as funding, raw materials, and human capital?
- Will the challenges posed by the changing environment require radically different transformation processes to generate and sustain the desired level of deterrence and combat capability?

The ability to answer these questions depends on how you frame organizational capability. If you view an organization as a structural design (e.g., a battalion), an organizational chart (e.g., a directorate in the Pentagon), a personnel roster (e.g., the comptroller shop) or a surrogate of military or industrial output (e.g., the 82nd Airborne or Boeing Aerospace) then you won't obtain an understanding how processes are translated into capability. You need to adjust your thinking to a systems perspective to bring out these dynamics.

From a systems perspective, organizations are collections of human and physical capital that exchange and process information, transform physical objects, and make decisions for the purpose of achieving some set of objectives related to their external environment. From this frame of reference, leaders can find ways to enhance existing processes in the organization, and identify the need for additional processes of environmental analysis to maintain the organization's survivability.

THE SYSTEMS PARADIGM AND STRATEGIC DECISION MAKING

Today, strategic leaders of competitive organizations face the challenge of using their organization's open systems capabilities to respond to present and future environmental challenges. This is a daunting task for any group of strategic leaders, regardless of their intelligence or experience. Leaders at this level are often overwhelmed by the quantity, as well as the VUCA aspects of environmental change. These conditions often place decision makers in situations that are beyond their expertise. In these situations, if a decision has to be rendered, leaders typically rely on their own scanning, analysis, and interpretation of data, albeit fraught with personal biases. Some leaders are effective using this technique but most strategic issues demand more rigorous approaches towards their resolution.

For the purposes of strategic decision making, organizations can be considered interpretation systems (Daft and Weick, 1984). Organizational interpretation is defined as "the process of translating events and developing shared understanding and conceptual schemes among members of upper management." Organizational interpretation about strategic issues is more than bureaucratic "staffing".

In general, members of organizations support strategic leaders' interpretations by: creating and maintaining the organization's capability to gather information about environmental threats and opportunities; and efficiently analyzing, evaluating and internally synthesizing this information to support the strategic decision making process. Organizational interpretation processes are valuable to strategic decision makers on two counts. First, they reduce the ambiguity of strategic issues by analyzing data from the environment. Next, these processes reduce the uncertainty associated with strategic issues. (For example, decentralized scanning performed by field organizations, lower level divisions, and individual specialists creates more insights to strategic issues in less time.) The ultimate benefit to strategic decision makers is that they can respond to strategic issues more quickly, with higher quality decisions.

If leaders permit their organizations to treat each confrontation with environmental change as a unique experience then, despite performance outcomes, these leaders are not deriving the full capability of organizational interpretation. When organizations develop the capability for systematic learning then successful and unsuccessful experiences will influence their future scanning and interpretation processes favorably.

ORGANIZATIONS AS LEARNING SYSTEMS

Learning, whether associated with people or organizations, is a set of processes that produce change. Edwin Nevis, Anthony DiBella, and Janet Gould from the MIT Organizational Learning Center define organizational learning as "the capacity or processes within an organization to maintain or improve performance based on experience." The purpose of this section is to identify ways leaders can influence these processes to promote learning and improve strategic leadership and decision making.

Earlier in this chapter we described the features of organizations as open systems. Two features among them were relevant to organizational learning:

- The capability of organizations to internally review the effectiveness of systems' processes against the dynamics of the environment and within the parameters of its core competencies.
- Cumulative process modification that results in the quantitative and qualitative growth of an organization's capability to respond to future environmental contingencies.

The first feature highlights the importance of organizational members dedicated to continuous process improvement. The phrase "process improvement" is overused, but it means that people should be constantly analyzing how they think, communicate, perform and add value to their organization. The first feature also implies that members need to have an intimate knowledge of the organization's core competencies, how their work contributes to the core competencies, and the environmental factors that are related to those core competencies.

Employees' level of understanding about the organization's core competencies is initiated and reinforced by leadership messages. When leaders communicate how the organization's core competencies are linked to the activities of different organizational subunits, then employees will understand how their daily efforts are translated into organizational capability. Moreover, when leaders communicate the organization's vision, and the values and ideology that support the organizational culture, they enhance employees' understanding of the organization's strategic objectives.

Organizational leaders must institutionalize the processes of knowledge acquisition. Knowledge acquisition includes activities such as customer surveys, research and development programs, demonstration projects, performance reviews, and the analysis of competitors' products. Informal sources for knowledge acquisition activities include trade publications, televised news and print media. The goal is for knowledge acquisition to be performed continuously as opposed to a singular response from a management inquiry. In an organizational learning system, knowledge acquisition is followed by information distribution. Organizational scholar George Huber from the University of Texas at Austin describes information distribution in the following way:

> Information distribution is a determinant of both the occurrence and breadth of organizational learning . . . organizational components commonly develop "new" information by piecing together items of information that they can obtain from other organizational units. . . . When information is widely distributed in an organization so that more and more varied sources for it exist, retrieval efforts are more likely to succeed and individuals and units are more likely to learn.

The activity of information distribution has even greater significance when it is performed by employees who are also knowledgeable about the organization's core competencies. At its best, information distribution in learning organizations involves purposeful exchanges of information among divisions in the organization that reduces the efforts of any single division to scan the environment. For example, in learning organizations, the supply division would know what information would be important to the marketing division, the production division, and the accounts division, and would route it to those divisions. Division personnel would also know when to modify the information it distributed, and to whom they distributed it as changes occurred in the organization's environment and in the organization's strategy. Again, organizational leaders can facilitate these communication processes.

Leaders can also establish interdepartmental working groups that have the assigned purpose of sharing acquired information to solve problems or develop strategies related to core competencies. Ultimately organizational leaders can make investments in human capital via training and development programs to standardize and improve "information-distribution" skills. Leaders can also invest in physical capital. They can create company-wide information systems that increase the ease and rate of information sharing among subunits.

ORGANIZATIONAL MEMORY

The second feature of open systems in learning organizations is process modification. This feature depends on organizational memory processes. An organization's capability to learn, and ultimately improve its future responses to the environment relies on processes that:

- Record organizational experiences that are relevant to strategic objectives
- Retrieve organizational experiences
- Apply those experiences to strategic decision making activities.

However, the processes that create organizational memory are frequently problematic. Many organizations have poor organizational memories because of a reliance only on employees' memories to retain, retrieve, and apply organizational experiences. This form of organizational memory is vulnerable to turnover and downsizing. Furthermore, organizations can have inadequate memories of success and failure because leaders develop processes to address immediate issues, but fail to evaluate if these processes have future value. Finally, poor organizational memories can result from the absence of organizational processes to: document and catalog organizational actions and outcomes; or, evaluate how past strategies can be applied to achieve new strategic objectives.

There are interventions that organizational leaders can make to improve organizational memory processes. For example, they have to determine how the current experiences of the organization are linked to the vision they have for the organization, the organization's core competencies, and strategic objectives. These actions help set up criteria for identifying which organizational experiences should be a part of organizational memory.

Next, leaders need to leverage their role as shapers of the organization's culture to inculcate employees' beliefs that organizational memory is a valuable tool, instrumental to goal achievement. When processes of creating memory become a part of the organizational culture they have a better chance for longevity in spite of employee turnover. The erosion of organizational memory can also be minimized when leaders formalize processes for creating and using organizational memory. Computer-based organizational memory can range from strictly archival systems to "memory banks" that continuously process information and form networks from organizational experiences and provide rapid access via search engines.

The bottom line is that organizational memory, like human memory, gets better with use. Strategic leaders must create the conditions and find methods to increase the relevance and capacity of organizational memory, and increase opportunities for members of the organization to use that organizational memory in either supporting strategic decision making, or in their strategic decision making processes.

CONCLUSIONS

This chapter has discussed a set of tools that leaders can use to make their organizations successful in VUCA environments. The systems paradigm is a "macro tool", providing an approach to analyze organizational capability through an understanding of processes that occur in organizations. This tool may be difficult for some to master but it has value for many organizational issues in the strategic environment. A tool within the systems paradigm that is particularly valuable is organizational learning. This set of processes has the potential to improve an organization's capability to respond to future environmental challenges and opportunities successfully.

By emphasizing these concepts as tools, greater responsibility is placed on leadership to use them to achieve strategic outcomes efficiently and favorably for the organization. In the chapters to follow there will be opportunities to refine your understanding of the systems paradigm and processes, and to expand your leadership style for personal effectiveness in strategic leadership and decision making.

3

FRAMING PERSPECTIVES

"You're wrong to say that you see nothing else. You see everything, although you may not be able to interpret it." Munoz didn't budge from where he was; he merely indicated the painting with a movement of his chin. "I think it comes down to points of view. What we have here are different levels, which are contained within each other: the painting contains a floor that is a chessboard which, in turn, contains people. Those people are sitting at a chessboard that contains chess pieces. The whole thing is contained in that round mirror to the left. And to complicate things further, another level can be added: ours, where we stand to contemplate the scene or the successive scenes. And beyond that there's the level on which the painter imagined us, the spectators of his work (Perez-Reverte 1994).

INTRODUCTION

The Pentagon's approach to change-its frame of reference-is evolutionary rather than revolutionary:

Without a peer in the world or the threat of global war, the American military still does its conventional war-gaming with planning models developed during the Cold War. It retains many of the weapons systems and structures initially designed to deter and combat a long-gone Soviet menace. The Pentagon's battle doctrines still rest fundamentally on notions of massing military might against the kind of sophisticated opposing army that went away with the breakup of the Soviet Union, although each of the military branches in exprimenting with new organizational forms and high-tech methods of warfare (Graham 1997).

The notion of framing something is to focus on a moment in time, a scene, or a set of ideas. It can involve deliberate use of psychological, and intellectual skills, on the one hand, or less conscious skills within a sense of perception. Framing is a set of skills employed to one degree or another by the politician, photographer, chef, advertising executive, historian, teacher, coach, artist, academic, author, and by ordinary people. Fcr example, the skill and depth used in appraising an event aid in helping to understand what might be taking place well beyond the limited knowledge of those who are involved in only part of the event itself. "The essential tool of the information manager is the ability to frame. To determine the entire meaning of a subject is to make sense of it, to judge its character and significance. To hold the frame of a subject is to choose one particular meaning (or set of meanings) over another. We manage meaning when we assert that our interpretations should be taken as real over other possible interpretations" (Fairhurst 1996).

The Quadrennial Review seems to be framed by using the traditions, experience, culture, and interpretations of the Department of Defense, and of the military services who are part of the DOD. But others might frame the same events from other points of reference or perspective:

21st-century military challenges will differ from past ones and so require changes in U.S. organization, weaponry, and fighting techniques" (Graham 1997).

This framing of the same set of data by those outside the Department of Defense or those in the Congress or academics leads to the debate about the future shape of national security. All parties frame what they see from their own unique set of experiences, tendencies, and interests.

FRAME OF REFERENCE

Frames originate as a result of both our nature, and the experiences we have that nurture us; some are natural (genetic), others are learned, and many revolve around the nature/nurture influence on how we see the world and its events. In addition, there are some frames that can be contrived, deliberately learned and used as a way of more consciously trying to interpret events.

The most common frame of reference is each person's way of observing, interpreting, and acting in the world. "One's frame of reference includes all that one believes or knows to be true of the worlds; the sorts of things that are in it, both animate and inanimate, and how they behave; what has happened in the past; and what is likely to happen in the future" (Moore, et al. 1985).

One's frame of reference carries with it limitations that can impair the individual in recognizing and dealing successfully with the environment.

There are gaps in our perception, knowledge, experience, ability to process information, and to report accurately on what we have seen or heard as, for example, a witness to an accident, or to a tale told by a colleague.

What did we really see, or hear, and how may it have been affected by prejudice, or a momentary distraction, or by some previous encounter with what looks much like the current situation, but in fact is different? The fact that we use a frame of reference, with all its limitations, as the basis for decisions and actions which may turn out to be false, is important at all levels of management and leadership.

Alexander George, in *Presidential Decisionmaking*, discusses a particular kind of limitation in a frame of reference which he calls attribution errors, the difference between a dispositional and situational frame of reference. In looking at a situation, George suggests that we are inclined to view our own attitudes favorably, those of an antagonist in a less favorable way; this is his notion of disposition. The situations in which we find ourselves also affect what we do. A simple example: we most often believe that our "home" athletic team plays fairly and competitively, while our opponent's players are disposed to play "dirty."

SENSEMAKING

"In real world practice, problems do not present themselves to the practitioners as givens. They must be constructed from the materials of problematic situations which are puzzling, troubling, and uncertain. In order to convert a problematic situation to a problem, a practitioner must do certain kind of work. He must make sense of an uncertain situation that initially makes no sense" (Weick 1995). Situations involving spousal abuse (unexplained bruises, absences from work, mood swings, and the like), child abuse, alcoholism, rumors of unethical conduct, or even the Unabomber, represent a phenomenon in which a set of discrepant clues are spotted but sensible connections are not immediately made.

Sensemaking takes time. It arises out of an accumulation of barely perceptible items, of plausible speculations, on information gathered from sources not part of the current situation, and on contradictory issues of reputation associated with a respected profession (e.g., military or the clergy). It is the task of the leader to interpret or translate this complex of information, to unravel the ball of twine, to make sense of the situation.

The role of the leader is to interpret, on the one hand, and to alter or guide the manner in which his followers understand the world by giving it a compelling "face." A leader is one who gives others a different sense of the meaning of that which they do by recreating it in this different "face," in the same way a painter or sculptor or poet gives those who follow him or her a different way of "seeing." The leader is a sense-giver. The leader embodies the possibilities of "escape" from what might otherwise appear to be incomprehensible, or from what might otherwise appear to be a chaotic, indifferent, or incorrigible world over which we have no control. (Thayer, 1988).

The role of a strategic leader in a volatile, uncertain, complex, and ambiguous environment is to be a sense-maker of phenomena, to connect the dots of random events and activities, and to bring coherence to apparent disarray. Sherlock Holmes might be a worthy exemplar. He used a rigorous, determined method, plus his own ingenuity and sensemaking to solve the most complex crimes. Notes from a flute, or the dog 'not' barking, or a smudge on the inside of a glass were often enough. Scientists in studying the confusing deaths of African males in the 1980s ultimately made sense of what they were seeing, finally identifying the Ebola virus and the symptoms of AIDS. Their sensemaking provided a new frame of reference for identifying the medical mystery.

OTHER FRAMES

There are any number of other frames that are used , and they are simply mentioned here:

- Time is a frame of reference. The past, present, and future affect our way of looking at things. Age affects how we look at the world. Youth frames the world in optimistic terms; in middle age, people become more realistic and come to terms with the way things are. If we have 'little' time we frame what we are looking at with a sense of urgency, and may focus on things that apply only to the short term. In the absence of a crisis, we may be inclined to put off time, to procrastinate, and miss opportunities.
- A code of conduct, or a moral-ethical frame of reference, often frames our view of things. Such rules of behavior may incline us to see things in our terms of right and wrong, good and bad, and acceptable or not acceptable. Codes of conduct are often affected by larger questions of values, culture, religion, and ethnic contexts. A global frame of reference confuses the traditions, mores, and practices of the people of many nations.
- At a professional level, certain frames are introduced for participation in such fields as medicine, the military, or law, or in the political environment. For example, a particular school of economics might be more Keynesian than another; a school of political science might be more real-politik than another. Certain elements of the military profession might be more devoted to warfare than to logistics. Thus, professions give still another set of lenses through which to view the world.

THE USE OF FRAMES

Framing seems to be a useful stratagem to use in making sense of complex problems and conditions. The inclination and artistry that some have in recognizing patterns and putting things into perspective is useful in making fundamental and significant changes. Framing is a kind of orientation or mindset, a set of skills used effectively in addressing complex problems.

In terms of national security, a series of events flows from the end of the Cold War, and notions of a multi-polar, uni-superpower strategic environment. These concepts lead to a rethinking of national security interests, and of consequent changes in force size, budget, infrastructure, and the like. This rethinking is a reframing of the defense component of the United States, a restructuring of physical, human, and policy dimensions of the military. The Executive Summary of the monograph, "Restructuring for a New Era Framing the Roles and Missions Debate," provides this terse rendering of the issue: Today, the United States faces a major challenge: restructuring its defense establishment to function efficiently and effectively in a new, dynamic security environment. This paper offers a framework for meeting that challenge, and offers restructuring as the frame to use in dealing with the ambiguous and complex conditions and assumptions that now exist. Restructuring seeks to utilize a frame, to gain control of a very fractious and volatile environment.

CREATED FRAMES

Some frames can be created. Those in the book, *Reframing Organizations* (Bolman and Deal), suggest a useful set of four frames to consider in analyzing organizations, their environment as a whole, or even individual events within their environment: The Structural Frame, the Political Frame, Human Relations Frame, and the Symbolic Frame. Each of the frames has a particular salience in itself; their combination into a multi-frame approach is perhaps their greatest strength.

Structural Frame. The Heritage Foundation, a conservative think tank in Washington, D.C., recently announced a budget proposal that would cut more than 500 billion dollars in spending over the next five years, while leaving Social Security untouched, cutting taxes by nearly $200 billion, increasing defense spending by $123 billion, shutting down the Rural Utilities Service, consolidating 160 federal job training programs, and trimming "corporate welfare."

Perhaps the most dramatic part of the proposal is the reduction in the number of cabinet-level agencies from the current 14 to only five: the departments of State, Defense, Treasury, Justice, and Health and Human Services. Three new bureaus would be created as independent agencies-Agriculture, Natural Resources, and National Statistics; and there would be some number of other independent agencies (Chandler 1997).

This structural frame addresses fundamental questions of national organization, how and where and why responsibilities are assigned, what connections and relationships are explicit, what certainty there is about the mission and aims of the organization, and the specific ways and means designed to help the organization achieve its goals. Every organization develops a design, and a set of mechanisms to cope with its environment. Businesses, military units, governments, and public or private associations all have structure and organization as a visible frame for their operational philosophy and processes.

The structural frame is based on scientific principle, and on the work of industrial psychologists like Frederick W. Taylor, or sociologists like Max Weber. These theoreticians espoused such ideas as time and motion studies, and the division of work into clear manageable units. This frame also is associated with the notion of bureaucracy, and depends on rationality and the sense that any problem can be solved by any group of people if it is simply organized into the most appropriate structural frame.

According to Bolman and Deal, the structural frame has these assumptions:

- Organizations exist primarily to accomplish established goals.
- For any organization a structural form can be designed and implemented to fit its particular set of circumstances

(such as goals, strategies, environment, technology, and people).

- Organizations work most effectively when environmental turbulence and personal preferences are constrained by norms of rationality. (Structure ensures that people focus on getting the job done rather than on doing whatever they please.)
- Specialization permits higher levels of individual expertise and performance.
- Coordination and control are essential to effectiveness. Depending on the task and environment, coordination may be achieved through authority, rules, policies, standard operating procedures, information systems,, meetings, lateral relationships, or a variety of more informal techniques.
- Organizational problems originate from inappropriate structures or inadequate systems and can be resolved through restructuring or developing new systems. (Bolman and Deal, 1991).

These assumptions and structural frames are reflected in organizational charts, or wiring diagrams, which spell out relationships between and among components of an enterprise, and the people who inhabit various 'boxes'. The structure usually contains a carefully crafted set of tasks within each sector of the organization, along with the procedure and protocols used to accomplish the mission.

Political Frame. The D.C. Board of Education announced that it would close 16 schools to eliminate excess space in the school system and generate millions of dollars for repairs. The Emergency Transitional Education Board of Trustees met to consider the proposal. The proposed changes have already been denounced by some parents, community leaders, D.C. Council members, and members of the elected Board of Education. Critics have said officials are moving too quickly and not consulting parents enough. In addition, the mayor, the Teachers Union, and other organizations indicated their displeasure with the idea. Previous efforts to close schools in the District have failed. The structural frame is ordered and rational by nature. This structured organization is, in the end, overtaken by the implicit, informal, machinations of office politics, of the exercise of power that works outside the formidable walls of the bureaucracy. It is aptly illustrated as the phenomenon of the water-cooler, that proverbial meeting place where people talk over what is really going on, and decide how work will or will not get done.

Bolman and Deal describe this as the political frame, a "screaming political arena:" Five propositions summarize this perspective:

- Organizations are coalitions composed of varied individuals and interest groups (for example, hierarchical levels, departments, professional groups, gender and ethnic subgroups.).
- There are enduring differences among individuals and groups in their values, preferences, beliefs, and perceptions of reality. Such differences change slowly, if at all.
- Most of the important decisions in organizations involve the allocation of scarce resources: they are decisions about who gets what.
- Because of scarce resources and enduring differences, conflict is central to organizational dynamics, and power is the most important resource.
- Organizational goals and decisions emerge from bargaining, negotiation, and jockeying for position among members of different coalitions (Bolman and Deal 1991).

These political polarities are represented in global terms by such distinctive classifications as labor and management, separate military groups, and different branches of government. The reality of tension between and among parts of an organization, and the complex nature of that tension, underscores the condition that not all who are part of an enterprise see the structure in the same way. However, a strategic leader does have a considerable number of tools at his disposal; the office does confer some positional power which allows for setting agendas, taking initiatives, and co-opting the activities of others.

Furthermore, strategic leaders can form coalitions with others, network informally, and negotiate and bargain to achieve agreement on certain plans of action. The leader, even with a structure of advisors and officers, a budget and other resources, may not be able to achieve as much success as he or she might wish,despite having the legal power. Others are able to utilize other forms of power, including public opinion and political influence to achieve what they might want, which could be contrary to what the leader desires.

Human Relations Frame. Organizations are formed to meet certain objectives for their members: workers in a corporation or other business, graduate students in a university, sailors in a navy, or youngsters who want to play baseball in a community. An organization provides the setting where participants gain access to training, education, sports, labor, or resources.

There is an implicit, if not explicit, connection between an organization and the people who belong to it. On the one hand, the organization has the potential to bring some good to its members, but it also has the potential to "use" and even abuse its workers, students, or citizens at various times. And, while people can contribute to an organization through their energies, ideas, skills and talents, as citizens of a community, it sometimes happens that many ignore service they can perform on behalf of others and 'take' what they can from the organization.

The human relations frame has certain assumptions:

- Organizations exist to serve human needs (rather than the reverse.)
- Organizations and people need each other. (Organizations need ideas, energy; people need salaries, work opportunities.)
- When the fit between the individual and the organization is poor, one or both will suffer; individuals will either be exploited, or will seek to exploit the organizations, or both.

- A good fit between the individual and the organization benefits both: human beings find meaningful and satisfying work, and organizations get the human talent and energy that they need (Bolman and Deal 1991).

The human relations frame suggests the most valued asset an organization has is its people: "By showing trust in and respect for all employees, managers can empower people to do their jobs to the very best of their ability. . . . By cultivating and investing time in employees, managers strengthen the foundation of the entire enterprise" (Augustine 1997). The human relations frame advances the notion that the structure of an organization may be a gleaming but empty shell if it does not serve to enhance the people who are part of the organization, or conversely if it does not allow the people to contribute their energy, ideas, talents, and enthusiasm to the organization.

In addition to the premise that man is by nature gregarious, that he seeks to join with others in social enterprises, the human relations frame suggests that there is a more fundamental notion, that of human need. The psychologist, Abraham Maslow, posits a hierarchical set of human needs, with the higher needs being able to be satisfied only after lower needs are met. Maslow organizes the hierarchy as follows:

1. Physiological needs, such as food and water
2. Safety needs, such as being free from fear
3. Belonging and love needs; positive relations with others
4. Esteem needs valuing self and others
5. Self-actualization and developing to one's fullest.

The U.S. Army's slogan, 'Be All You Can Be," Jesse Jackson's mantra, "I am somebody," or the challenge of many educators, "All Children can Learn," addresses self-actualization and the implied satisfaction of all the other needs.

There is a discernible orientation toward human relations awareness in organizations of all kinds. Structure has changed, often because of economic considerations. This has led to more participative management, an implicit sense that bringing people together to solve problems can lead to improvements in quality, increases in productivity, decreases in time lost because of injury, illness, or other negative influences. Specific negative attributes in the workplace are forcefully addressed as issues of human and/or civil rights, equal opportunity, sexual harassment, gender opportunity, health, training, etc. A broad democratization of workplaces, both public and private, classrooms, and athletic teams; and, components of industry and the defense department are defining a different human relations environment with more accountability, quality, zero-defects production, self-managing work teams, and project management.

More recently this notion of fit or compatibility between the organization and the individual has been described by Professor Ouichi in his Theory Z, a management philosophy successfully blending Japanese and American approaches to management. Theory Z reflects the central assumptions of the human resources frame: that individuals want their productive time to be a rewarding experience, that they want to contribute to the success of whatever enterprise they may be associated with, and that if the structure is engineered appropriately they will be able to achieve those goals. Theory Z suggests that humanized working conditions not only increase productivity and profits to the company but also to self-esteem for employees. What Theory Z calls for is a redirection of attention to human relations in the corporate world as well.

Symbolic Frame. *Sotuknang destroyed the world because the Hopis forgot to do their duty. They forgot the songs that must be sung, the pahos that must be offered, the ceremonials that must be danced. Each time the world became infected with evil, people quarreled all the time. People became powaqas, and practiced witchcraft against one another. The Hopis left the proper Road of Life and only a few were left doing their duty in the kivas. And each time, Sotuknang gave the Hopis warning. He held back the rain so his people would know his displeasure. But everybody ignored the rainless seasons. They kept going after money, and quarreling, and gossiping, and forgetting the true way of the Road of Life. And each time Sotuknang decided that the world had used up its strit and he saved a few of the best Hopis, and then he destroyed all the rest. Lomatewa stared into the eyes of the Flute Clan boy. "You understand this?" I understand," the boy said* (Hillerman, 1988).

There is this symbolic frame, or lens, to view an organization, a most unconventional one to those who see the environment as organized and structured, rational and linear. In an environment, though, that is volatile, uncertain, complex, and ambiguous, the ordinary frames may not fully explain the course of events as they cascade through the chasms of history. Rather than idyllic and placid streams, leaders experience wild, unpredictable, and even contrary currents. Rather than looking at things through the eyes and careful measurements of a time and efficiency expert, for example, we often seem to be viewing a world epitomized by symbols of ethnicity, tribalism, religion, or even myth. This so-called symbolic frame is based on a set of things embedded in the 'culture' of organizations. Rituals, protocols and manners invite us to look beyond visible and tangible elements to find out what really might be important; unlike the political frame it does not smack of cynicism, but provides an insight to persons or events invested with 'magical' power. The symbolic frame is based on the following assumptions:

- What is most important about any event is not what happened, but what it means.
- Events and meanings are loosely coupled: the same events can have different meanings because of the way individuals interpret their experiences.
- Many of the most significant events and processes in organizations are ambiguous or uncertain, it is often difficult or impossible to know what happened, why it happened, or what will happen next.
- The greater the ambiguity and uncertainty, the harder it is to use rational approaches to analysis, problem solving, and decision making.
- Faced with uncertainty and ambiguity, human beings create symbols to resolve confusion, increase predictability, and provide direction. Events may remain illogical, random, fluid, and meaningless, but human symbols make them seem otherwise.

- Many organizational events and processes are important more for what they express than for what they produce: they are secular myths, rituals, ceremonies, and sagas that help people find meaning and order in their lives (Bolman and Deal 1991).

The symbolic frame looks at events-what people do, how they form and organize themselves, how they govern, how they reward and punish-and tries to discern what that means. It gauges the importance and significance of the symbols, rituals, customs, practices, and traditions of a particular organization. Anyone observing the Congress of the United States, for example, recognizes a set of protocols and observances that lend civility, order, and dignity to the complexity of lawmaking: people are addressed in certain ways, despite heated emotions; seniority is revered and acknowledged in itself before it becomes a factor in naming Committee Chairs; elaborate rules govern debate and discussion; and rituals abound, such as a phone call to the President of the United States by the Speaker of the House that closes a session of the Congress.

SYSTEMS FRAME

As something of a final thought Bolman and Deal suggest the presence of a "fifth" frame that combines elements of each of the other frames. Based on systems theory and cybernetics, the fifth frame suggests, in effect, the use of all the frames in looking at, or trying to gain the most appropriate frame of reference to use in analyzing a particular situation.

For example, on June 25, 1996, a terrorist truck bomb exploded outside the northern perimeter of KhobarTowers, Dhahran in Saudi Arabia, a facility housing U.S. and allied forces supporting the coalition air operation in northern Iraq. There were 19 fatalities and approximately 500 wounded. The perpetrators escaped. There have been a series of investigations revolving around such questions as to whose responsibility it was to provide security, whether that was adequately provided for by the base commander, what cultural and other issues might have been factors, and what role the United States should have in continuing operations in Saudi Arabia.

The structural frame would analyze the physical attributes of the base, the procedures that were in place, the security precautions that had been implemented, and the like; this frame could trace the series of meetings and understandings on what was to be done to protect the American base from terrorists. The human relations frame would reveal the extent to which the base commander considered and communicated the dangers of threats to those stationed there, and communicated the steps that were in place to protect them. The political frame might reveal the major constituencies, leadership, and the management of disagreement; further more, leaders might have decided not to push, or to move more slowly in implementing certain things because of sensitivity between components of the Air Force, elements in the Saudi Government, the Central Command, and others who might have had differing views about threats of terrorism, and adequate protection. The symbolic frame might be particularly relevant in the sense that perceptions of the threat, and adequacy of protection, and even the kinds of protection might have been perceived differently by Americans and by the host Saudis.

USE OF THE FRAMES

While we may have an inclination to use one frame over another to look at a situation, we might not make full sense of a situation by doing so. If nothing else, knowledge of the frames should alert the strategic leader of the importance of applying all the frames to a situation in order to leverage the best possible solution.

Some frames may have more relevance in certain situations than others. In a scenario in which employee morale is poor, the human relations frame might have more significance. Rather than reorganize and restructure to improve production or conditions, it may be more important to find out what is really bothering the employees, and then include them in the process.

A familiar argument among leaders is whether a review of policy or practice should be a "top-down" or a "bottom-up" process. From a more traditional and structural frame, the inclination is that it be studied by senior managers, perhaps supported by consultants hired by the leadership, with the results implemented based on the recommendations; a top-down approach. On the other hand, the political frame would argue that change might best be done by a review of things by those who are closest to the problem. Workers, for example, might decide that they could be more efficient if the lighting was improved, or if certain pieces of equipment were rearranged in the work area. This is a bottom-up approach. The symbolic frame suggests that the best way to show an interest in real reform is not to isolate it to either bottom or top, but to include both ends in the process. The role of the strategic leaders is diverse enough for them to be at various times an architect (structural frame), catalyst (human relations frame), advocate (political frame), prophet and poet (symbolic frame) (Bolman and Deal 1991).

SUMMARY AND CONCLUSIONS

Frames can be differentiated as natural, learned, or created. Frames can be used effectively to address most problems, and the more complex the problem, the more points of view and frames of reference have to be employed. Some frames of reference contain bias or misperceptions or prejudice, even when done in good faith; how else to explain the imprisonment of large numbers of Japanese and Italian Americans in the Second World War, or the Tuskegee experiments on black Americans? Some frames of reference are flawed due to the lack of information about the fundamental problem and their second, and third and fourth order impacts. Some frames are overused; how else to explain the tendency of leaders to revise the structural frame when coming into an organization? Some frames, such as the human relations frame, may be underused; how else can you explain the failure to include employees, or students, or citizens in matters that concern them?

Making sense of the environment is one of the critical tasks of the strategic leader. Awareness of the value of framing (and reframing) as ways of looking at the world, and skill in using sensemaking techniques, are critical to success at the strategic level.

4

STRATEGIC LEADER PERFORMANCE REQUIREMENTS

Officers who succeed at three and four star levels have the individual capacity to cope with complexity, amorphousness, and uncertainty. They do not have to have everything laid out for them. They have the resiliency and ingenuity to adapt to new and different circumstances.

A Four-star Flag Officer

Among performance requirements at the strategic level, there is a critical requirement for strategic vision. Most of what we know about strategic leadership performance requirements comes from three sources: Stratified Systems Theory (SST), outlining how complexity-handling skills requirements must grow with organizational level; a 10-year research program on senior officer leadership conducted by the U.S. Army Research Institute; and general literature on executive leadership.

STRATEGIC LEADERSHIP

Leadership is an interactive process, the collective energy of a group, organization, or nation is focused on the attainment of a common objective or goal. Through leadership, clarity of purpose, direction, and means is achieved. There is also a perception of shared commitment by members. However, leadership tasks at the top of a large-scale organization are different from those at lower levels because the nature of work changes as an individual moves up through the hierarchy of an organization.

Most large-scale organizations have three broadly defined parts: the top levels ("strategic"), the middle levels ("organizational") and the bottom levels ("production" or action-oriented).

Leaders at the lower levels are responsible for getting things done; they are action-oriented. Compared with leaders at topmost levels, they have little discretion about the

decisions they make, the procedures they use, and the degree of innovation they may implement. They may improvise but they rarely *invent*, because, at their level, consistency of action is important.

The mid-levels are responsible for setting near- and mid-term goals and directions, and for developing the plans, procedures and processes used by the lower levels. (Plans, procedures, and processes are major tools for coordinating effort, particularly in large-scale organizations with many interdependent parts that must act in a coordinated way.) The mid-levels are also responsible for prioritizing missions and allocating major resources to tailor capability at the lower levels. This includes formulating intermediate-range resources allocation plans that implement concepts developed at higher levels, as in the Planning, Programming, Budgeting and Execution System (PPBES).

Top-level leaders are responsible for the strategic direction of their organization within the context of the strategic environment-now increasingly global. The term "strategic" implies broad scale and scope. It requires forward vision extending over long time spans-in some cases 50 years or more. So strategic leadership is a process wherein those responsible for large-scale organizations set long-term directions and obtain, through consensus building, the energetic support of key constituencies necessary for the commitment of resources.

The major functions performed by increasingly higher levels of the organization are increasingly indirect, complex, and ill-defined. The lower levels deal with well- understood procedures. The resource requirements are modest, and expectations of performance are clear. Leadership is "direct"; leaders are expected to influence the course of events by their own actions. At higher levels, requirements are less clear, problems are less defined, and there are situations where developed procedures or precedents do not exist. Leaders at higher levels must be creative in problem solving, more innovative in their thinking. They must also be more proactive, in the sense of looking further forward more perceptively to set directions that play out over long periods.

INTEGRATING THE LEVELS OF LEADERSHIP

FUNCTION	STRATEGIC LEADERSHIP	ORGANIZATIONAL LEADERSHIP	DIRECT LEADERSHIP
VISION	CREATE THE VISION	CREATE THE PLANS	EXECUTE THE PLANS
TEAMWORK	INTEGRATE STRUCTURE/ PURPOSE	DESIGN INTER-DEPENDENCIES	FORGE TEAMWORK
VALUES	ARTICULATE CULTURAL IMPERATIVES AND VALUES	SET COMMAND CLIMATE	MODEL AND REINFORCE VALUES
INFORMATION	ESTABLISH CONCEPT BASE FOR INFORMATION SYSTEMS	ENGINEER INFORMATION SYSTEMS	GENERATE/ APPLY INFORMATION

The critical functions of higher levels are increasingly conceptual (abstract) in nature. The lower levels are more concerned with hands-on operations. Tanks are maneuvered. Ships are driven. Aircraft are flown. There are rules and procedures that make tasks clear and unambiguous.

The midlevel of the organization is where procedures and practices used by the lower levels are generated. Leaders no longer deal "hands-on" with weapons systems; they deal indirectly with organizational systems, and thus must deal conceptually, using analytic procedures, because they are allocating finite resources to competing demands. Their thinking skills must be rational, critical, and discerning.

At the topmost levels, there are more conceptual requirements. Analytic skills alone are not enough because of long-time horizons and the massive scope and scale of resources being committed. To build long-term vision of where an organization must move over the next 15 to 30 years, leaders must be creative (e.g., exercise creative thinking skills). Creative thinking is very different from critical thinking. The creative process demands synthesis skills, a willingness to take moderate risks, and a degree of personal comfort and confidence in decision making when exploring the uncertain and unknown.

The functions of higher levels require increasingly long time frames for their execution. There are three reasons why this is so. The first is that the resources committed by consequential decisions are much greater. All organizations have "sunk" costs. They exist in research and development, equipment, training, and operational procedures. The cost of an aircraft carrier, for example, must be amortized throughout a life-cycle covering decades; the concepts giving rise to this type of system must have arisen out of strategic vision extending over 35 to 40 years or more. A second reason is that the uncertainties of implementing strategic vision are very great. Research and development on a new system may extend more than a decade. For example, the F-22 will have been in development for perhaps a dozen years when the first aircraft flies. Will it be needed? If so, in what quantity? Finally, every organization has both a culture and a well-established set of operating practices and functional roles. They are based on extended training of organization members and long periods of operational experience, incurring both human and dollar costs. Any change in practices and procedures, if necessary, not only creates resistance from members who, by nature, do not like change, but also increases the financial cost of both re-training and subsequent operations.

The effectiveness of long-term vision is crucial to the long-term health of any organization. At all levels, leaders must make trade-off decisions, generally with the use of resources. Critical trade-offs reflect a choice between current effectiveness and projected future effectiveness , whether to do more research and development on a future, qualitatively superior weapons system, or to buy more of the available system; whether to make the investment in current technology or wait for the next quantum step. Each decision is surrounded by risk, imposed by cost and the uncertainty of future developments. Strategic leadership is a balancing act, a thin line between maximizing present effectiveness, and maximizing future effectiveness, decisions that, to some extent, are mutually exclusive. Resources expended today in the wrong direction become a loss. This is why strategic vision is crucially important to organizations and to the national interest.

Strategic leadership is a risky business. Strategic decisions are rarely clear-cut. There will always be uncertainties and often ambiguities. Contributing to the uncertainty is the fact that decisions must be made with some set of presumably valid assumptions in mind. However, strategic decisions may play out over long time spans: 10, 15, 20 years-or more. It is almost certain that very long time frames will see change in some or many of the assumptions on which such decisions were based. The decisions themselves may thus become flawed over time-overtaken by events through no fault of the original decision maker. Another uncertainty is that the support of constituencies for the decision may change with changing circumstances. And the risk is compounded by the fact that strategic decisions almost always call for major commitment of scarce resources. "Opportunity cost" is created when commitment of resources to one option precludes the exercise of other options. Consequential strategic decisions- those committing very large resources to very long term courses of action-may also prevent reconsideration of other options. A risky business indeed.

An additional source of strategic risk is that top-level decisions will almost always have both direct and indirect effects. Where decisions impact globally, even the direct effects may be uncertain. The probable actions of competitors/ adversaries may not be understood when prediction must take into account other cultures, themselves understood only dimly. And there may be missing information. In the Cuban missile crisis during the Kennedy administration, the Executive

Committee members were quite uncertain what the response of the Russians would be to the various options discussed. It is now known the Soviets had over 150 nuclear warheads in Cuba, including tactical nuclear weapons that might have been triggered by any direct assault on the island.

However, direct uncertainties may be minimal compared to indirect outcomes of decisions that involve long-term, irretrievable commitment of mammoth resources. An indirect effect occurs when a decision creates a direct effect that produces additional ripple effects. In complex systems, second-, third-, fourth-order effects are common. And the further removed they are, the harder they are to anticipate.

Two examples illustrating this are the North American Free Trade Agreement (NAFTA) and the impending decisions about medical care in the United States. The results of these system changes will play out over a 20- to 50-year time frame, intermixed with changes resulting from other decisions. Not only are indirect effects hard to anticipate, but also in some cases it may not be clear what actually did/will cause them.

For all these reasons, strategic decisions need to be systematic, rational (to the extent possible), based on well understood and articulated assumptions, and broadly supported by those involved in their implementation.

Consensus team decision making is a process that can produce decisions of this nature; however, not all decisions at the top require this process. First, not all decisions are resource intensive.

Those, by their very nature, are less risky because they do not create "opportunity costs." Second, not all decisions deal with long time horizons. Some of what is in a flag rank officer's in-box is due out within hours or days, so effects can be examined and "mistakes" quickly rectified. (However, if the leader is adding value to the organization, even short-term decisions will be considered within the context of strategic objectives.) And, finally, not all top-level decisions are complex. The time and resource costs of consensus-team decision making may not be warranted.

STRATEGIC TRADE-OFFS: BALANCING PRESENT AND FUTURE EXPECTATIONS

Strategic leadership involves making choices between competing alternatives that are, to some extent, mutually exclusive. Sometimes, one choice commits resources that cannot later be allocated to another. This is "opportunity cost." At other times, opportunity has a sharply defined window, demanding quick initiation. Then there is no later opportunity for another choice. Trade-offs between a course of action that will pay off maximally in the short term, and one that will pay off maximally-if it pays off at all-in the long term contribute to the complexity of strategic decisions. Among them are:

Differences in needs and expectations must be assessed and balanced among the various constituencies that have a critical interest in decisions. Members of one's own organization and key external constituencies such as the Congress, the media, and the citizens who are served by the military must be considered. This has substantial implications for making strategic decisions and constructing strategic plans. For example, each service has its own concept of its strategic mission, and how it should contribute to joint operations. These expectations may be at odds. Effective strategic leadership required understanding these different expectations,and an ability to balance them in creative and non-destructive ways. *Desert Storm* provides an illustrative example. Political considerations governed selection of the ground forces to "liberate" Kuwait City, and determined the selection of forces that were to cross the Iraqi borders.

Decisions are required on the number and types of subordinate and lateral organizations that must be brought together around a single set of understandings and purposes in order to achieve unified action. This issue derives from different cultural understandings, even among the services. Language used and understood by one might not have the same meaning to another. Frames of reference will differ enough to require tradeoffs between what is optimum as a 108 course of action, and what is feasible, based on current skill levels, training, concepts of employment,etc. *Desert Storm* provides an example here also. Coordinating the action of multi-national forces was daunting. There were enormous differences in equipment and languages. The anticipation was that communication problems would be massive. However, a staff member suggested that Special Forces soldiers (trained in the language and customs of the multi-national combatant forces, but equipped with U.S. equipment and concepts) would be an effective interface. This proved valid.

There is an influence of forces external to the organization which the executive may or may not be able to anticipate or control. For example, in the current media-dominated world, actions that might appear straightforward in the absence of public scrutiny may become untenable. Regardless of the merits of any public event today, there can be no doubt that its outcome will be influenced by public opinion. Its importance may be media generated, and its eventual defusing will require delicate decision-making by top officials. Other force influences, both internal and external to the organization, for one reason or another, cannot be fully known. If greater clarity cannot be obtained on these forces, the executive may have to "live with them." First, understanding that these influences exist in a complex situation suggests that time should be spent looking for contingencies whenever strategic decisions or plans are being constructed. Second, understanding that change probably is inevitable as the course of action unfolds suggests that tolerance of uncertainty and/or ambiguity is an important part of the psychological make-up of any strategic leader.

THE JOINT, UNIFIED, AND COMBINED PERSPECTIVE

The importance of a joint/combined perspective is reflected in the extent to which strategic leaders must operate outside a narrowly defined single service (or single nation) environment. The complexity created by the requirement to interface outside single service boundaries is twofold. First, communication is complicated by the need to understand the different cultures and languages of the other participants, including the members of other U.S. service branches. Accurate, effective communication requires understanding the frames of reference of other organizations' listeners, not just one's own. Second, subordinates, e.g., in a joint command, may not be totally subordinated in the same sense as in single service organizations. Other leaders, and the forces they command, might be nominally under your command. Nonetheless, they retain at least some of their allegiances and lines of authority to their own-service commanders, reducing the likelihood that your command influence alone will produce committed, unified action.

JOINTNESS

ONE REASON THE MILITARY SERVICES HAVE TROUBLE OPERATING JOINTLY IS THAT THEY DON'T SPEAK THE SAME LANGUAGE. FOR EXAMPLE, IF YOU TOLD NAVY PERSONNEL TO "SECURE THE BUILDING," THEY WOULD TURN OFF THE LIGHTS AND LOCK THE DOORS. THE ARMY WOULD OCCUPY THE BUILDING SO NO ONE COULD ENTER. THE MARINES WOULD ASSAULT THE BUILDING, CAPTURE IT, AND DEFEND IT WITH SUPPRESSIVE FIRE AND CLOSE COMBAT. THE AIR FORCE, ON THE OTHER HAND, WOULD TAKE OUT A THREE-YEAR LEASE WITH AN OPTION TO BUY.

Strategic leaders must also be skillful at working in a collegial, but, at the same time, competitive environment where each member bids for a share of limited resources. Although they compete with one another, they also rely on each other to reduce uncertainty, and to build consensus and shared vision in these complex environments.

MULTINATIONAL AND NATIONAL ENVIRONMENTS

The requirement to operate effectively in a multinational environment demands an international perspective — understanding the political, economic, and social factors in other countries. Leaders responsible for developing and sustaining the coalitions and alliances central to our national defense strategy must have an in-depth understanding of the other cultures involved. This is an essential part of the strategic frame of reference to make clear the meaning of actions taken, words spoken, and, perhaps more important, words and expectations unspoken. Lacking this, negotiation well encounter obstacles that impede progress.

A past Supreme Allied Commander, Europe, explained some of his decision processes. His position demanded that he have a profound understanding of the national cultures, proclivities, and interests of all the NATO nations. First, a decision taken by NATO had to be unanimous, so patience was a valuable attribute for decision makers. Second, he had had to make decisions contrary to the interests of the United States when U.S. interests were not representative of the best interests of the NATO nations. Balancing the sense of "what's best for all combined" against "what's best for the U.S." was a delicate task, given that he had to answer ultimately to critics in the U.S. who felt their national interests had not well been represented.

An equally profound national perspective is required for testimony to Congress, and interactions with executives of federal agencies, state and local authorities, the media, and other leaders of political and social opinion who influence national attitudes toward the military. This awareness of the outlook, values, and priorities of others requires a deep understanding of American society, including its culture and values, and differences in the interests of its key groups. This leadership perspective is necessary not only for public representation, but also for shaping the culture and values of our military institution as an integral part of the total society.

Because strategic leaders must proactively influence their constituencies as well as respond to their concerns, both national and international perspectives are used in two ways:

- To influence opinion and build understanding in external audiences of needs and purposes of the military.
- To interpret the outside environment in order to aid the formulation of internal policy and decisions, and to guide organizational direction.

Defense needs, goals, or objectives may be in conflict with those of other departments, because all elements of government compete for resources within an increasingly constrained and ever-less munificent fiscal environment. In addition, public sentiment may be activated by either the media, other organizations, or members of government to swing the perception of the national interest in one direction or another, thus changing the relative importance of needs, goals, and objectives of any given agency or department. One key role of strategic leadership is to understand this competition, and to participate at senior levels in ways that represent his/her institution effectively in the public eye. Strategic leaders are responsible for achieving such shared understanding-both by representing defense views to external audiences and by explaining external views to internal audiences. Understanding then serves as a basis for the formulation of the military services' strategic direction that accurately reflects national policy objectives.

STRATEGIC RESPONSIBILITIES

Within the DoD, strategic leadership responsibilities are broad and varied. Four areas of concern to strategic military leaders and their civilian counterparts stand out.

The first strategic responsibility is managing the relationship between the nation's total defense force and the overarching national policy apparatus:

- Interpreting national policy guidelines and directives.
- Providing advice and counsel in national policy formulation.
- Planning jointly for the maintenance of the U.S. military's capability required to implement national policy.
- Presenting the organization's requirements for resources and capability.
- Developing competitive strategies.
- Bridging the gap between political decisions made and individuals who ultimately carry out those decisions.

The second strategic responsibility is representing the organization in its relationships with the larger society:

- Regularly communicating with the Congress and other branches of government, to ensure understanding and appreciation of service traditions, values, and needs.
- Acting as a spokesperson for the organization with other federal agencies, the media, significant influential forces at the national level, and the public at large, to enhance appreciation and respect for the role of the military in society and in the global environment.
- Building and maintaining a network of information sources that can be used to understand and influence the military environment.

The third strategic responsibility is creating the future operating capability of the military to meet worldwide contingencies:

- Assessing threats to national interests, to include regular re-assessment of current assumptions and of the probable nature of future war.
- Developing a concept base for future force structure, equipment, and operating doctrine.
- Creating components of force structure, defending and supporting research and development activities extending into the far term as necessary.
- Developing operational concept plans to meet threats.
- Commanding and controlling joint forces.

The fourth strategic responsibility is managing joint and combined lateral relationships among the Services and with representatives of other countries in both peace and war.

- Creating understanding and acceptance of both institutional goals and national objectives, and, in turn, understanding goals and objectives of other national forces.
- Creating the consensus required to enable joint and combined action to be undertaken in pursuit of shared goals and objectives.
- Maintaining the knowledge and resource base needed to envision desired future outcomes and negotiating to make them happen.

STRATEGIC PERFORMANCE REQUIREMENTS

The systems led by strategic leaders are ponderous and complex; they change slowly and only with great expenditure of energy. Within this protracted time horizon, strategic performance requirements include:

- Envisioning the roles the military can and should play in furthering national policy objectives both in the near (3-5 years) and far (20 or more years) term.
- Envisioning the future operational capability required to discharge responsibilities inherent in projected roles.
- Envisioning program efforts necessary to gain future capability, within the constraints of available resources and tolerable risk, while protecting a capability to perform defined roles.
- Building consensus within the organization, and with appropriate federal and international agencies, as necessary, to gain support for program efforts to enhance future capability.
- Achieving the commitment of the organization, federal agencies and the Congress to provide continued support for program efforts, and working to maintain that level of commitment.
- Initiating programs with far-distant completion dates that must be approved, funded, and institutionalized to be achieved.

STRATEGIC SKILLS AND ABILITIES

- Leaders at all levels require skills and abilities in three broad areas:
- Technical knowledge and skills required in the position, especially about executive information systems.
- Interpersonal/communication knowledge and skills.
- Conceptual skills which allow the strategic leader to make decisions and cope with the level of complexity associated with a particular position.

Specific leadership tasks to be performed differ from level to level in organizations. More importantly, the balance between technical, interpersonal/communication, and conceptual changes across levels, as shown in the figure above.

TECHNICAL SKILLS

Technical skills are required at all levels. However, at the lower levels, technical skills consist of using or operating a system; at upper levels, technical skills are more about employing systems within systems in order to create synergy. For example, at the lower levels, automation-technical skills might consist of what is required to install and maintain a network of computer systems. At the strategic level, they might be what is required to achieve the integration of an extensive automation system, e.g., WWMCS, into a multiservice command and control architecture. At the direct level, technical focus is on solving well-defined problems, and performing specific tasks and missions. At the strategic level, the focus is on solving ill-defined problems-dealing with intangibles and indirect effects that can impact on the organization. Many of the technical decisions facing these senior leaders require the assessment of organizational capabilities and an understanding of the intricacies of resourcing the total organization.

Structuring and re-structuring includes responsibility to develop new kinds of systems and organizations to provide future operational capability. These strategic decisions require major resource commitments that cannot easily be reversed (e.g., the decision to build an aircraft carrier). They also require calculation of the tradeoffs between opportunity and risk, with the knowledge that if decisions are wrong, the defense posture may be weakened.

New organizations may be developed in response to changing threat capabilities, technological enhancements, or resource changes. Within the Air Force, the development of composite wings is an excellent example. Within the Army, the creation of light divisions is another. Light divisions were formed to deal with a part of the spectrum of war that was not sufficiently covered, as well as to increase flexibility and mobility. However, such decisions carry substantial opportunity costs. In this case, the light divisions cost some heavy divisions.

INTERPERSONAL SKILLS

Because the relationships at the strategic level are much more lateral and without clear subordination than at lower levels, the interpersonal skills involved in persuasion, negotiation, and collaboration are more crucial. These processes operate on a base of effective reasoning and logic. Strategic leaders — especially when consequential decisions are being made — must be able to build the perception that their ideas are rational and deserve support. This demands that a consensus be built among contemporaries of equal rank and tenure, who might have competing interests and ideas of their own. To a very great extent, the capacity to build consensus depends as much on interpersonal skills as on political and conceptual skills.

The ceo must be able to lead subordinates who disagree with each other, and with him, while he retains his own convictions about the desirable direction for the corporation. This conviction may be tested over several years by the skepticism and dissent of other senior officers. But if the ceo and those who agree with his ideas for new direction are persistent, and if they are correct in their decisions so that improved results become apparent to others, then gradually they can rebuild a consensus about the "rightness" of the new ideas, and these will be incorporated into management's beliefs.

CONCEPTUAL AND DECISION SKILLS

Environmental Scanning. Scanning is purposeful search in the environment for relevant information. The skill lies in knowing what may be important, where to look, who to ask, and what to ask, to obtain needed information. Not all environmental scanning is done by strategic leaders. In today's environment, the task has such enormous scope that whole departments, branches, or organizations maintain environmental scans. For example, environmental scanning is one of the most central missions of the CIA.

In any organization the leader's unique capacity to commit the resources of his/her organization, opens many doors. One way a leader may add value is by using this "source mobility" to scan, interpret, and understand what is going on elsewhere that may have future relevance to his/her organization. Because many strategic courses of action require huge investments, they may unfold over substantial time frames. Therefore, to the extent early sensing of important events might allow timely action to gain a competitive advantage, the value of strategic scanning may be enormous.

Decision Making. In most strategic decision making where options are consequential, situations may not have clear cause-and-effect outcomes. Also, plausible courses of action may not yet have been developed or identified. In such cases, decision makers must isolate and identify key issues, visualize and predict potential problems, and formulate least-risk solutions. Additionally, at the strategic level, some problems may be so poorly structured that even one clearly workable course of action is not apparent. The complexity may be too great, and the consequences of possible courses of action too uncertain. For these complex and ill-structured problems, most organizations make use of an executive team, composed of the leader and his/her advisors. The assembled wisdom of the team members enables a broader scope to be considered, and permits a more careful analysis of the information relevant to the issue.

Reducing Complexity. The complexity and uncertainty of the strategic environment exceeds that which can be tolerated at the lower levels. Decision makers at these levels- nominally the mid-levels-develop concrete plans for allocating resources to operations. For example, the PPBES process is located at the mid-level of the various services; this process allocates major fiscal resources to long range concrete plans. However, this kind of resource allocation cannot be done intelligently without concept guidance from higher levels. The strategic role is to comprehend the complexity and uncertainty in the strategic environment, and then to set understandable azimuths for the mid-levels of the organization that can be used as a rational basis for resource allocation to operational units.

Systems Understanding. This is a capacity to visualize the interactive dynamics of large systems, including interdependencies, so that decisions taken in one area will not have adverse impact in another. Strategic decisions must balance conflicting expectations, requirements and values, over time. Systems-by virtue of strategic leadership-must deal with current requirements, conceive future requirements, and balance these requirements with current and future resources.

Understanding Indirect Effects. A strategic leader's frame of reference and vision must be broad enough to predict the indirect-second-, third-, and fourth-order effects of decisions. Without this capacity, changes in policy, regulation, or action may produce effects neither anticipated nor desired.

Future Focus and Vision. Strategic leaders must not only be future oriented, but must have a "sense of time" to envision long-term system-wide programs and schedules for their implementation. Time horizons from 12 years (for the Extended Planning Annex) to 20 years (for programs requiring major capital resources, such as the force modernization programs of the various services) are common in peacetime. The importance of vision at this level is that it provides the umbrella for defining specific and detailed programs at the organizational. As one four star general put it: It seems to me that you need a long range planning effort that is visionary (20-25 years). You would not want to commit yourself that that is the way it is going to look out there. But if you force a group to philosophize and postulate about what it will be out there, then it causes dialogue. ... Pretty soon, as you work down, you find yourself arriving at a consensus of what that vision might be, and it influences what your middle term goals might become.

Proactive Reasoning. Although strategic leaders must react to immediate, near-term events, they reduce the surprise factor by maintaining a "proactive stance." Being proactive is more than just seeing the future relevance of present-day events. In this proactive process, strategic leaders use their frames of reference as a tool to:

- Assess current position.
- Envision desired future capabilities.
- Determine the difference and define steps to close the difference.

- Initiate the future program.
- Monitor progress.

The Army's force modernization program is an example of executive action that illustrates this five-step process. To accomplish this task, senior leaders had to understand how to initiate and institutionalize a desired set of objectives so their successors would continue toward attainment as a natural course of events. Its prime initiator said it would not be fully complete "within the service lives" of the graduates, predictably an additional 10 to 15 years. His time horizon was a minimum of 20 to 25 years at the time the program was institutionalized.

This program was not formulated in response to a requirement. Rather, it was envisioned as a necessary step to create a force that could deal with future contingencies. It was a proactive effort requiring consensus for initiation, and a program for creating the critical mass of resources to get it started.

5

THE STRATEGIC LEADER AS AN INDIVIDUAL

DEVELOPING STRATEGIC LEADERS

Times of great change create an enduring need to do more leader development, more often. *—Sullivan and Harper*

DEVELOPMENT

An excellent concept of development comes from George B. Forsythe's article "The Preparation of Strategic Leaders." Forsythe argues that one's definition of development depends on the way one frames the concept. One frame is to take a learning perspective, and to consider leader development as "the acquisition of knowledge, skills, and values associated with-effective leadership." This type of development is "adding new tools to the tool box." When we identify strategic performance requirements, using this approach, we are specifying the new knowledge and skills strategic leaders will need.

But leadership at the strategic level is more than the acquisition of knowledge and skill; it consists of "qualitatively different ways of doing business." There is a second frame, and that is a developmental perspective. This perspective concentrates not on the knowledge acquired, but how to interpret it and what to do with it. "The developmental approach is concerned more with who the leader is and how the leader makes sense out of the world. It thus is concerned more with expanding frames of reference, perspective taking, building mental maps, and the development of conceptual capacity rather than with the acquisition of skills and knowledge. This process of leader development involves adaptive change in the leader's frame of reference as he or she advances to higher levels in the organization."

What provides the impetus for this adaptive change? Most often, it is the recognition that existing frames of reference are not sufficient to deal with the performance demands placed on the individual.

Think of it as being "outside your comfort zone." When a leader is confronted with VUCA characteristics of the strategic environment that existing frameworks cannot explain, there is an impetus for development and adaptive change to develop frameworks which can deal with the demands. How does one go about developing the new frames of reference and increased conceptual capacity? It involves two steps: self-assessment and development planning. Self-assessment will be discussed in the next chapter.

Development planning and self-assessment provide the insights that lead to adaptive change. Feedback from self-assessment either confirms things you already knew about yourself, or provides you new insights. If you stop at that point, however, you have not begun the process of growth and change. It's only when you commit to development that the real value of the assessment process is realized. The critical question to focus on is: *"How can I maximize my personal and professional growth?"*

Development involves life-long change, with each part of life having attendant satisfaction and challenges.The first step in planning for development is self-assessment. The self-assessment process, however, goes beyond the use of feedback assessment instruments. When you engage in self-assessment, look at all the areas of your life. The rationale is simple: your life is an integrated whole, a system. Your goals, aspirations, challenges, and opportunities in one area will have an impact on other areas. One key question to address in development is, "How can I achieve a balance in my life?"

PROFESSION

What is going on in your professional life? That you have been selected to attend ICAF means that you are among the high performers from your service or agency. You are well established in your profession, and have moved into the middle management ranks.

Most of your experience has been at the direct leadership or "operator" level. By direct leadership we mean the level of leadership where interactions are at the personal, face-to-face level. In the services, direct leadership extends up through the lieutenant colonel/commander level. When you can interact with members of your command, you're operating at the direct leadership level. Many of you also may have had staff assignments or assignments in a functional area of expertise (such as maintenance or logistics). Most of you will not have had the opportunity to serve at the strategic decision making level in major commands or on joint staffs. Having reached the top of the direct level of leadership, you need to be ready to transition to a higher level.

There are two different areas where the road may take you in the near future in your profession. Some of you will go on to command at the colonel/captain level, which may mean moving into a more indirect leadership role. At this mid, or organizational, leadership level, the performance requirements and demands of the position are often different than at the direct level (think back to Stratified Systems Theory). Many of you also will be operating on a high level staff such as a major command staff, a DOD agency, or on the Joint Staff at the strategic level. Part of your development must prepare you to operate at this level.

Civilian students may have had a different career path up to this point, but also are at a transition point. Many have been functional specialists. Those who are acquisition specialists, logistics specialists, budget analysts, or systems analysts may have spent careers in a narrow specialty. You also are at a transition point because you need to move to a higher organizational level, advance in your profession, and broaden your frame of reference.

SELF

What are you likely to be going through, individually and personally, at this stage in your life? Gail Sheehy's fascinating and insightful book, *New Passages: Mapping Your Life Across Time*, is organized around the stages of life and the passages that occur between those stages. One of her assertions is that the traditional life cycle we took for granted does not apply today. There have been such dramatic changes in how long people live that the old markers of age are outdated. To understand what is likely to be occurring in your life at a particular age, your frame of reference has to be your generation. You can't judge what is happening in your life by examining your parents' experiences; yours will be entirely different.

Sheehy predicts that at about age 45 most of us will go through a transition from what she calls First Adulthood to Second Adulthood. She calls this transition middlescence, in a play on words on adolescence. Her theme is that with increasing longevity, those in their 40s can look forward to an entire new adulthood from 45 to 85+. Ms. Sheehy views this move into second adulthood as an opportunity for tremendous growth and development. No longer should we view reaching our late '40s as the beginning of a long decline into old age, but rather the beginning of a new adult life that can be just as productive as our first adult life.

BALANCE

"How can we achieve a balance in our lives?" What should have emerged from reflecting on what is going on in your life is that there are multiple demands, challenges, and opportunities. How can you pursue multiple goals in different life areas simultaneously? The answer is, you can't. What normally happens is we pursue goals in one area at the expense of the other areas, and our lives get out of balance in either our profession, family, community, or self.

The balance most of us find the hardest to achieve is the balance between profession and family. The demands of the profession for many are such that there is no time left to spend with one's family, or at least not sufficient quality time. You may be experiencing a problem of balance at ICAF. This year represents an opportunity to reflect, learn, and grow. But you also may have had expectations that you could take time off from the demands of your normal jobs and get reacquainted with your families this year. How do you achieve a balance, take the opportunities this year provides for professional growth, yet also grow in other areas? The only way to resolve this dilemma is through prioritizing. Establish goals in each of your life areas, then determine which are the most important. If you find that your life is out of balance, trade offs in one area may provide the opportunity for achieving goals in other areas.

SOME KEY QUESTIONS

In addition to asking yourself how you can achieve a balance in your life, there are some key questions. One of these is, "What are the major challenges I will face in the future?" A large part of development is preparing yourself to face anticipated major challenges. For example, we have suggested that one major professional challenge may be to prepare yourself to operate in the strategic arena at a higher organizational level. An example of a major challenge in the family area may be caring for aging parents. An essential first step in planning for development and growth is anticipating the challenges one will face in the future.

Another question to ask is, "What can I control?" Some things in your life are out of your control. You can't reverse the aging process. However, you definitely can make lifestyle choices that can slow down (or accelerate) how rapidly you age. And, in the professional area, you may not have much say about where you will be assigned, but you can control how well prepared you will be for a particular assignment. An essential part of development planning is determining where you have choices and when you can exercise some control over your life.

LOOKING INTO THE FUTURE

"Where do I want to be in the future?" This is the second step in planning your life journey: envisioning the future. Shift your attention to tomorrow. Look to the future, and ask yourself,

"Where do I want to be in 5 years? In 10 years? In 20 years?" Remember Sheehy's conceptualization of the Second Adulthood as extending from age 45 to 85+. What do you want to do in your second adulthood? Essential to the successful passage into second adulthood is viewing the passage as opening up possibilities and choices, not limiting opportunities and restricting choices.

Increasing longevity has given us opportunities that our parents never had: the time to build an entire second productive adult life. This provides tremendous opportunities for growth, if we can only avail ourselves of those opportunities. Determine where you could be in five or ten years, or where you would like to be.

Skeptics are saying, "Why envision a future that you can't achieve?" If envisioning the future is dreaming about unachievable outcomes, then it is a waste of time. But if you look more closely at those who achieve their dreams, you will find that they didn't stop with dreaming about where they'd like to be in the future. They asked themselves, "What can I do to get there and reach my goals?" They then developed and implemented a plan to achieve what they wanted to accomplish.

COMMITTING TO DEVELOPMENT

This brings us back to a few more critical questions you need to ask. First, "Do I really want to commit to development?" There are substantial opportunities for growth and development during your year at ICAF. McCall, Lombardo, and Morrison, in *The Lessons of Experience: How Successful Executives Develop on the Job,* present a model for development which involves three choices.

The first choice is to recognize your shortcomings or identify areas where there is room for growth and improvement. All of us have strengths and weaknesses, and if we're going to overcome our weak areas and our shortcomings, the first choice we must make is to identify those weaknesses. Figure 1: the authors believe that sooner or later you will be forced to confront your weaknesses, because they eventually will be revealed in one way or another.

CHOICE: Finding out about shortcomings.		<——> AVOID
Wait for a castastrophe to reveal a weakness	**OR**	**Actively pursue an accurate protrait of self**
- SOONER OR LATER (BIG MISTAKE).		- JUMP INTO NEW SITUATIONS
- SOONER OR LATER (MISSED		- DIG FOR INFORMATION.
PROMOTION, NEGATIVE		- SEEK FEEDBACK
APPRAISAL, DEMOTION,		- INTROSPECT
TERMINATION).		

The second choice is to accept responsibility for your shortcomings. If you deny any responsibility for your weaknesses, then there's no reason to try and do anything about them. You must accept responsibility for your weaknesses and determine their causes if you're going to overcome them.

CHOICE: Accepting responsibility Diagnosis of Shortcomings		<——> DENY
RESULT OF A LACK OF	OR	RESULT OF PERSONALITY, LIMITED
KNOWLEDGE,		ABILITY, OR SITUATIONAL MISFIT?
EXPERIENCE, OR SKILLS?		

The third choice is what to do about your weaknesses. The authors suggest four types of strategies based on the diagnosis of why the weakness exists: build new strengths, anticipate situations, compensate, and change self.

CHOICE: What to do about it about <—>IGNORE

build new strengths	anticipate situations	compensate	change self
find situations where learning new things is essential.	ask "dumb" questions.	avoid certain situations.	intensive counseling, coaching.
find ways to get help and support while learning.	seek advice, counsel.	delegate to others.	personal change effort.
	spend time learning.	choose staff who cover weaknesses.	change just enough to get by.
	use others' expertise.	change the situation.	

Committing to development means recognizing areas for development, taking responsibility for growth in those areas, and forming a plan on how to effect that development. If you are committed to development, the final two questions are:

- How can I best use my year at ICAF?
- How can I maximize my opportunities for personal and professional growth?

The answers you reach to these questions will determine if this year really becomes a year of transition, growth, development, and change.

CONCLUSION

As we stated at the beginning of the chapter, the ICAF experience is about development. As you've gone through the chapter, we hope it stimulated some thought about development, and helped you think about the question we initially asked you to focus on: "How can I maximize my personal and professional growth during my year at ICAF?" As you continue through the Strategic Leadership and Decision Making Course and the ICAF year, we hope you will continue to focus on development, and take every opportunity you can to truly maximize your professional and personal growth.

EXECUTIVE ASSESSMENT

In the small unit he had commanded, everyone knew him, loved him, and trusted him, and he was a success at his work. But with a larger unit, his mistrustfulness, his air of gloom, and his silence prevented him from being successful. Events proved clearly that he was only another example that every leader has his limitations, which are fixed not only by his intelligence and his learning, but to a great extent by his personality.

First, organizational effectiveness springs from an executive ability to adapt to a strategic environment and integrate functions and processes within the organization. Second, effective executive performance is a function of executive flexibility. This flexibility emerges from the integration of cognitive, behavioral, and dispositional characteristics. The individual qualities necessary for leadership success at the strategic level are grounded in high information-processing demands and the social complexity that define the domain of organizational leaders.

The intended outcome of integrating an individual's cognitive, behavioral, and dispositional characteristics is to provide a mosaic of strengths and weaknesses, juxtaposed with performance requirements specified by Stratified Systems Theory (SST), to provide a clear picture of developmental growth.

While tactical and technical, interpersonal, and conceptual skills are required at any level of leadership, conceptual skills and flexibility overshadow all other skills necessary at upper levels of management (Katz & Kahn 1978).

EXECUTIVE ASSESSMENT PROGRAM

The executive assessment program at ICAF includes four major sources of information. Each source provides one view of important attributes, views, orientations, or preferences. When the separate pieces are integrated, they provide a basis-a personalized mosaic-for assessing where you are in your development. This facilitates charting a course that will accelerate your developmental process. A broad overview of these four sources of information follows.

MYERS-BRIGGS TYPE INDICATOR (MBTI[r]). Leaders have preferences for certain types of information for sources they trust to give that information, and for processes they use to come to a decision. Some prefer to deal with hard facts (what you see is what you get) and to come to a decision quickly (figure it out and get on with it). Others prefer to probe for underlying dynamics, to understand the "big" picture, and to look for contingencies before executing a given course of action.

These preferences differ, although it may not be evident how big these differences are, how they influence the decision making process, and how well a unit's people communicate with one another. The MBTI[r] will provide important insights in this area.

STRATEGIC LEADERSHIP DEVELOPMENT INVENTORY (SLDI). The SLDI provides you a thorough assessment of three broad areas (by former superiors, former peers, and former subordinates) important to strategic leadership effectiveness: *cognitive skills*, *positive personal attributes*, and *negative personal attributes*. SLDI highlights the importance of cognitive skills in dealing with the volatility, uncertainty, complexity, and ambiguity of the strategic environment.

A high ratio of positive to negative personal attributes facilitates trust and loyalty among leaders and subordinates at all levels. A low ratio of positive to negative is a barrier to effectiveness that may be hard to overcome. The SLDI will give you some insights as to how you see yourself, and how others see you in these three areas.

MANSPEC. The MBTI(r) measures preference for information source and how judgments are made. The SLDI is designed to provide feedback from others on conceptual factors that are important for success. But, there are other important factors, factors that fall into what we call "personality." There is ample evidence that personality traits influence strategic leadership potential and ability.

While personality is probably not as important as conceptual skill, personality deficiencies can be fatal if they interfere with an ability to forge strategic consensus and broad-based support for decisions. In recent years, evidence has accumulated in regard to personality dimensions. There is every reason to believe they are important for strategic leaders (McGee, Jacobs, Killcullen, & Barber 1996).

MANSPEC (MANDATA, 1994) is a battery of several tests designed to assess personality dimensions important to interpersonal skills, conflict handling, and for determining how to function as a member of a group. The MANSPEC themes are remarkably close to the "Big Five" dimensions (see Barrick & Mount, 1991; McCrae & Costa, 1987; Costa & McCrae, 1992; Hogan, Curphy, & Hogan, 1994).

CAREER PATH APPRECIATION (CPA). Career Path Appreciation (CPA) is a one-on-one interview to tap conceptual skills and to predict future growth of conceptual skills. Originally developed by Stamp (1978; 1988), it provides two estimates: One is current conceptual capacity or ability; the second is potential for growth in conceptual capacity or ability.

Administering a complete CPA is time and labor intensive. For those reasons, ICAF developed and uses a modified version of the CPA. Although not as comprehensive, the MCPA is valid and reliable. If you would prefer the more comprehensive assessment provided by a CPA, see your instructor.

THE "BIG FIVE"

SURGENCY: A COMBINATION OF ASSERTIVENESS, PERSISTENCE, AND DOMINANCE.

AGREEABLENESS: INTERPERSONAL EFFECTIVENESS, ABILITY TO INTERACT

HARMONIOUSLY WITH OTHERS.

CONSCIENTIOUSNESS: RESPONSIBLY DEALING WITH OBLIGATIONS, BOTH STATED AND IMPLICIT.

EMOTIONAL STABILITY: STABILITY OF AFFECT UNDER PRESSURE OR IN CRISIS SITUATIONS.

INTELLECTANCE: OPEN-MINDED ATTITUDE, CONCEPTUAL GRASP, CAPACITY FOR CREATIVITY, ORIGINALITY, AND/OR RISK TAKING.

THE MYERS-BRIGGS TYPE INDICATOR(r) (MBTI(r))

One of the most widely-used and best known assessment instruments, the MBTI(r), measures personality preferences in four areas:

- Extraversion-Introversion. This defines the focus of interests, and where to look for mental stimulation. A score strongly toward the E side of the distribution indicates a *preference* for externally generated stimuli. Other people and groups of people are a source of energy. A strong I score, on the other hand, indicates a preference for contemplation and reflection. A strong E is characterized by breadth of interests, while a strong I is characterized by depth of interests.

- Sensing-Intuitive. This describes a preference for gathering information, becoming aware of things, and seeing what is in a specific situation. A strong S is interested in what is real, immediate, practical, and observable- what can be seen, touched, and examined- the evidence of the senses. By contrast, a strong N is future-oriented, conceptual — interested in theory, possibilities, and the meanings in patterns of events.
- Thinking-Feeling. This describes a preference for the method information is used to make decisions. A strong T is detached, logical, analytical, and task-oriented. A strong F approaches decisions with a concern about other persons who may be impacted by the decision. A strong T is likely to emphasize task and mission; a strong F is likely to emphasize people concerns.
- Judging-Perceiving. This describes a person's preference for dealing with life events, including decision making situations. A strong J values orderliness, careful planning, scheduling, and moving quickly to a decision- in general, behavior that introduces structure, reduces uncertainty, and brings closure to open-ended situations. A strong P, on the other hand, is curious, flexible, and spontaneous, preferring less structured situations that present a variety of options.
- Preferences on these four dimensions affect how decision makers approach their work. As the strategic environment is characterized by volatility, uncertainty, complexity, and ambiguity-and since many strategic decisions have a high risk-the application of some of these preferences may seriously impair the effectiveness of decisions.
- E-I. There seems to be equal advantage to strategic leaders from both extroversion and introversion, although extraversion is slightly favored. About equal numbers of each appear in the highest ranks of large scale organizations. And the data from ICAF's administration of the MBTI(r) suggests a roughly symmetrical distribution of E-l scores in former classes.

Scores have been converted to a single dimension around a center point of 100. For example, an E score of 20 would be shown as 80 in the E-I preference figure. An I preference of 20 would be shown as 120.) There is evidence in the strategic leadership literature suggesting an advantage from some degree of preference on the other dimensions.

- S-N. A preference for S clearly should be advantageous at lower organizational levels, where leadership tasks are direct and "hands on" in nature. It seems logical that some preference for N would be an advantage at the more senior levels, and might be critical for strategic decision making. This preference is associated with future-orientation and interest in possibilities, concepts, and intangibles. This is descriptive of the strategic envionment.
- J-P. A strong J preference has high survival value at lower organizational levels where there is low uncertainty, high structure, minimal decision discretion, and frequent time pressure. However, it has decreasing value at higher levels, because uncertainty, complexity, and decision discretion all increase. A strategic leader must be able to close decisively when the situation demands, yet, until then, remain open, curious about all possibilities and alternatives. As in T-F, it would appear that a balance-a flexibility in the approach as situations differ from one another-would have good survival value. But an examination of the distribution of student scores from previous classes shows a bias toward the J end of the dimension (17 points below the theoretical midpoint of 100) that is almost as strong as the bias toward T, but with a strange twist: the class mean is biased toward the low (J) end of the distribution, but the really extreme scores are at the high (P) end. This suggests development needs at both ends of the curve. Those at the low end need to learn to withhold closure a bit longer (e.g., remain open to new, possibly conflicting information); this is the *divergent* part of strategic decision making.

Those at the high end need to learn how to manage time so as to reach closure at the point of peak action; this is the *convergent* part of strategic decision making.

IMPLICATIONS-DEVELOPMENTAL NEEDS. It is not surprising that there is a bias toward S, T, and J. Leadership performance requirements experienced by the vast majority of students have been oriented toward "hands on," direct responsibilities.

However, the future will hold different requirements. There are several implications for planning future development. First, it is likely that the former classes are representative of future classes. This means that there will be a number of students with extreme scores. A student with an extreme score (35 points below or above the midpoint of the scale) on any dimensions should re-evaluate his/her flexibility to deal with situations demanding actions contrary to the student's expressed preference. Vulnerabilities indicated by strong preferences would include the following:

- Strong E. A possible lack of focus to achieve depth in a technical area, particularly one that requires intense individual study effort.
- Strong I. A possible deficiency in interpersonal skills, coupled with a possible assessment by others of cold interpersonal relations andinteraction, if coupled with a strong T.
- Strong S. A possible tardiness in developing the abstract conceptual thinking skills and complex frames of reference required in mid- and top-level assignments. Possible assessment by others of a lack of depth. Tendency to micromanage, if coupled with a strong T.
- Strong N. Possible deficiency in situational sensitivity, required to deal decisively with developing situations. Possible assessment by others of a lack of focus, and less than desired reliability in completing assigned tasks.
- Strong T. Possible over-emphasis on mission at all costs, coupled with assessment by others as uncaring. Tendency to micromanage, if coupled with a strong S.

- Strong F. Possible over-emphasis on people concerns, with possible assessment by others as not being "tough" enough.
- Strong J. Possible over-emphasis on scheduling and conformity to set procedures; tendency to come to a decision too quickly without considering contingencies or exploring options. Possible assessment by others, if coupled with a strong S, as being rigid and not very creative.
- Strong P. Possible vacillation in a decision situation, considering options until the point of decision has passed. Possible assessment by others as not being sufficiently focused on task completion.

The issue is not that any one pattern of preferences is either "good" or "bad" but rather that extreme preferences indicate a lack of balance, constituting vulnerability. The developmental objective is to identify any lack of balance and formulate a plan that will result in skill-building. A large part of the SLDM course is focused on how to use self-assessment information for this purpose.

THE STRATEGIC LEADER DEVELOPMENT INVENTORY (SLDI)

Except for the SLDI, all of the assessment instruments described in this chapter rely on your assessment of yourself. The Johari Window illustrates the challenges to communication effectiveness, and thus to the potential for strategic consensus, that blind spots might create.

THE JOHARI WINDON

	YOU KNOW	YOU DON'T KNOW
I KNOW	Potential for rational discussion/ negotiation	Potential for self-concealment/mistrust
I DON'T KNOW	Potential for Avoidance/Poor communication	Potential for Blunder

SLDI CONTENT. The SLDI measures three broad categories of factors: conceptual skills and abilities, positive attributes, and negative attributes. Each is important in its own right because, as critical leadership tasks become more complex at more senior levels, leaders must encourage and empower teamwork among subordinates and contemporaries in conceptual capacity and skill.

The factor structure of the SLDI is discussed in detail in *A Guide to the Strategic Leader Development Inventory* (Jacobs 1996).

Three perspectives are important when interpreting the SLDI. One is how you stand in relation to others in your self-assessments. A second is how your self-assessments compare with those of others, particularly if one "source" is substantially higher or lower than the others. A third is whether there are "peaks" and "valleys" that might indicate particular strengths or weaknesses.

FACTOR STRUCTURE

1997 STRATEGIC LEADER DEVELOPMENT INVENTORY

Conceptual Skills and Abilities	**Positive Attributes**	**Negative Attributes**
Professional Competence	Interpersonal Competence	Technical Incompetence
Conceptual Flexibility	Empowering Subordinates	Self-serving/ Unethical
Future Vision	Team Performance Facilitation	Micromanager
Conceptual Competence	Objectivity	Arrogant
Political Sensitivity	Initiative/ Commitment	Explosive/Abusive
		Inaccessible

MANSPEC

MANSPEC (MANDATA 1994) is an assessment system with an integrated battery of questionnaires and tests. The system provides automatic scoring and interpretation of results. In the interpretation, it integrates the assessment results and yields a range of objective, jargon-free reports. This was a part of the automated battery you took at the beginning of your ICAF year, and will be a part of your individual feedback, providing information on:

- The roles (e.g., consulting, new ideas) you prefer for yourself in team decision manking.
- Your preferred operational style-how you go about doing business (e.g., planning).
- How you handle conflict (e.g., challenging, resolving, defusing).
- Where you see yourself in dimensions such as risk avoidance, ingenuity, and persistence.
- Your professional/managerial style-a "suitability for high levels of management" scale.
- The kinds of vocational activities (e.g., persuasive, analytical, creative) you find most attractive.

In condensing the number of personality variables, five major patterns,, derived from a factor analysis are reflected in the MANSPEC (MANDATA, 1994) data. These patterns may be interpreted as the "Big Five" personality factors: Surgency, Intellectance, Conscientiousness, Agreeableness, and Emotional Stability.

Surgency. This pattern consists of high scores on driving, dominance, challenging, and professional/managerial style, as well as low scores on supportive traits. Surgency is significantly related to MBTI(r) preferences -introversion and thinking.

SURGENCY

- HIGH ON DRIVING
- HIGH ON DOMINANCE
- HIGH ON CHALLENGING

- HIGH ON PROFESSIONAL MANAGERIAL STYLE
- LOW ON SUPPORTIVE
- RELATED TO INTROVERSION
- RELATED TO THINKING

This pattern identifies a strongly competitive person who may or may not be a team player, but who wants to win. This person may not be sympathetic with someone who needs personal support. The strength of a person with this pattern is that he or she is strongly motivated to get to the top, and will drive relentlessly to get there. However, there may also be vulnerabilities. A person with this pattern may pursue win-lose (as opposed to win-win) strategies; win-lose is detrimental to team building or consensus decision making. This pattern also may produce a leader who drives his or her subordinates too hard and for too long, or for the wrong reasons. By contrast, the reverse of this pattern may identify a leader who avoids risk; for example, when competing for resources for his or her unit.

Intellectance. This pattern consists of high scores on creative activities, new ideas, ingenuity, and catalyst, coupled with a low score on practical attributes. This factor is called openness or open to experience. Intellectance is related to the MBTI(r) preferences-intuitive and perceiving.

INTELLECTANCE

- HIGH ON CREATIVE ACTIVITIES
- HIGH ON NEW IDEAS
- HIGH ON INGENUITY
- HIGH ON CATALYST
- LOW ON PRACTICAL
- RELATED TO INTUITIVE
- RELATED TO PERCEIVING

Someone with this pattern can think "outside the box" and enjoys doing that. He or she looks for new experience, is open to options, and can handle a degree of uncertainty. This pattern also identifies a leader who is likely to be successful at higher levels. The strength of a person with this pattern is the ability to see options others might miss-to create a longer-range vision of where the organization should be going. A possible vulnerability is a tendency to miss details.

Conscientiousness. This pattern identifies a person who is systematic, cautious, and possibly rigid. It consists of six MANSPEC (MANDATA, 1994) scores: planning, stimulus control, serious-mindedness, risk control, persistence, and details. Conscientiousness, sometimes referred to as methodical, is related to the MBTI(r) preferences- introversion, sensing, and judging.

CONSCIENTIOUSNESS

- HIGH ON PLANNING
- HIGH ON STIMULUS CONTROL
- HIGH ON SERIOUS-MINDEDNESS
- HIGH ON RISK CONTROL
- HIGH ON PERSISTENCE
- HIGH ON DETAILS
- RELATED TO INTROVERISON
- RELATED TO SENSING
- RELATED TO JUDGING

A leader with this pattern wants a high degree of predictability in his/her environment. Extensive and detailed plans are one way to get it. Leaders with this pattern are hard workers. The strength of a person with this pattern is a determination to get the job done. A vulnerability is a tendency toward micromanaging the work of subordinates, a fault visible to peers and subordinates alike.

Agreeableness. Five MANSPEC (MANDATA, 1994) scores contribute to this pattern: high on affiliation, high on caring activities, high on persuasive activities, high on consulting, and low on critical judgment. Agreeableness is related to the MBTI(r) preferences-extraversion and feeling.

This pattern could be called "likes people," and suggests a person who has high regard for and enjoys being with other people. A strength of a person with this pattern is outgoing behavior and inter-personal interaction, a necessary part of consensus building. A possible vulnerability is that this person may not focus on the task at hand.

AGREEABLENESS

- HIGH ON AFFILIATION
- HIGH ON CARING ACTIVITIES
- HIGH ON PERSUASIVE ACTIVITIES
- HIGH ON CONSULTING
- LOW ON CRITICAL JUDGE
- RELATED TO EXTRAVERSION
- RELATED TO FEELING

Emotional stability. Three MANSPEC (MANDATA 1994) scores contribute to this pattern: high on openness, high on energy, and high on mood stability. A person scoring high on these three MANSPEC (MANDATA 1994) variables is likely to be objective and helpful in facilitating the work of his/her organization. This factor sometimes is called "even-tempered." Emotiontional stability is related to the MBTI preferences-extraversion and thinking.

EMOTIONAL STABILITY

- HIGH ON MOOD STABILITY
- HIGH ON OPENNESS
- HIGH ON ENERGY
- RELATED TO EXTRAVERSION
- RELATED TO THINKING

A strength of a high scorer would be that subordinates would keep him/her better informed, whether the news is good or bad. There is no apparent vulnerability to high scores. A clear vulnerability with low scores is the perception of being arrogant, self-serving, and possibly unethical.

Developmental Implications. The table of strengths and weaknesses is a good guide for how to use MANSPEC (MANDATA, 1994) information (see following page). Strategic leaders must be competitive. They also must be creative, providing new ideas and creative vision to inspire and stimulate their organizations toward future objectives only dimly seen. (To some degree, they must be methodical but creativity and visioning skills are more important than being methodical.) Finally, strategic leaders must genuinely like people. They will have an advantage in building consensus decisions if they are even tempered.

MODIFIED CAREER PATH APPRECIATION (MCPA)

A complete CPA is a work sample in the sense of observing how decision making is being exercised. A CPA assesses how the person is coping with complexity. The CPA taps into thinking processes, concept formation, comfort with ambiguity and uncertainty, insight and intuition, characteristic strategies, and feelings about work.

The MCPA was developed at ICAF as a labor-saving surrogate for the CPA. The MCPA uses the part of the CPA (Phrases) which accounts for the largest amount of significant variance in the CPA rating of conceptual capacity of senior service college students.

What good is the MCPA? Stamp (1988) reported a longitudinal study of 182 lower and middle level managers who were followed up 4 to 14 years after initial assessment. The initial assessment predicted their current level within their organizations with a correlation of .79, proving this assessment has significant predictive validity of strategic leadership potential. This strategic leadership potential is based partly upon the ability to cope with complexity, concepts, formation, ambiguity and uncertainty.

CONCEPTUAL CAPACITY IS STRONGLY RELATED TO:*

- CREATIVITY
- GENERAL INTELIGENCE
- PROBLEM-SOLVING ABILITY
- INTELLECTANCE
- EMOTIONAL STABILITY

- MBTI(r) INTUITIVE
- MBTI(r) PERCEIVING

* Reported in McIntyre, et. al. 1993

A person with high levels of conceptual capacity-a key dimension of strategic leadership ability-will be intelligent, intuitive, open-minded, flexible, and emotionally stable. These personality traits will yield problem solving abilities within a VUCA environment.

FOCAL POINTS FOR INDIVIDUAL DEVELOPMENT. The study of the leader as an individual is based on the premise that growth in both mental capacity and problem-solving skills continues for most people throughout their adult lives. This development depends on clear self-understanding of strengths and weaknesses and the motivation to grow.

MENTAL MAPS. The decision maker's mental map (frame of reference) is an important tool. Complex mental maps are like brick buildings. Each piece of information and experience placed within an overarching structure provides strength. Several elements of the ICAF self-assessment point to mental map-building. They are the MBTI(r) S-N and J-P scores (moderate N and P), the SLDI (all the conceptual skills factors), and MANSPEC (in particular, intellectance and emotional stability).

Clearly, motivation is very important. If the assessment process shows low inclination toward activities that build complex mental maps, it is time to re-think professional and life objectives. Uncomplicated mental maps make for uncomplicated lives, but neither is characteristic of the strategic environment and strategic leader performance requirements. This is where motivation comes in.

SKILL BUILDING. Strategic leaders are extraordinarily well-rounded in the skills they bring to the demands of their jobs. It is a mistake to think they were born that way. They have worked long and hard to develop the tools and skills they are using, focusing not only on what they started out with, but also on what new ones they needed to become more proficient. For example, writing is a skill. Some find it easier than others to write well. But, everyone can develop better writing skills with motivation and practice. So it is with all the skills of strategic leadership.

The essence of skill building is identifying experience, activities, or studies to develop weak skills. In all cases, the most important ingredient after an area of skill deficiency has been identified, is commitment to improve in that area.

SUMMARY AND INTEGRATION: DERAILMENT

What happens if you don't respond to the results of your executive assessment in terms of your subsequent professional development and leadership performance? It will be a phenomenon called "derailment." Derailment can take many forms-dismissal, transfer, early retirement, plateauing, or death. The causes of derailment are linked to failures to develop executive flexibility. Evidence of these failures include:

- Cognitive versus Technical Skills: Technical achievement at lower levels becomes a weakness at higher levels if it leads to over-confidence and arrogance. Unsuccessful executives are unable to shift from technical skill requirements to cognitive skill requirements at the strategic level. Successful executives have a broader perspective when dealing with complex strategic problems.
- Emotional Stability: Executives who derail are less able to handle pressure, are prone to moodiness and angry outbursts, and are inconsistent in their behavior. Successful executives are calm, confident, and consistent during crises.
- Interpersonal Skills: Executives who derail tend to be insensitive, abrasive, selfish, inconsiderate, manipulative, offensive, and/or intimidating. Successful executives are sensitive, tactful, diplomatic, and considerate.
- Defensiveness: Executives who derail tend to be more defensive about failure. They try to cover up mistakes and/or blame other people, especially subordinates. Successful executives admit their mistakes, accept

responsibility, fix the problem, and move on without dwelling on the failure.

- Integrity: Successful executives have strong integrity. In contrast, derailed executives are too ambitious about advancing their own careers at the expense of others or the organization. They are considered less dependable because they betray a trust or break a promise.

RESULTS OF DERAILMENT

- DISMISSAL
- TRANSFER
- EARLY RETIREMENT
- PLATEAUED
- DEATH

When you have completed your individual feedback session with an SLDM faculty member, you should have gained an excellent foundation for understanding yourself, your strengths and weaknesses, your professional and life goals, and your developmental needs. Your development should be aimed at:

- BROADENING YOUR FRAMES OF REFERENCE FOR STRATEGIC DECISION MAKING AND HOW YOU VIEW THE DECISION ENVIRONMENT.
- CONTINUALLY GAINING GREATER INSIGHT INTO YOUR OWN THOUGHT PROCESSES .
- DEVELOPING MODELS AND LANGUAGE FOR "THINKING ABOUT HOW YOU THINK."

STRATEGIC LEADERSHIP: SOME KEY POINTS

(Thurman, 1991)

- "BRIDGE" ACROSS AMBIGUITY AND UNCERTAINTY ...
- Analytic work not enough.
- Synthesis skills are essential.
- BE VERY AWARE OF SELF AND OTHERS AROUND YOU ...
- People process information differently.

- SENSE ORGANIZATION AND PERSONAL DYNAMICS ...
- Relationships with others.
- Expectations of others for you.
- ABILITY TO CONCEPTUALIZE ...
- Essence of the process.
- Step back — get the meaning.
- SEEK BROAD CONSENSUS, CONFLICTING ADVICE ...
- More workable decisions.
- Better prepared for disagreement.
- People of good will have differing opinions.
- HAVE BAG OF SKILLS AND COMPETENCIES ...
- Sense of personal efficacy.
- Appetite for knowledge.
- Competence on the boundaries.
- ABSOLUTE PERSONAL INTEGRITY ...
- Total reliability as seen by others.
- Unquestioned ethics.
- PRESUMPTION OF GOOD INTENT ...
- Conflict abounds everywhere.
- Understand where people are coming from.
- Must understand transient events.
- BE DECISIVE IN THE FACE OF UNCERTAINTY ...
- When in charge, take charge.
- Have faith in the people around you.

6

STRATEGIC THINKING

PERSPECTIVE

How do executive-level leaders regard decision making and thinking at the strategic level?

At this level, there is a great premium on anticipation. If I am not drawing on my experiences and an intuitive sense of understanding of the situation, then I am not functioning as a four-star. One of my first requirements is to be a good anticipator. Number two is that at the four-star level, if I am anticipating right, I can shape issues, rather than issues shaping me. When anticipating, I have to have an intuitive judgment that says, "These things are important." The anticipation and shaping (of) issues are what this job is all about (Stewart, 1993).

Officers who succeed at the three- and four-star levels have the individual capacity to cope with complexity, amorphousness, and uncertainty. You do not have to have everything laid out for you. You have the resiliency and ingenuity to adapt to new and different circumstances (Franks, 1994).

The most important phase in the exercise of strategic leadership is the front-end work. The in-depth, serious thinking by a leader and his or her team results in the creation of an intellectual framework for the future. Imaging the future first takes place in the mind of the leader and then must be communicated throughout the organization. Intellectual change guides the physical changes that manifest transformation. Without the tough up-front work of intellectual change, physical change will be unfocused, random, and unlikely to succeed (Sullivan & Harper, 1996).

Bloom's Taxonomy of Learning

UPPER LEVEL THINKING SKILLS

- EVALUATION
- SYNTHESIS
- ANALYSIS

LOWER LEVEL THINKING SKILLS

- APPLICATION
- UNDERSTANDING
- KNOWLEDGE

This is your last educational opportunity before entering the strategic leadership environment, and your best opportunity to explore the vast strategic environment that lies before you. This SLDM curriculum is designed to help you develop skills for thinking and functioning in an environment where there are no right answers, and only a range of solutions, some of which work better than others when implemented. Your focus is on developing your higher order thinking skills.

The strategic environment requires leaders to develop both individual and team thinking skills. It is important to differentiate between individual and collective thinking. In the Consensus Team Decision-Making Model (CTDM), you will find a paradigm for a team approach to strategic thinking. This collaborative problem-solving approach is what you will participate in and manage as your careers progress. A group/team approach to decision making requires you to adopt a different frame of reference about your own work in relation to others'.

CAPACITIES VS. KNOWLEDGE AND SKILLS

The hypotheses for understanding executive development was presented at a U. S. Army Conference on Strategic Leadership. This theory suggests that executive development should be divided into two major areas. The first area accents technical, intellectual, and inter-personal knowledge and skills. The second area, one that is of particular interest to us, stresses capacities. Capacities include perspective-taking, visioning, and metacognition.

Traditional military education emphasizes knowledge and skills as most important.

This focus may just be the primary reasons for the huge success of leadership at the direct leadership level in the defense community. However, research evidence suggests that capacities are essential for the executive leader at the strategic level. This is not to say that knowledge and skills are unimportant, only that the importance of capacity increases significantly at the strategic levels.

SELF-AWARENESS

Executive development efforts such as the SLDM course are designed with the belief that enhanced self awareness leads to higher levels of performance.

Self awareness is defined as the ability to reflect on and accurately assess one's own behaviors and skills as they are manifested on the job. It is an important ability for achieving leadership excellence.

Rarely are self assessments and assessment by others completely congruent. We call the lack of agreement between self assessment and assessment by others "the coefficient of self delusion." This coefficient can be positive (when others' ratings are higher than self ratings) or it can be negative (when others' ratings are lower than self ratings).

The positive coefficient of self delusion occurs with people who either are genuinely humble or may be trying to avoid over-inflating their self ratings for a variety of reasons.

The negative coefficient of self delusion usually occurs with people who are not conscious of the impact of their behaviors on others or they have an inflated sense of self. In either case, it is important to investigate why the assessment gap exists and reflect upon ways that it can be narrowed, perhaps even closed.

*EXECUTIVE DEVELOPMENT AREAS**

KNOWLEDGE AND SKILLS	CAPACITIES
TECHNICAL EXPERTISE	BREADTH OF
TACTICAL EXPERTISE	PERSPECTIVE
KNOWLEDGE OF THE ENVIRONMENT	FRAME OF REFERENCE
COMMUNICATIONS SKILLS	METACOGNITION
DECISION MAKING SKILLS	SELF-AWARENESS
PROBLEM-SOLVING SKILLS	VISIONING
MOTIVATING SELF AND OTHERS	POLITICAL SENSITIVITY
	INTEGRATIVE CAPACITY
	JUDGMENT CHARACTER

*Adapted from "The Preparation OF Strategic Leaders" (Forsythe 1992).

METACOGNITION

As you begin to understand what influences your decisions, it is also critical to understanding of metacognition so that you are better able to control and influence your own thought processes. Metacognition is a key variable which differentiates effective thinkers from less effective thinkers.

Cognition is the mental faculty or process by which knowledge is acquired through perception, reasoning, and intuition. The basic process of acquiring knowledge is simply learning. This includes the creation and management of aggregated knowledge in the form of complex cognitive structures or mental maps.

Metacognition is cognition directed at monitoring and controlling the process of cognition. Metacognition is thinking about thinking. The result of metacognition is the conscious regulation and rearrangement of how you think in the face of complex problems requiring novel solutions.

Metacognition is both a process and a skill. As a *skill*, metacognition is about self-awareness and strategic management of self. As a *process*, metacognition involves conscious, self-directed investigation of one's mental process. This includes perception and understanding of context as well as the notions of perspective-taking and multi-frame thinking-walking in another's shoes. Therefore, the process of metacognition often involves temporarily suspending assumptions, including one's own values and belief systems. This also can be construed as placing self in perspective, or "decentering."

Argyris' (1977) notion of double loop learning is a nice analogy for comparing and contrasting cognition and metacognition. Construe the smaller, inner circle as cognition and the larger, outer circle as metacognition. The ball in position A orbits in the realm of acquiring knowledge-cognition. If, for some reason, the ball breaks its smaller orbit and gets out on to the larger, outer circle-say, in position B-the ball can look down and into the smaller, inner circle.

This is the process of metacognition-getting out on the outer circle, then investigating from a higher position the cognition going on the smaller, inner circle. The benefits of metacognition would be realized when the ball returns to the smaller, inner orbit and manages itself in a new way, appropriate to the times and situation.

If double-loop learning doesn't work for you, Markessini (1990) developed a model which juxtaposes metacognitive processes with cognitive processes. It construes metacognition as an umbrella or executive control function under which cognitive functions occur. A third analogy for metacognition comes from models of information processing. Human information processing occurs at two levels. At the "lower" level, a closed system accepts input, processes it, and produces output without any feedback. At the "upper" level, a control system acts as a feedback processor with a capacity for both rewriting the rules used at the "lower" level and providing feedback to the "lower" level. The action process, cognition, merely executes, resets, and executes again. The executive process, metacognition, can edit or adjust the action process after considering feedback.

Unless you master metacognition, you will not be able to manage your personal development as a strategic thinker and leader. Conceptual capacity is a good indicator of how capable you currently are at monitoring and managing your thought processes.

CONCEPTUAL CAPACITY

One of the basic principles of Stratified Systems Theory (SST) is that leadership performance requirements change at higher organizational levels. The first implication of SST, however, is that leaders must be able to make choices about decision alternatives and problem solutions at all levels. Further, SST states that at higher organizational levels, problem types and decision choices become more ambiguous, less structured, and more differentiated. The complexity of the organization-environment interaction requires more productivity and planning within longer time frames that add to the cognitive demands of senior leaders.

An effective executive-level leader is expected to have a high level of conceptual capacity. If you are working for an executive-level leader and you have considerable conceptual capacity, you stand a better chance of understanding the issues and problems at that level, and a higher probability of being a valued asset.

What if you aspire to be an executive-level leader and you are not satisfied with your current level of conceptual capacity? The good news is that conceptual capacity increases with age. The bad news is it may not increase at a rate that will equip you to function effectively at the strategic level. Conceptual capacity can be boosted by developmental experiences (e.g., attending a senior service college), by assignments (e.g., working for a strategic leader or serving on a special high level planning group), and by broadening your professional reading program.

EXECUTIVE FLEXIBILITY

High levels of conceptual capacity are associated with higher levels of executive flexibility. Being flexible allows you to see problems from more than one perspective, allows you to reframe complex problems so that solutions become clearer, and allows you to accommodate seemingly ambiguous solutions. Being flexible allows you to question underlying assumptions about a problem and facilitates the generation of an array of possible solutions. Being flexible also is related to an individual's disposition to work at the strategic level.

COMPOSITE INDICATOR OF EXECUTIVE FLEXIBILITY

SOURCE	CONSTRUCT
MBTI	NT VS SF
MANSPEC	CATALYST PERSISTENCE INGENUITY
SLDI	INTERPERSONAL COMPETENCE
MCPA	CONCEPTUAL CAPACITY

There are several ways to measure executive flexibility. We can use behavioral measures, cognitive measures, and/or dispositional measures. Re-searchers at ICAF are involved in investigating these approaches, trying to determine an integrative measure of executive flexibility.

Results of the composite measure of executive flexibility used at ICAF are directly related to indicators of conceptual competence, vocational interests, and style of creativity. The composite measure also is inversely related to mental rigidity.

CREATIVE AND CRITICAL THINKING

Creative thinking and critical thinking are two sides of the same coin. Both are important skills in strategic decision making. Your careers, to this point, focus mostly on the critical thinking side of the coin. You may not have spent much time generating solutions to complex problems.

For some, creativity remains a mysterious gift, an elusive phenomenon that defies scientific description. For others, it provides an opportunity to use their decision-making ability. Over the years different theories of creativity have placed varying degrees of emphasis on the personal characteristics of creative individuals, or the dynamics of the social and motivational forces influencing creativity. Some theories stress personal growth or self-actualization, while others stress the historical views of human behavior. Nevertheless, one tenet seemed common to all-creative thinking skills can be developed or learned.

INDICATORS OF RISK TAKING AND RISK AVERSION

SOURCE	CREATIVE THINKING	CRITICAL THINKING
MBTI	E (EXTRAVERSION) N (INTUITIVE) P (PERCEIVING)	I (INTROVERSION) S (SENSING) J (JUDGING)
MANSPEC	CATALYST CREATIVE INGENUITY NEW IDEAS PERSUASIVE EXECUTIVE DISPOSITION	ADMINISTRATIVE DETAILS PLANNING PRACTICAL RISK CONTROL STIMULUS CONTROL
MCPA	HIGHER LEVELS OF CONCEPTUAL CAPACITY	LOWER LEVELS OF CONCEPTUAL CAPAPCITY

One ideology involves the cognitive, rational, and semantic approach to understanding the creative process. The first element, cognition, refers to creativity as an intellectual activity, thoughtful in nature. Rational implies that the activities and skills involved in the creative process do not just happen. A variety of methods and techniques can be used to assist creative efforts. Semantic merely emphasizes that language is a powerful tool to assist in creative learning and the problem-solving process.

Creative thinking is associated with the divergent phase of problem solving. In the divergent phase of problem solving, we seek to generate or create as many possible alternatives. We can take existing alternatives and tinker with them to see if we can adapt something that already is working to the problem at hand. People who exhibit this creative style generally are called adaptors. Or, we can start with a clean sheet of paper. People who exhibit this creative style are called innovators. People who tend toward the MBTI(r) N (intuitive) and P (perceiving) preferences elect the innovative creative style. People who tend toward the MBTI(r) S (sensing) and J (judging) preferences elect the adaptive creative style.

RISK TAKING

The strategic environment rewards or punishes risk taking and quickly sensitizes decision makers to resource issues. This resource-constrained environment demands that leaders must do more with less, and often increases the risk of failure to achieve the desired end state. Because the strategic environment is rapidly changing, decision makers must learn to think smarter and more creatively in order to get the most out of dwindling resources. Creative solutions are not achieved without taking risk, and often deviate sharply from known ways of doing things.

There are several indicators of creative thinking ability and critical thinking ability. It is important not to focus on any one of these indicators. Rather, you will find it useful to integrate all of these indicators into a mosaic of your creative and critical thinking abilities.

CONCLUSION

A leader can develop more effective strategic thinking skills. This is done by exploiting any opportunity to better understand yourself, how you think about complex problems, and how to go about making decisions. This understanding of yourself is critical, since this information that forms the foundation for developing your strategic thinking capabilities necessary in the strategic environment. The more you understand yourself, the more control you have over both the process, and the products you produce.

Virtually all of you will be required to serve in strategic environments. This means there will be many opportunities for you to function as a strategic thinker or advisor. You must, therefore, continue to develop a new and broader set of thinking skills. The SLDM course, and the overall ICAF experience have been designed to help you understand and develop effective strategic thinking skills to solve the complex, fast changing, unstructured problems you will soon encounter.

7

TEAMS AND DECISION MAKING IN THE STRATEGIC ENVIRONMENT

CREATING AND MANAGING TEAMS

Despite America's individualist ethos, American managers appear to have an insatiable appetite for information about teams. Since the mid-1980s, there has been an exponential growth in the number of articles published on teams in the workplace. The internet reveals endless numbers of consultants offering techniques to create teams out of "ordinary" workers or enhance the productivity of existing teams. Many of these articles on teams only advocate the use of teams as a solution to the new challenges confronting organizational leaders, and most authors fail to explain *how* leaders can successfully create teams.

Creating and managing teams in the workplace can lead to effective outcomes, but the success and longevity of teams in organizations will depend on how thoroughly organizational leaders understand how to extract the gains teams can provide. If leaders don't understand the skills they need to possess, as well as the group processes that are required to create and maintain teams, then teaming will be destined only to be the management fad of the 90's.

Should you care about this? Absolutely!! First of all it's a matter of competitiveness. As leaders from your host organizations you should be trying to use high-performance teams to create and sustain competitive advantage. At a time when downsizing and consolidation decisions are followed by the statement, "doing more with less," leaders should be looking at every way to derive synergy from the organization. Leveraging human capital as teams will be one of the strategies that leaders have to try to *gain and sustain* advantage over competing nations, competing industries, and competing organizations.

Many of you may be comfortable with creating and managing teams in your service branch or agency, but you need to realize that creating and managing interservice and interagency teams present unique challenges and requires different leadership techniques. Chances are that leaders of these kinds of teams will have a harder time developing a common definition of issues and acceptable solution options among members. Furthermore, team members' commitments are often divided between their home agency and the interagency team. The results of competitive team dynamics can be reduced efficiency in achieving goals, watered down recommendations in an attempt to address all issues or, if the issue is too contentious, disbanding the interagency team.

Knowing when to use teams and how to manage them are techniques supporting this strategy. This chapter and the three that follow are intended to broaden and deepen your conceptualization of what constitutes a team and team decision making.

TEAMS ARE COMPLEX

Most of us have been members of a group that we've labeled a team, whether it was a sports team, a committee, a task force at work, or an advocacy group in the community. Essentially the label of team is given to a group of people who interact well. But it is important to use a more precise definition of a team for two reasons:

- We can discern the features a team possesses that distinguish it from a group.
- We can identify the features of a high performance team.

Groups are "an expression of the needs and aspirations of the people who comprise them" (Walton and Hackman). Teams, on the other hand are a special kind of group, with *three* additional characteristics.

First, teams are typically formed by management directive.

Second, team members share responsibility for the specific outcomes and operations.

Third, teams typically exist in an empowering work context. That is, teams are found in organizations that "emphasize the mutuality of interests between employers and employees . . . [where] all members, not just managers, have means to influence work related decisions . . . [where] there is open information and two way communication about organizational policies and practices; and hierarchical differences are minimized in ways that encourage all to feel that they are full members working together toward shared objectives"(Walton and Hackman).

All teams are not alike.

First, they can differ on the type of outcomes they've been organized to achieve.

Some teams, such as advisory panels, committees and employee involvement groups are assembled to provide advice and involvement to managers in the organization.

Another type of team, the projects and development team, is an assembly of professionals who work on assigned or original projects. Finally, teams can be created to produce an outcome that is organized action. This type of team includes: sports teams, negotiating teams, expedition teams, and surgery teams.

Teams should be properly configured and managed for the type of organizational output that they are intended to produce.

Overall, teams in organizations create outcomes that exceed the collective capability of individuals who work within the formal line structure of an organization.

For example, the Department of Defense benefits from the productivity defense contractors generate through teams. Honeywell Corporation, a subcontractor for the Air Force's B-2 bomber, is a case in point:

TYPES OF WORK TEAMS AND THEIR CHARACTERISTICS

TYPE OF OUTCOME AND EXAMPLES	COMBINATION OF MEMBER EXPERTISE	TEAM'S DEGREE OF INTEGRATION WITH OTHER WORK UNITS	TEAM'S WORK CYCLE
ADVICE AND INVOLVEMENT *Advisory Panels* *Committees* *Employee Involvement Groups*	Low Differentiation of Expertise Among Members	Low Level of Integration	Can Vary in Length
PRODUCTION OR SERVICE *Assembly Teams* *Maintenance Crews* *Flt Attendant Crews*	Low Differentiation of Expertise Among Members	High Level of Integration	Work Cycles Typically Repeated or Continuous; Cycles Often Briefer Than The Team Life Span
PROJECT *Research Groups* *Task Forces* *Architect Teams*	High Differentiation of Expertise Among Members	Low Level of Integration	Work Cycles Typically Differ For Each Project
ORGANIZED ACTION *Sports Teams* *Negotiating Teams* *Expedition Teams* *Surgery Teams* *Cockpit Crews*	High Differentiation of Expertise Among Members	Low Level of Integration	Brief Performance Events, Often Repeated Under New Conditions, Requiring Extended Training and/or Preparation

Adapted from: Sundstrom, E., DeMuse, K.P, and Futrell, D. (1990) Work teams. *American Psychologist* 25, no. 2, 120-133.

In 1992, Honeywell's defense avionics division in Albuquerque reorganized their entire 1800 person organization into multifunctional teams. Division management searched among their supervisors for people who could facilitate loyalty, communication and decision making within a group and completed the change in six months. According to the division's general manager senior management "took a 'burn the bridge' approach because we wanted people to know we were serious. If we hadn't made a big fuss, this would have died a natural death."

One of the successful teams developed a data storage systems for the Northrop Grumman's B-2 bomber. The team leader managed the group by taking actions that created team loyalty and focused their effort on the Air Force's needs. The leader saw his job as helping the team "feel as if they owned the project by getting whatever information, financial or otherwise, they needed. I knew that if we could all charge the hill together, we would be successful" (Caminiti 1995).

Honeywell's strategy can be instructive in developing work teams. Senior management essentially bet the farm by ushering in a complete organizational transformation within 6 months. They wanted people to know they were serious. Next they diligently searched for employees who had the skills to work in teams. Senior management didn't organize teams and then wish for success. They carefully identified employees who would maximize the chances that their teams would be successful. Finally, team leaders reinforced a strong sense of members who possessed a sense of ownership about their project and loyalty.

Team members can also be expected to demonstrate two types of loyalty and identification: (1) loyalty to other team members and identification with the group for effective group interaction; and (2) loyalty to the organization and identification with organizational objectives for effective task accomplishment. Recent research in teams and task groups suggest that these outcomes are the product of two coincident group processes.

LOYALTY TO TEAM MEMBERS AND IDENTIFICATION WITH THE GROUP. The interpersonal processes among team members culminating in loyalty and group identification are normal to group development. Connie Gersick's research on a variety of task groups and teams is an example of recent research findings. She found that the orientation groups took toward completing a task was established in the group's first meeting. Gersick reported:

> ...lasting patterns can appear as early as the first few seconds of a group's life...The sheer speed with which recurring patterns appear suggest that they're influenced by material established before the group convenes. Such material includes members' expectations about the task, each other, and the context, and their repertoire of behavior routines and performance strategies (Gersick 1988).

Only later, at the midpoint of the group's lifespan, did strategic *reorientation* to norms and task accomplishment take place. Gersick's research reveals that from the opening moments of a group's existence its members are simultaneously developing strategies for task accomplishment and developing the structure and processes for interpersonal relationships.

Gersick's findings also suggest that leaders need to create immediately the conditions for team members to generate team identity and loyalty such as: establishing open communication, developing trust, and generating a sense of camaraderie. Trust, loyalty, open communication and camaraderie are the group characteristics that we typically associate with successful teams' efforts in sports and in combat units. Team efforts are the synthesis of two processes; one part interpersonal (among team members and groups external to the team) and the other part, task directed. Consequently, leaders' creation of conditions that facilitate positive interpersonal processes will also facilitate the task directed decision making process.

To reap the benefits of teamwork, one must actually build a team. Calling a set of people a team or exhorting them to work together is insufficient. Instead, explicit action must be taken to establish a team's boundaries, to define the task as one for which members are collectively responsible and accountable, and to give members the authority to manage both their internal processes and the team's relations with external entities such as clients and co-workers (Hackman).

THE OTHER SIDE OF THE COIN: THE TEAM'S LOYALTY TO THE ORGANIZATION AND ITS

IDENTIFICATION WITH ORGANIZATIONAL OBJECTIVES. The team's loyalty to the organization and identification with organizational objectives are essential. Without loyalty to the organization, the team will fragment as team members pursue their individual interests. Also, teams that lack identification with their organization's objectives are not likely to produce outcomes of value.

Team loyalty to the organization is a consequence of the rewards leaders use to manage individual performance in the organization:

(1) Visibly and verbally reward productivity and innovation

(2) Downplay status differences between management and non-management employees

(3) Consistently demonstrate how organizational membership is instrumental to employees achieving their own goals.

How are you going to implement these techniques in your organization, and can you practice your strategy? Ideology must be translated into action on a daily basis so that members of the organization have solid evidence that they are partners whose efforts are recognized as instrumental to the organization's success. Daily actions that exemplify the core values of trust and interdependence are critical for laying a solid foundation for employees to develop allegiance to their organization. Roger Hallowell's research on Southwest Airlines illustrates how this firm turns concepts into action.

Southwest Airlines has demonstrated its superior comprehensive strategy by (1) being the only major United States airline to earn a profit throughout the early 1990's, (2) having one of the most successful airline stocks, and (3) being the only airline to win the industry's "triple crown" measures of customer satisfaction . . . Southwest's success may be due largely to its unusual focus on creating value for employees. "LUV" and "FUN," the cornerstones of Southwest's employee-relations approach, represent concern and respect for the individual, as well as the consensus creation of the environment that encourages all employees to have fun on the job . . . LUV refers to one of the company's core values involving the way individuals treat each other. LUV includes respect for individuality and genuine caring for others . . . FUN is exactly what its name suggests . . . FUN occurs throughout the company through jokes, parties, and generally entertaining behavior. A front-line manager notes, "We're kind of a big family here, and family members have fun better. Herb Kelleher sums up FUN at Southwest in saying "We demonstrate by example that you don't have to be uptight to be successful . . . LUV and FUN are embedded into the Southwest culture and reflected in the company's operating policies . . . FUN and LUV produce commitment that changes employees' perception of their relationship with the airline (Hallowell 1996).

Southwest Airlines' practices for developing loyalty provide some substance to the ideas that are circulating about transforming organizational culture. Would Southwest's techniques work in the federal government? The bottom line is that if you want to insure team success in your organization you have to think hard about the ways you can reinforce or transform your organizational culture so that it communicates an ideology of partnership and collective gain to employees.

The effort of leading teams to identify with the organization's objectives is as challenging as efforts to develop team loyalty. When teams identify with the organization's objectives, members' conceptualization of problems and their solutions have a better chance of being consistent with the strategic objectives of the senior decision makers. This is a matter of a team members actually understanding the top management's strategic frame of reference.

Senior decision makers can reveal their frame of reference for organizational issues when they imbed answers to "why" questions in their assignments to their teams. Answers to "why" questions create clarity. With clarity of purpose there is a better chance for team members to develop a common understanding of issues, and to adopt unified approaches to solutions. Researchers Carl Larson and Frank LaFasto, who interviewed members of mountain expedition teams, executive management teams, GAO and Congressional investigation teams, provide insight to team clarity: Examples of goal clarity are literally everywhere in our interviews with leaders and members of effective teams....Captain William Bauman, a staff writer for the [Challenger disaster] investigation team, identified goal clarity as one of the primary explanations for the success of the team, one of the most effective Presidential Commissions in recent history. The mission of the Rogers Commission was to investigate the Challenger disaster and determine the cause within 120 days. . . . The team was under considerable pressure from the public and media to assess blame. . . . But what was needed immediately following the disaster was a clear determination of cause. What caused the disaster? What were the major contributing factors? And what specific recommendations would grow from these determinations? The report of the Rogers Commission never deviates from the question of what happened and why. The mission was clear and concrete, and the team was able to execute it effectively (Larson and LaFasto 1989).

Their interviews also revealed that clear communication of the team's purpose lead to successful team outcomes in mergers and acquisitions. Another interviewee, Anthony Rucci, one of the leaders of the team that implemented the largest merger of the health care industry, provided the following insights: The first and most important step is to define the objective clearly. In fact Rucci believes it is important to be able to visualize the result and describe what that result will look like once it is accomplished. For Rucci, the vision includes imagining what excellence would look like in achieving the result. "It's getting the results in a way that hasn't been done before. It's achieving the results in a way that set a standard, a higher standard for how you can get something done"(Larson and LaFasto 1989).

Each of these examples reinforces the earlier points made about ways leaders can develop a team's loyalty to organizational objectives. If team members know why the specific issues that the team is to address are important to senior management then they can see how their efforts will be integrated into the organization's strategy.

THE CHARACTERISTICS OF HIGH-PERFORMANCE TEAMS

High-performance teams may be appealing to think about because they conjure images of organizational teams operating with the precision of a drill platoon, the efficiency of an Indy race car pit crew, or the effectiveness of a police SWAT team; images synonymous with capability and productivity. These images are useful for picturing how teams could operate, but leaders need more insight about high-performance teams if they are going to create them.

Jon Katzenbach and Douglas Smith provide a description of high-performance teams based upon their research on teams in a wide variety of organizations:

Strong interpersonal commitments drive a number of aspects that distinguish high-performance teams. Fueled by interpersonal commitments, team purposes become even nobler, team performance goals are more urgent, and team approach more powerful. The notion, for example, that "if one of us fails, we all fail" pervades high-performance teams. In addition, mutual concern for each other's personal growth enable high-performance teams to develop interchangeable skills and hence greater flexibility. High-performance teams also share leadership within the team more than other teams. And, not significantly, high-performance teams seem to have a better developed sense of humor and more fun (Katzenbach 1993).

High-performance teams seem to possess the characteristics of other organizational teams. However, this type of team also displays: (1) higher levels of camaraderie; (2) increased levels of interdependence; (3) greater collective learning and adaptive capabilities; and, (4) closer identification with team outcomes than the average team. Are high-performance teams a chance occurrence? It will appear that way if you only look at a team's output. The success-failure records of teams, especially those operating in highly competitive environments, will fluctuate over time. How many sports teams can be considered dynasties?

At the core of a high-performance team's capability is the team members' ability to use interpersonal relations to facilitate team learning and performance. Team members forge and maintain high levels of camaraderie and appear to leverage these personal processes to: (1) accelerate members' ability to learn from each other and from their collective experiences; and, (2) efficiently focus members' efforts on accomplishing their objectives. Descriptions of high-performance teams consistently mention team members' emphasis and maintenance of strong team identity. This team also vigilantly minimizes internal politics by agreeing to place high value on the team's collective goals.

How do leaders encourage collective action?

- Leaders need to establish a set of fundamental standards: individual commitment, motivation, and self-esteem.
- Leaders must establish team norms that require team members to be accountable to the group for their performance.
- Leaders must require the team to exert pressure on itself to constantly monitor its performance against goal achievement and to adjust their team processes when warranted.

CREATING AND MANAGING TEAMS AT THE STRATEGIC LEVEL OF ORGANIZATIONS

Whether they are used in employee involvement groups, assembly teams, maintenance crews, or research groups, many organizations have benefited from the higher quality output of teams. In the early 1990's Motorola's CEO and Prudential Insurance Company's CEO offered the following perspectives on top management teams:

In my mind, there is a definite parallel between the self-managing worker teams we are trying to develop across the baseline of the organization and our top management group. We are really trying to create the same behaviors of openness, collective problem solving, multiple leadership, and mutual trust and respect in both situations. So there are important parallels. But somehow it is still different and more difficult at the top. —George Fisher, CEO Motorola

I know teams work. But I'm still not convinced it is worth the time and effort to push further in the direction of making our executive office into a team....The essence of the issue is defining a set of team goals for ourselves as a group beyond dealing with the broad strategic and leadership issues of the corporation. And so far, it is not evident to me what those would be. I must admit, however, I am intrigued by the possibility.
—Robert Winters, CEO,

The Prudential Insurance Company of America

Why is it so difficult to create or even visualize a top management team? Part of the answer lies with the job demands of senior executives. Senior executives are paid to confront the VUCA environment. Under complex conditions they generate ideas for the organization's future and translate them into initiatives, often resolving policy conflicts through negotiation. Other aspects of the strategic leaders' responsibilities include conceptual tasks such as solving short term problems for which answers are derived through staff analysis or team consensus.

Strategic leaders make the greatest contributions to their organizations by generating decisions on issues for which there are no right answers. Here, top management teams can be of great assistance, because their members can reduce the uncertainty surrounding strategic issues by incorporating additional sources and types of information in all deliberations. Executive team members can also reduce complexity surrounding strategic issues by offering interpretations that are based on different frames of reference that can stimulate sophisticated analyses, and provide more comprehensive solutions.

Executive level decisions are also guided by multi-agency teams, comprising either strategic level executives themselves or senior staff representatives from organizations that have a stake in the issue. The Department of Defense is increasingly engaged in interagency operations. "Deep VUCA" issues ranging from drug interdiction policies, to peace keeping operations, to nuclear weapons control policies are all viewed from a multi-agency perspective. A benefit with multi-agency teams is that decision outcomes will be endorsed by those organizations that have a stake in the issue.

Can teams be organized at the strategic level to achieve gains discussed earlier? Yes, but only if challenges to developing team consensus about long term issues are overcome. The strengths of top management team members also create multi-agency liabilities in the form of each executive's perceptual filters (Starbuck and Milliken 1988). Different terms pertain to each executive's personalized model for interpreting VUCA issues, and these personalized models can be based on organizational culture, professional norms, individual preferences, or personal life experience. Regardless of the basis of executives' approaches to interpretation, the success of team processes will depend on how the team manages conflict during their attempt to reach consensus.

Executive team interactions that contain too much conflict result in polarization or fragmentation within the team. Donald Hambrick, a researcher on executive teams from Columbia University conducted in-depth interviews with 23 chief executives from major corporations in the United States and Europe (Hambrick 1995). Among his findings were examples of how fragmentation occurs:

In our zeal to give autonomy, we've created a bunch of fiefdoms. Everyone's pursuing their own objectives. Right now, there's very little natural, informal communication or collaboration among these folks. We're facing some new marketplace shifts which affect the whole company, and unless we can get our act together, we will be passed by.

We're not running on all cylinders. Communication is slow and spotty. As a result, we've had things drop between the cracks. I'm trying to figure out whether this is a matter of group "chemistry", group process, or what.

Team? How do you define a team? When I think of a team, I think of interaction, give and take, and shared purpose. Here we're a collection of strong players but hardly a "team". We rarely meet as a team-rarely see each other, in fact. We don't particularly share the same views. I wouldn't say we actually work at cross purposes, but a lot of self-centered behavior occurs. Where's the "team" in all this?

These kinds of problems are not restricted to corporate teams. There are numerous examples of how excessive, dysfunctional conflict among the military services, and between the military and other government agencies, have led to suboptimal results. Richard Gabriel analyzed military operations such as the Sontay Prison raid, the Mayaguez rescue mission, the Iranian hostage rescue attempt and the Grenada invasion. Gabriel links many of these failures to breakdowns in interservice decision making at the executive level.:

> A number of the key decisions seem to have been made on the basis of interservice rivalry, bureaucratic consensus, and political criteria rather than operational requirements. There seems to have been a bureaucratic imperative to give each service a role, regardless of whether it could best contribute to the success of the mission. In some instances, this imperative ruled even when a course of action seemed to work against the chances of success.

PRODUCTIVE CONFLICT

There is a third category of interaction, productive conflict, that seems best suited to the goal of strategic decision making teams. L. D. Brown describes productive conflict as follows:

> Productive conflict at agency or cultural interfaces involves perceiving and explicitly recognizing cultural differences, encouraging communication about those differences, when relevant, and encouraging representatives to resolve differences without escalation.

Leaders must initiate and manage productive conflict in executive teams in two ways: through the techniques they use to unify team members' commitment to strategic objectives; and through the rules of operation they establish for their teams. Jon Katzenbach and Douglas, in their book, *The Wisdom of Teams*, provide a set of guidelines that leaders can follow when establishing rules of operation for executive teams. They include:

- Carve out teams assignments that tackle specific issues. Team members will be able to connect their efforts in the top management team with a stream of tasks that can be linked to organizational change.
- Assign tasks to one or more individuals for later integration by the entire team in subsequent working sessions. This technique causes members to do real work together beyond full team meetings, allowing team involvement and accountability to grow outside the context of team meetings.
- Determine team memberships based on skill not position. Skill based membership relieves the difficult constraint of hierarchically imposed membership that also bring a political dimension to team meetings. This approach allows the option of multiple smaller teams, constituted to address particular issues.
- Require all members to do equivalent amounts of real work. Each member's sweat equity in the work product will insure that they have first hand knowledge of the output.
- Break down hierarchical patterns of interaction. Work assignments and the contributions to be made should not be only related to hierarchical position. Without a consistent flow of contributions that go beyond hierarchical roles, each person is deprived of the opportunity to do real work on behalf of the team.
- Set and follow rules of behavior similar to those used by other teams. Senior management teams can facilitate a greater degree of mutual accountability by setting and following the same rule of conduct that help teams at all levels of the organization provide focus, avoid, and promote openness, and trust.

CONCLUDING COMMENTS ABOUT TEAMS

This chapter has presented a discussion about work teams that provides you with the tools to analyze how teams operate in a variety of contexts. Ordinary work teams can be configured to produce different outcomes and it is up to organizational leaders to match the right kind of team with the desired output. High-performance teams are not found in ordinary organizational contexts. Instead, they embody a team capability that is necessary for success in highly demanding, nonroutine tasks. Executive level teams confront VUCA issues. But they can be hampered by the challenge of trying to develop team consensus among different individuals who may interpret strategic issues differently.

Effective teams do not exist because leaders hope they will exist. They exist because leaders possess the ability to analyze accurately when teams can be effective in the organization, and because leaders know how to manage team processes to produce high-quality results.

8

CONSENSUS TEAM DECISION MAKING

The Westerner and the Japanese man mean something different when they talk of "making a decision." In the West, all the emphasis is on the answer to the question. To the Japanese, however, the important element in decision making is defining the question.

The crucial steps are to decide whether there is a need for a decision and what the decision is about. And it is in that step that the Japanese aim at attaining consensus. Indeed, it is this step that, to the Japanese, is the essence of decision.

The answer to the question (what the West considers the decision) follows from its definition. During the process that precedes the decision, no mention is made of what the answer might be. . . . Thus the whole process is focused on finding out what the decision is really about, not what the decision should be (Drucker 1974).

INTRODUCTION

A strategic leader can utilize decision-making teams as a powerful asset in successfully coping with the enviornoment. Such teams improve their decision making by using a process of consensus, a process useful when developing national security strategy, military strategy, or strategic planning in other public or private sectors. Knowing how to forge consensus for policy development and implementation is critical to successful management and leadership.

STRATEGIC LEADERS AND TEAMS

Why be concerned about consensus team decision making at the strategic level? What is so important about that approach to policy making? Consensus decision making offers the benefit of using more fully the experience, judgment, perceptions, and thinking of a team of people. To those who have not participated in consensus decision making, the process may seem frustrating. But, mastery of small group consensus decision making processes may be the key to achieving a successful resolution of whatever crisis appears in this complex environment. Because of the nature of modern issues in the global environment, strategic decision makers must rely on teams to solve problems and to make policy recommendations. A high performing team can be a positive force in assessing strategic situations and formulating national policy.

LONG-TERM VISION. Effective strategic leaders employ a strategic team to help them in the visioning process. This team "sees" the strategic environment from various frames of reference, visualizing the effectiveness of proposed strategies over time. Teams help leaders to understand a complex situation and gain insight into how to achieve long-term objectives, allocate resources and integrate operational and tactical decisions into strategic plans.

CONSENSUS STYLE. Effective strategic leaders know how to get everyone involved in policy making and build consensus in the process. Within large complex organizations, whether public or private, consensus is the engine that sustains policy decisions. No strategic leader can succeed unless he or she can build such consensus. Thus, the search for consensus among peers, allies, and even competitors becomes a requirement for shared commitment to a national policy, and to corporate, business policy.

TEAM BUILDING. Successful strategic leaders use their knowledge and skills to structure and lead high performing teams. Strategic teams that perform with unity of purpose contribute to the creation of strategic vision, develop long-range plans, implement strategy, access resources, and manage the implementation of national policy. Given the nature of the strategic environment and the complexity of both national and global issues, strategic leaders must use teams. They cannot do it alone.

CHALLENGES TO DECISION MAKING TEAMS

Strategic decision makers regularly use teams to solve urgent problems such as in the drug wars where both civil and military assets, and federal and state resources are jointly employed. Most strategic-level decision-making teams exist for brief periods to resolve a major problem or to develop national policy and strategies to meet future challenges. While these teams carry great responsibilities, they are often "ad hoc" in nature.

A team leader has two overriding responsibilities: First, the leader is accountable for the effective functioning of the team. The leader monitors team performance and takes action to improve team effectiveness. Teams tend to perform best when responsibilities are shared and leadership tasks are distributed among members. Empowered team members are more likely to take responsibility for team success. Second, the leader is responsible for developing a stable leadership structure. Many decision-making teams tend to be more effective when the framework for leadership is clear. These teams tend to work more efficiently, have fewer interpersonal problems, and produce better outputs. Common observations of the strategic decision making process that contribute to the leadership challenge include:

- Diverse Team Membership. There are often several agencies involved, each having different terminology, goals, and priorities. Members may lack understanding of various agency roles and contributions to the issues. And, members have different perceptions about how the government works.
- Lack of Policy Guidance. Strategic-level decision-making teams often are not given clearly defined policy guidance from above due to politics or concerns about media scrutiny. This often leads to involvement in undesirable arenas.

- Low Team Authority. The framework for getting things done is either ambiguous or nonexistent. Nobody is in charge of the process. The "lead agency" concept is confusing and agencies are designated without specific guidance. Standard military formats and structures are not useful.
- Internal Politics. Bureaucratic bias impedes team performance. Team member mindsets emphasize agency goals and programs at the expense of overall government objectives. There is a strong preference for agency autonomy due to narrow budget constraints and rigid resource controls. A powerful bias against adapting and integrating operations precludes coordinated implementation.
- Organizational Inertia. There is strong inertia toward familiar situation assessments and courses of action. Members resist change or divergence from existing policies.
- Lack of Integration. Sub-groups produce uncoordinated products because they work in parallel, even when dealing with sequential tasks. There is no coordination mechanism to integrate subgroup work while in development. In the end, the team staples together disconnected subgroup products for implementation.
- Gaps and Ambiguities. In interagency teams, the economic component and the private sector often have no spokespersons. The resource dimension security is often lacking, and team assessments in this area are absent, weak, or wrong.

Given these difficulties, it should be no surprise that team meetings can be a journey into foreign territory for each team member. By adopting a "consensus style" of leadership, some of these problems can be eliminated.

CONSENSUS IN STRATEGIC DECISION MAKING

Decision making at the strategic level hinges on the ability of decision-making teams to forge consensus for action. No team can succeed unless it is strong enough to sustain decisions through bureaucratic politics, interest group resistance, media criticism, and implementation. Consensus acts as the "power plant" within the national security decision making system, or the private sector, to sustain policy decisions through implementation either in the government bureaucracy, or in the market place.

WHAT IS CONSENSUS?

Strategic decision-making teams work to build consensus in solving critical problems. Some of the critical tasks requiring consensus are:

- Assessment of the strategic situation
- Identification of critical policy issues
- Articulation of policy objectives
- Determination of a strategy
- Execution of strategy.

A strategic team's goal is to make decisions that best reflect the thinking of its members, thus 'forging' consensus. One can easily confuse what consensus is and isn't. Here are some guidelines (Scholtes 1988):

- Consensus is both process and outcome. Consensus is a process in which everyone has their say. Divergent views are fully addressed and resolved by the group. A satisfactory level of convergent individual opinion emerges in the search for general agreement.
- Consensus is agreement, but not necessarily complete agreement. It is an outcome which is "close enough" to be acceptable. All or most team members can support it, and few or no members totally oppose it. Usually, when a team achieves general agreement, no one is completely satisfied, but everyone accepts or "lives with" the group's prevailing view.
- Consensus is not authoritarian, perfect, conformist, or bland.
- Consensus is not the team leader imposing decisions and tem members complying, as in a command situation.

Hierarchical decisions do not reflect the thinking of the group. Hierarchial decisions usually do not implement the alternative that all members agree is best and that everyone can support.

- Consensus is not a perfect team agreement representing first priorities of all team members. Everyone will not be totally happy with the consensus.
- Consensus is not a unanimous decision. This essentially gives each team member veto power.
- Consensus is not majority vote. This is faulty consensus, since it only reflects what the majority is happy with. The minority is forced to comply with a decision it doesn't want, which is not what consensus is all about.
- Consensus is not "groupthink," the desire of cohesive teams to conform and make close-minded decisions, disregarding critical examination, divergent opinions, or debate.
- Consensus is not a bland, watered-down proposal having no substance, and entailing no risks.
- Effective consensus falls somewhere on a continuum between perfect agreement and total discord. Poor strategic decisions emerge at either extreme (Priem 1990).
- Some teams get bogged down trying to achieve perfect consensus, essentially giving each member veto power over any team decision, wasting time and provoking harmful interpersonal conflict. In many cases within government, teams find themselves at the other extreme-their search for consensus produces bland, watered-down initiatives that have little impact on strategic problems.
- A consensus decision is one that all team members can support. It may be, but is not necessarily, the alternative most preferred by all members. When true consensus is reached through a process in which everyone participates, the output is usually a superior quality decision. Moreover, it is a decision having widespread

acceptance and support for implementation. Most important, team members are motivated to see the decision through to completion (Brilhart and Galanes 1989).

THE POLITICAL FRAME OF REFERENCE

This frame emphasizes both forms of consensus: a shared vision for change and common ground found through understanding and negotiation. The political frame suggests a three-step strategy for political action:

- Set an agenda for change.
- Build networks and coalitions.
- Conduct bargaining and negotiations.

An effective leader must create an agenda that has a vision of what can and should be the long term interests of the parties involved. The leader must also have a strategy that considers relevant organizational and environmental forces in building a network to achieve goals. Most important, the team leader must negotiate differences based on a shared vision of the future.

BUILDING THE MODEL

The Consensus Team Decision Making Model (CTDM) identifies factors that distinguish high-performing teams from less productive ones:

- High Conceptual Level
- Prudent Consensus Approach
- Vigilant Decision Management.

The Consensus Team Decision Making Model portrays a thinking, collective group capable of high performance. Within the three pillars, there are 14 success factors critical to excellence in team decision making. Consensus, however, is not always present.

I was surprised that critical deliberations were taking place with no preparation or follow-up planned . . . the Oval Office debate was a free-swinging affair, and the freest swinger of all was the President's Chief of Staff, John Sununu. . . . He cut people off in mid-sentence and pursued his pet tangents, a behavior . . . that did not seem to bother the President. Bush listened, spoke little . . . repeated that the plotters had to express a clear intention to restore democracy . . . and then brought the meeting to a close (Powell 1995—418).

Strategic decision-making teams must operate at the proper conceptual level. This means employing multiple frames of reference and "staying out of the weeds." They search for consensus among themselves, within their organizations, among interested groups, and with the public. Finally, strategic teams avoid consuming limited resources or prolonging action, thereby missing strategic opportunities.

- What is the success factor?
- Why is it critical to strategic teams?
- How do high-performing teams exercise the factor?
- How do less productive teams fail to apply the factor?
- What methods help strategic teams improve?

We can analyze and evaluate every team, even low performing teams, in terms of these success factors. All teams display them in varying degrees. The best teams, however, appear to make a conscious commitment to monitor team performance in terms of the factors. This commitment to excellence differentiates and defines the high-performing team.

PILLAR ONE: HIGH CONCEPTUAL LEVEL

This dimension of consensus team decision making views the team as an intelligent entity, one that thinks rationally, analyzes the situation, synthesizes information, evaluates alternatives, and makes decisions. The team's objective is to find the highest quality solution to a complex strategic problem and minimize risk of failure.

Consider the example of a joint team of planners tasked to recommend a National Military Strategy for approval by the Chairman, Joint Chiefs of Staff. The team's objective is to develop an effective strategy that meets future threats to our nation's security. The team must address many complex issues.

These include world security threats, international agreements, domestic priorities, regional military powers, current political realities, and even contemporary social, economic, and environmental trends. The success of the team in developing an effective National Military Strategy depends in part on their collective capability to understand and integrate these diverse and complex strategic perspectives. Pillar One factors:

- Envision goals
- Design process plans
- Achieve situation assessment
- Expand frames of reference
- Focus time horizons
- Clarify value trade-offs
- Detect gaps and ambiguity.

ENVISION GOALS. Envisioning team goals is especially important where bureaucratic conflict can destroy team effectiveness. In this situation, team goals serve the purpose of establishing a sense of shared mission. Goals encourage team members to rise above parochial positions and commit to the team's higher mission. The team leader is responsible for articulating these team goals. He or she should state goals in language that all team members can easily grasp:

- Explain how the team's mission fits into the larger picture.
- State major tasks the team must accomplish and products it must deliver.
- Ensure a shared understanding of desired outcomes.
- Describe outcomes that would count as team failure.
- Provide a basis for determining priorities.

DESIGN A PROCESS PLAN. A team's process plan describes how the team will approach its work: a sequence of steps and a delegation of responsibilities. This process of deciding how to decide is "making a meta-decision." Meta-decisions are more important in group decision rnaking than in individual decision making. While an individual who has started in the wrong direction can turn around and go back to square one, a group moving in the wrong direction will have a tougher time undoing agreements and expectations among members in order to change course. The process plan should:

- Specify how the team will resolve conflict.
- Get going quickly.
- Establish checkpoints.
- Recycle issues as appropriate.

ACHIEVE SITUATION ASSESSMENT. Seeking divergent viewpoints provides a broader understanding of the strategic situation. Divergence enables teams to better assess the effectiveness and risks of strategic plans. Each team member has unique experiences which can be captured with free and open discussion. To realize the group's collective conceptual power, the team cannot merely tolerate different viewpoints. Instead, they must seek all member viewpoints to broaden the team's assessment.

Teams operating at a high conceptual level encourage diverse viewpoints and dissenting opinions rather than suppressing them as unwanted complications. Commitment to divergence is so strong, teams employ a variety of techniques such as devil's advocate when they do not uncover divergent viewpoints.

EXPAND FRAMES OF REFERENCE. A frame of reference is a perspective or mental map used by a strategic decision maker to make sense of events. Frames are both windows on the world and lenses to bring the world into focus. Multiple frames are helpful in understanding a complex strategic situation. For example, a strategic decision maker may find political and military frames of reference only to be inadequate in understanding the situation in Bosnia. Rather, decision makers must expand their frames of reference to include historical, social, legal, and religious perspectives in order to better understand the conflict.

High-performing teams expand their frames of reference to make sense out of the complex strategic environment. This includes not only numerical expansion, but also qualitative amplification of existing frames of reference. This expansion results in increased understanding of interdependent systems, a wider set of causal factors, and an expanded number of affected groups. With a broader understanding of the strategic situation, high-performing teams then focus their information resources to clear up ambiguities and build alternatives that integrate key issues emerging from these various perspectives.

FOCUS TIME HORIZONS. Time horizon describes the focal distance a team perceives in a strategic situation. A team may see tasks in terms of either current results or long-term changes. Appropriate time horizon is a function of the strategic situation and the team's mission. For a crisis response team, the time horizon could be 24 to 72 hours into the future, depending on the nature of response options. But for other strategic planning tasks, the time horizon could be 10 to 20 years. Establishing the appropriate focal point is a matter of insight—balancing near-term actions and future objectives.

Focusing the time horizon presents a challenge for strategic decision-making teams. Various federal departments routinely make strategic decisions within different time horizons. DOD normally uses a long-term planning horizon of six years. In contrast, other departments, such as Justice or Treasury, plan about one year in advance. Obviously, the problem of coordinating a national drug interdiction strategy among these three departments creates difficulties for an interagency team. The same problem occurs when teams are composed of federal, state, and local officials.

CLARIFY VALUE TRADE-OFFS. Strategic decisions, by their nature, are value-laden. For example, the decision to partially lift the ban on homosexuals in the military deals with one's values about military readiness and one's values about the civil rights of American citizens. Such decisions present difficult value conflicts to the team. Few strategic teams perform very well when attempting to resolve value conflicts through internal debate. Moreover, teams find value conflicts are not easily solved by objective analysis. Yet, value conflicts remain a central feature of strategic decision making.

High-performing teams recognize most strategic decisions have important value tradeoffs, some involving serious moral implications. These teams search for and clarify value conflicts. High-performing teams develop policies and actions to resolve value conflicts, thereby providing moral power to their decisions.

DETECT GAPS AND AMBIGUITY. Gaps usually emerge because the team is too homogeneous, not having the sufficient diversity among members to identify important strategic issues involved in the decision. In assessing the effectiveness of military operations, a naval officer offers one perspective, while Army and Air Force officers provide different ones. The lack of any of these perspectives could be a gap in assessment. Gaps are hard to detect since teams rarely realize something is missing.

High-performing teams work to detect gaps in information by examining and clarifying assumptions about the information base. When they detect gaps, these teams attempt to fill them rather than continue operating without needed information. If the gaps cannot be filled, the team notes missing information so that planning and decision making continues, but, with this problem in mind.

High-performing teams also watch for ambiguities carefully. These teams even check out questioning expressions of team members, for example, to determine whether an apparent visual ambiguity is simply a misunderstanding or a genuine inconsistency. Less productive teams fail to clarify obvious misunderstandings. Skilled teams don't allow themselves to be paralyzed by ambiguity; if an ambiguity cannot be resolved, they incorporate it as a qualifier to plans and actions. Sometimes, the ambiguity is due to different interpretations of the strategic situation. In this case, effective teams remain aware of these assessments.

PILLAR TWO: PRUDENT CONSENSUS APPROACH

After the inauguration, the Clinton national security team gathered . . . for the first time. The issue was Bosnia. . . . Tony Lake, the new National Security Advisor, sat in the chairman's seat, but did not drive the meeting. Warren Christopher, the Secretary of State, sat on one side of Lake, somewhat passively ...

lawyerlike, simply [waiting] for his client group to decide what position he was to defend. Les Aspin [Secretary of Defense] flanked Lake on the other side.

He did not try to lead either, and when Aspin did speak, he usually took the discussion into tangents to skirt the immediate issue. Vice President Gore arrived after we had been talking for over an hour, and we had to shuffle around the table to find a chair for him. . . . The President showed up a little later. . . . At subsequent meetings, the discussions continued to meander like graduate-student bull sessions or the think-tank seminars. . . . Backbenchers sounded off with the authority of cabinet officers. I was shocked one day to hear one of Tony Lake's subordinates, who was there to take notes, argue with him in front of the rest of us (Powell, 1995).

This component of consensus decision making views the team as a mediating entity; one that consists of people with competing interests and conflicting preferences. Accordingly, the team's task is to resolve conflicting viewpoints and build consensus.

Consider a joint team of planners tasked to develop a recommendation concerning allocation of service roles and missions. The team's objective is to allocate various roles and missions to ensure U.S. forces have superior military capabilities while avoiding redundancies and wasting resources. Pillar Two factors:

- Strengthen team identity
- Control internal politics
- Foster competitive debate
- Forge consensus for action

Success of a joint team in developing a consensus recommendation depends on the group's ability to identify as a team, control politics, and mediate conflict among its members. Teams in the joint/interagency arena are not likely to be "normal" teams. Their members represent real, usually entrenched, organizational interests. They feel an obligation to fight for those interests.

STRENGTHEN TEAM IDENTITY. Team identity describes the extent to which members see the group as an interdependent team, and operate from that perspective. Team members with weak identity participate as separate individuals, having no linkage or commitment to the group. Each must rely on his or her own individual skills. In contrast, members of a team with strong team identity capture the power of the group's shared expertise. The quality of a team's identity can be defined by how well team members use the following activities:

Defining Roles and Functions. Team members perform key roles and functions. All team members relate their roles and functions to one another. This shared understanding of interrelated roles and functions enables team members to integrate their work, anticipate what should occur when the unexpected happens, and react accordingly. With this knowledge, team members can assess whether functions assigned to specific members are being accomplished properly. They adjust their workload and assist one another when the need arises.

Engaging. Team members contribute to team success by participating actively in the execution of assigned roles. Each team member is a valuable resource. Team member contributions are secured through active participation and commitment. Low performing teams have members who express their disengagement in a variety of ways. A few may say, "Just tell me what you want me to do and let me get on with my job." Others are silent participants. Some fail to advocate a coherent position. Nearly all disengaged members show a lack of will to voice concerns with the direction their team is headed. High-performing teams recognize disengaged members and try to bring them back into the team.

Compensating. Team members contribute to success by stepping outside of their assigned roles or functions and helping other team members who are overcommitted or absent. When a team comes under pressure, some members may be unable to handle their functions. A high-performing team encourages its members to step outside their roles in order to help teammates.

A high-performing team understands it is not enough for team members just to compensate when problems arise. The team also learns what caused the problem, such as an uneven distribution of workload or an unwise employment of a member's expertise. In these cases, a high-performing team will even-out the work load, allocate appropriate resources to deal with a sudden turn of events, or realign team responsibilities according to member skills and expertise. Strong team identity is especially important to the success of a decision making team.

CONTROL INTERNAL POLITICS. Controlling politics is critical to team decision making because internal politics produce poor team performance and jeopardize organizational effectiveness. Politics consumes team members' time. Politics distracts team members and dissipates their energy. Strategic team members are busy people, and politics draws them away from their responsibilities. Another reason politics leads to poor performance is that politics restricts information flow within the team. Politics entices team members to withhold information from one another in order to "jockey for position."

Strategic decision making is inherently political. It involves complex issues with high stakes, conflicting viewpoints, and uncertain outcomes. However, not all joint/interagency teams engage in politics. In the Cuban missile crisis, President Kennedy's advisory team relied on open and forthright discussion with full access to information in group meetings. Although there was substantial conflict within the team, there was little evidence of politics. Internal politics are defined as tactics and covert ploys team members use to enhance their power to influence decisions. These actions include off-line lobbying, withholding or manipulating information, controlling agendas, or behind-the-scenes coalition building. In contrast, a lack of internal politics within teams is demonstrated by open and frank discussions, with a full sharing of information, and in meetings open to all team members.

The team leader is responsible for controlling internal politics. The first and perhaps most important step for reducing politics that results from conflicting aims or purposes is to understand that information hiding, deception, and games are part of organizational life. Techniques for controlling internal politics include:

- Conduct open and frank discussions.
- Fully share information.
- Make meetings open to all members.
- Avoid micro-management.
- Empower team members.

FOSTER COMPETITIVE DEBATE. Competitive debate describes how decision-making teams manage the conflict inherent in strategic decisions. Conflict within a decision making team is inevitable.

It can be healthy and useful, provided it is structured, focused, and conducted in the spirit of mutual respect. Failing that, conflict can be counterproductive and damaging to the team's mission. Consequently, it is prudent for teams to skillfully foster competitive debate of the issues.

High-performing teams encourage competitive debate—open and frank combative dialogue. Major points of difference and conflicting views are discussed among all team members in open forum. Teams compare different assumptions, facts, and reasons used to support conflicting positions. They focus debate not on bureaucratic "posturing," but on reasons, facts, and assumptions. Skillful teams establish important "ground rules" to promote productive debate:

- Include all affected team members in the debate.
- Adhere to norms for proper conduct and protocol.
- Employ neutral, appropriate language and nontechnical terminology.
- Discourage the use of "we-they" discourse.
- Avoid old grievances about historical injustices.
- Provide full access to information.
- Keep communication channels open.
- Focus on interests and mutual problems instead of "positions."
- Avoid "winner take all" decisions.

FORGE CONSENSUS FOR ACTION. Decision making within government, among nations in alliances and coalitions, in the joint arena, or in public-private sector partnerships hinges on the ability of top decision-making teams to forge a consensus for action. A consensus building process may be slow, inefficient, and often frustrating. However, no team can succeed unless it can sustain its decisions through the difficulties of bureaucratic politics, interest group resistance, and public criticism.

High-performing teams approach the task by first strengthening team identity, controlling internal politics, and fostering competitive debate in an open, cooperative forum. With these conditions in place, these teams push for consensus by employing several tactics known to be effective in dealing with differences among team members.

High-performing teams take a prudent approach to building consensus. They know that gaining unanimous agreement on all issues essentially gives each member veto power, thereby trapping the team in endless discussion.High-performing teams use tactics and procedures that keep pace with the environment. Many successful teams use a two-step procedure called "consensus with qualification" to push for consensus. First, the team debates the issue and attempts to gain consensus. Second, if consensus does not emerge after everyone has had their say, the leader makes the choice, guided by input from the team. All may not agree with the decision, but everyone has a voice in the process.

PILLAR THREE: VIGILANT DECISION MANAGEMENT

Having suffered through endless, pointless, mindless time-wasters for years, I had evolved certain rules for holding meetings. First, everyone got a chance to recommend items for the agenda beforehand, but I controlled the final agenda, which I distributed before the meeting. Once a meeting started, no one was allowed to switch the agenda. Everyone knew that the meeting would last exactly one hour. The first five minutes and the last ten minutes belonged to me. In those first five minutes, I reviewed why we were meeting and what had to be decided by the end of the session. For the next twenty minutes, participants were allowed to present their positions,uninterrupted. . After that, we had a free-for-all to strip away posturing, attack lame reasoning, gang up on outrageous views, and generally have some fun. Fifty minutes into the hour, I resumed control, and for five minutes summarized everyone's views as I understood them. Participants could take issue with my summation for one minute. In the last four to five minutes, I laid out the conclusions and decision to be presented as the consensus of the participants (Powell 1995).

Vigilant decision management describes how a team monitors its activities and adjusts to improve performance. This component of consensus team decision making views a team as a self-correcting entity; one that identifies weaknesses and takes action.

Vigilant decision management focuses on a team's ability to evaluate its performance while working within its tasks. It is one thing to engage in the process of envisioning goals. It is quite another to sit back and assess whether all team members understand the goals. Only through vigilant decision management can a team fine tune its performance. Pillar Three factors:

- Keep pace with the environment.
- Manage time.
- Adjust and self-correct.

KEEP PACE WITH THE ENVIRONMENT. Processes that once relied on careful analyses and broad-ranging strategic plans are no longer a guarantee to success. The premium is now on keeping pace with the environment and moving fast to seize opportunities, especially in crisis or highly competitive environments. The best decisions are irrelevant if it takes too long to make them.

How do high-performing teams manage to resolve competing and paradoxical tensions in strategic decision making? These contradictions include simultaneously:

- Deliberate and rapid decision making processes.
- Powerful team leaders and empowered team members.

- Bold, innovative decisions and safe,. incremental execution.

MANAGE TIME. Time management is the team's ability to meet team goals on schedule and to sequence subtasks so that output from one task becomes timely input to the next one. Effective time management requires skill and constant attention. Even teams with developed time management skills may fall victim to inconsistent monitoring of their schedules. They may work steadily toward their deadlines, only to realize at the last minute that various products of their deliberations don't fit well, or parts are missing altogether.

High-performing teams assign a "time keeper" or set "alarm bells" to alert them of approaching deadlines. These teams set time schedules and check periodically to see if they are meeting self-imposed deadlines. When the team sees they will not be able to accomplish all tasks, they re-order tasks so the most important ones can be completed. They also keep all team members informed of changes.

Protecting the last part of a work period to review the team's product and to complete final revision requires good planning and constant monitoring of a team's schedule. Allocating time effectively allows a team to review and refine its product. This skill is what distinguishes an excellent team product from a mediocre one. Without effective time management, teams crash with a flurry of activity just prior to a deadline. The result is that the team's product comes frustratingly close to high quality, but doesn't quite hit the goal.

To avoid a last-minute crash, high-performing teams build cushions into their time schedules, particularly when they are less experienced with the task at hand. They anticipate that unexpected additions to their tasks and unavoidable difficulties are common, and use this knowledge to gauge the size of the time-cushion they need.

ADJUST AND CORRECT. Adjusting and self-correcting is the essence of double-loop learning, and can be used to improve all consensus team decision making success factors.

Double-loop learning is the process of uncovering errors in fact. In a double-loop learning model, the smaller inner circle represents the actual decision making process. The large outer loop represents critical self-examination coupled with adjusting and self-correcting. The decision to get out on the outer loop and examine what is going on is the sign of a mature, high-performing team. Initially, the decision to get on the out loop will always be a conscious one. But, as the team matures and practices consensus decision making, the trip to the out loop will be automatic.

EVALUATING CONSENSUS TEAM DECISION MAKING PROCESSES. How do we know that the team is achieving its task; how do we provide meaningful developmental feedback to the team as a whole and to the team leader as an individual? If feedback is goinlg to be more than just a trendy catchword, the key words in the above question are 'meaningful' and 'developmental'. One of the ways to approach the question of evaluation is to see it in as a functional system consisting of four basic components:

- Inputs
- Process
- Output
- Feedback

Inputs are defined as the members of the team, including the team leader. Each team member brings with him or her a set of values, morals, skills, attributes, preferences, knowledge, experiences, and expectations.

Process is defined as how a team arrives at a decision. This includes defining the problem, gathering information, building alternatives, evaluating alternatives, and choosing an alternative.

Output is defined as the goal or outcome of the decision making process. Historically, this is the part of the General Systems Model that, within highly structured organizations, gets total attention. The classic symptom of an output-oriented team is the almost instantaneous and heroic leap to a solution without the benefits of an effective consensus.

Feedback is information about the acceptability and effectiveness of the output. It is also information about the effectiveness and efficiency of the decision process. Explicit in the word feedback is the need for measurement and/or assessment. The feedback can be quantitative, that is, objective; or, it can be qualitative, that is, intuitive or subjective. The keys are how we measure or assess, and how we feed back measurement or assessment to the target. Within the context of consensus team decision making, there are two feedback targets: the team as a whole, and the team leader as an individual.

A FINAL WORD

In the final analysis, how you make decisions at the strategic level is just as important as the decision itself. The best decision in the world is nothing without a powerful consensus for action. The most perfect consensus in the world is useless unless it has produced a decision that is good for the organization. At the front end of the entire consensus team decision making process is something called "inputs." People who enter into a consensus decision making must come armed with critical and creative thinking skills that will allow them to efficiently and effectively function at the strategic level.

9

TEAM TACTICS AND TECHNIQUES

Strategic leaders need teams to solve problems and to develop policy alternatives to meet the challenges of working in "permanent white water." This is particularly true when dealing with policy issues and problems related to resource allocation decisions. A high-performing team will use, as one of several tools, a consensus process in estimating the situation and developing policy recommendations at the strategic level of government, business, or in other national or international organizations. The consensus team model uses a systems approach in dealing with strategic problems.

INPUTS

Inputs to the consensus decision making process include the leader, the team members, and other resources used to forge a decision. Clearly, the quality of the decision making process and the decision itself are affected by the quality of the inputs. This is especially true with regard to the team leader's contributions.

The leader of a strategic team has two critical responsibilities. First, the leader is accountable for the effective functioning of the team. Key to maintaining effective functioning is the team's ability to step back periodically and critically examine what is happening. Second, the leader is responsible for developing and maintaining a stable structure as the team engages in its work. This responsibility hinges on the team's meta-decision. A meta-decision is a front-end decision about how the team is going to reach consensus and make a decision.

Consensus acts as an energy force in developing unity of action and effort. Consensus involves both process and outcomes. It is not dictatorial, idealistic, conforming, bland, or sterile. Developing effective consensus has much to do with widespread participation, acceptance, and support for decision implementation.

PROCESS

The process is divided into Three Pillars:

- High Conceptual Level. Employ multiple frames of reference to develop high conceptual power. This means developing a "team mindset." Team members must think strategically to find the highest quality solution to a complex national problem, and to minimize risk of failure. Remember to stay out of the weeds.
- Prudent Consensus Approach. A high-performing team recognizes that effective team consensus does not emerge at the extreme ends of decision options. It usually falls between unanimous agreement and profound conflict. Successful strategic teams develop strong team identity, co_rol internal politics, foster competitive debate, and forge consensus for action.
- Vigilant Decision Management. Effective strategic teams monitor their activities and make necessary adjustments to improve performance. The team is a self-correcting entity that develops capability to assess performance and take corrective action. The critical element here is that team members collectively take responsibility for both identifying and implementing changes to achieve success.

OUTPUT. High-performing teams employ consensus decision making. Common purpose and goals, shared leadership roles, personal and mutual accountability, and collective work products are the values gained from this consensus approach.

FEEDBACK. Strategic leaders have an opportunity to expand power through the feedback process in the model. The most dynamic aspect of the consensus team approach may be in employing feedback effectively to both team members and the team leader. Meaningful feedback is essential to making this process work.

A FINAL WORD. How you make decisions at the strategic level is just as important as the decision itself. The best decision in the world is nothing without a powerful consensus for action, and useless unless it has produced a decision that is good for the organization. Decision makers must come armed with critical thinking skills that will allow them to efficiently and effectively function at the strategic level.

TACTICS AND TECHNIQUES

In addition to the CTDM Model, there are a number of other tactics and techniques that can enhance the decision making processes of strategic leaders. Tactics and techniques are instruments to use to achieve some desired end. We measure a piece of lumber before cutting it to a precise length and angle to fit it in a structure. We choose a particular iron to approach the green given certain wind conditions. We know what we want and we choose our tools from experience, or the practices of others. Techniques are methods a person uses to complete the technical requirements associated with a particular role. Techniques represent knowledge of specialized methods and the skill to apply them. Tactics are more like plans and procedures that would be used to achieve some objective. For example, a leader might use as a tactic the CTDM, and use evaluation of the work as a technique.

Some techniques and tactics break down into simple lists of things that leaders have used successfully. Retired General Colin Powell, former Chairman of the Joint Chiefs of Staff, developed a collection of 'rules' which he kept very much in evidence on his desk:

1. It ain't as bad as you think. It will look better in the morning.
2. Get mad, then get over it.
3. Avoid having your ego so close to your position that when your position falls, your ego goes with it.

4. It can be done!
5. Be careful what you choose. You may get it.
6. Don't let adverse facts stand in the way of a good decision.
7. You can't make someone else's choices.
8. Check small things.
9. Share credit.
10. Remain calm. Be kind.
11. Have a vision. Be demanding.
12. Don't take counsel of your fears or naysaysers.
13. Perpetual optimism is a force multiplier.

The following six sections develop the processes of team tactics and techniques.

SECTION 1: Leader Planning and Preparation

The team leader is responsible for laying the groundwork for team activities. A joint/interagency team leader has several issues to consider before his or her team gets down to business.

1. Clarify the team's identity and charter.

Establish a close working relationship with the Executive Sponsor-the strategic decision maker empowering the team. The Executive Sponsor will guide team efforts and maintain liaison with the other strategic decision makers. This reduces the amount of mixed guidance to the team and clarifies the reporting relationship between the team and strategic decision makers. Clarify and gain agreement on the following issues (Clark and Wheelwright 1992):

- The name of the team.
- The name of the Executive Sponsor.
- The Executive Sponsor's objectives, intent, and guidance.
- The team's purpose and assigned tasks.
- A description of the desired product-what is a quality product?
- Set boundaries on the magnitude of the desired outcome.

- The users and the uses of the team's work.
- Team composition.
- Advisors & experts available to the team.
- The team's scope of authority.
- The Executive Sponsor's milestones.
- The Executive Sponsor's reporting requirements.

2. Understand the complexity of the problem.

Do not go into your first meeting cold. Track the history of the problem and related policy decisions. Develop your intuition about how the policy has taken shape, how the problem evolved to its present state, and how organizations have responded. Understand the stakeholders, their interests and their competitors. Get an accurate view of how stakeholders will react in team activities. Clarify the Executive Sponsor's current political agenda. What perceived need inspired the decision to form a team? What are the risks and consequences of team failure? In the end, what really matters to the strategic decision makers?

3. Write out the team's mission.

Define the team's mission-when, who, what, to do what and where.

4. Determine the conceptual framework.

Most problems lend themselves to a conceptual framework for resolution. In many cases, the systems approach is very useful. Once identified, a conceptual framework serves as a basis for designing the team's process plan. For example, the Framework for Grand Strategy suggests that the team should first assess the international environment, and then assess the current U.S. domestic situation. Overall, the conceptual framework guides the work of the team.

5. Envision goals (Zsambok, et al. 1992)

- Identify the team's specified and implied tasks. State team goals in specific, concrete language:
- Consider how the team's purpose fits into the larger picture.

- State the tasks and products that you must deliver.
- Think about outcomes that would count as team failure.
- Provide a basis for deciding priorities.

6. Determine needed functional expertise to fill gaps.

The conceptual framework may also indicate information needs. These gaps may require the team to rely on outside experts or use of a "fact-finding" subgroup. Consider how the team will fill its information needs.

7. Keep pace with the environment (Eisenhardt, 1990).

You may have to deliver a product quickly. Keeping pace may require "fast decision making." Before you design your team's process plan, you may need to employ tactics to accelerate the team's decision making processes:

- Initiate procedures to track real time information on the environment and current operations. Hone your understanding of what is going on and what works. Do not completely rely on long-term, general performance trends.
- Anticipate that while the team is doing its work, it will need to build several alternatives, using the team's intuitive understanding of the situation and diversity of experience. Even include options that may not have widespread support. Shape alternatives as more information is available. Rely on the power of comparisons in reflective debate to sharpen preferences and team member efforts.
- Seek outside advice. Rely on an experienced counselor to act as a sounding board for ideas or to provide insight into a variety of issues. Be selective in choosing an advisor-a team is best served by a trusted counselor who is respected by his or her colleagues.
- When it's time to decide, include everyone. Use a two-step procedure called "consensus with qualification" to push for consensus. Debate the issue and attempt to forge consensus. However, if consensus does not emerge the leader makes the choice. All may not agree with the decision, but everyone has a voice in the process.

- Integrate policy and tactics. In deliberations of strategic options, discuss required tactical moves in a "quick and dirty" fashion. Refine options as necessary. Do not complete elaborate, detailed tactical planning during deliberations.

8. Design a process plan (Zsambok, et al. 1992).

Describe how your team will approach its work-the sequence of steps and delegation of responsibilities. Consider the conceptual framework you identified to solve the problem in laying out the major steps in the team's process plan. Make sure your plan reflects the sequential step-by-step nature of tasks.

Establish checkpoints in the process plan to review team progress. Plan on periodically checking to see if the team is still on course. Be prepared to recycle on certain issues. Use checkpoints to adjust the team's process.

Write out a team process plan and allocate time available. Frequently, the structure of most "unstructured" strategic decisions involves three basic phases:

- Identification: assess the situation and identify problems.
- Development: search for alternatives and build decision options.
- Selection: evaluate & choose an option, and authorize actions.

9. Manage time (Zsambok, et al, 1992).

Do not go further in your process planning without properly allocating time available to each portion of the team's process plan. Outline a time schedule. Include periodic "alarm bells" to alert the team to approaching deadlines. Protect the last part of a work period to review the team's product and to complete final revision. This requires constant monitoring of a team's schedule. To avoid a last minute crash, build cushions into time schedules.

10. Structure the team.

Consider tasks that need to be done and tailor the team to get the work done. Use designated subgroups as necessary, such as a fact finding subgroup. Be careful that you properly integrate the work of a subgroup into the team's process plan. Make sure that you do not employ subgroups in parallel when their products are sequential in nature.

11. Determine assignment of member roles and functions.

Define team member roles and functions. There are a few key functions that must be assigned initially.

These include time keeper, recorder, spokesman, and chart maker/report writer. Relate team member roles and functions to one another. This understanding of interrelated roles and functions enables team members to integrate their work, anticipate what should occur and, when the unexpected happens, react accordingly.

12. Plan to control internal politics (Eisenhardt, and Bourgeois, 1988).

Control internal politics by empowering team members. When the leader empowers members, most see little need or have any desire to engage in politics.

13. Plan for reflective debate.

- Establish important ground rules to promote productive policy debate(Yates, 1987):
- Include all affected team members in the debate.
- Adhere to norms for proper conduct and protocol.
- Employ neutral language and ordinary, nontechnical terminology.
- Discourage the use of "we-they" discourse.
- Avoid old grievances about historical injustices.
- Provide full access to information.
- Keep communication channels open.
- Focus on interests and mutual problems instead of "positions."
- Avoid "winner take all" decisions.

Encourage team members to speak their minds. Recognize that if debate is left unstructured, there is a high cost to team unity. Unstructured debate can get emotional. Lingering rivalries are possible. Do not allow extreme and strident voices to dominate discourse and obstruct the team's process. Employ proven methods that improve the quality of strategic decisions: include Dialectic Inquiry and Devil's Advocate.

The Dialectic Inquiry method is useful in paring down and producing a high quality assessment of the situation. The Devil's Advocate method is useful in producing a high quality ccurse of action.

14. Plan for forging team consensus.

Consider how you plan to build consensus on situation assessment and your team's proposed recommendation. The basic idea is that everyone must have their say. If push comes to shove, consider using the two-step procedure called "consensus with qualification" to push for consensus.

15. Lay out the agenda for the first meeting.

- The goals of your first team meeting should focus on three themes:
- Strengthening team identity.
- Understanding the rationale for forming the team.
- Starting work on situation assessment.

There is always a temptation to plunge into the problem. Your team will do better in the long run if you spend equal time on all three aspects, especially at the first meeting.

16. Arrange details of first meeting.

Let team members know the following details of the team meeting so they can prepare:

- Organizational sponsor.
- Name of the team meeting.
- Date, time, duration, and location.
- Purpose & desired product.
- Attendees.
- Preparation tasks (if required).
- Resource requirements.

SECTION 2: A General Team Process Plan

A team process plan describes how a team will sequence steps and delegate responsibilities. The team also should gain consensus on a procedure that resolves conflict quickly.

SESSION	TOPICS FOR DISCUSSION
1a Initial Meeting	Team goals, ground rules, member roles, etc. Conceptual framework and process plan.

If you need a conceptual framework, use the tried and true "systems approach" to gain insight into what is happening. A systems approach enables the team to identify key components and how they interrelate. Identify cause-and-effect patterns. Then the team can better understand how possible decisions are likely to turn out.

1b. Problem Awareness: Historical view, key trends, major issues.

Start with a historical frame of reference. Track the evolution of the problem and related policy decisions. Discuss how the policy has taken shape, how the problem evolved to its present state, and how organizations have responded.

2. Stakeholders: Stakeholder views.

Understand the interests of the stakeholders and their competitors; obtain an accurate view of how they have reacted to policy decisions. Consider the stakeholders' frames of reference and perspectives. Search for a shared vision of the future—identify the stakeholders' "common ground."

- Identify external forces and critical trends.
- Listen to stakeholder perspectives on the problem.
- Clarify stakeholder concerns and needs-no debates.
- Identify common concerns among stakeholders.
- Describe a vision for the future that addresses the common concerns and needs of the stakeholders (Weisbord 1992).

3. Assess the Situation (Zsambok): Frames of references, time horizon.

- Expert opinions.
- Functional considerations.
- Gaps and ambiguous information.

Using the systems approach, reframe the problem using more frames of reference-political, structural, symbolic, human resources, economic, military, social, or religious to make sense out of the complex strategic situation. This includes not only a numerical expansion, but also a qualitative amplification of existing frames of reference. Seek all viewpoints to broaden the team's situation assessment. Even under severe time pressure, remain aware of dissenting perspectives and weigh team assessments accordingly.

4. Clarify the Problem: Confirm team goals & debate the issues.

Encourage reflective debate. An open, frank, and combative dialogue on major points of difference and conflicting preferences can be constructive. However, recognize that unstructured debate carries a high cost. Do not allow extreme and strident voices to dominate and obstruct the team's process.

Ensure all members have a shared understanding of the problem before proceeding. Reassess a situation when information changes. Analyze whether new information calls for modifying plans. If so, ensure the team members understand changes in the team's assessment.

5. Create Alternatives: Brainstorm & create strawmen alternatives.

Start by brainstorming solutions to the problem. After everyone has given their input, group the solutions and list the various approaches to the problem.

6. Screen Alternatives: Discuss feasibility and desirability of alternatives.

Request team members review and assess the alternative approaches individually according to their agency/functional perspective. Suggest a simple rating scheme such as:

- Workable and preferred
- Workable but less preferred
- Difficult but preferred
- Not executable (state rationale)

Be careful not to exclude some good alternatives. The screening process enables team members to gain insight into other member perspectives and how each function would have to change to implement a decision. This step is crucial in gaining a broad perspective on how the U.S. Government works and the need for joint/interagency cooperation.

7. Develop Decision Options: Formulate choices for decision

Develop a few decision options in concrete terms. Assign someone (who has a good understanding of the team's mission) to build a few strawmen. Use concrete strawman proposals to discuss, compare, modify, and to chose from. In developing options, consider various stakeholder perspectives.

8. Assess Decision Options: Compare and debate the choices

Here are some important questions to answer in assessing decision options:

- What is the objective we hope to achieve with the decision?
- Have we considered all means available?
- Can or will this option achieve the objective?
- What are the costs-according to each frame?
- Are the desired gains and risks of failure clarified?
- What are the value tradeoffs incumbent with the decision?
- Will the public support the decision?
- Will the situation be altered later?
- What are other possible outcomes-short & long term?
- What will it take in "political capital" to implement?

When assessing decision options, use a devil's advocate or "war gaming" model to search for gaps in a proposal. In war gaming, team members "play out" a decision option against probable threats or simulated opponents, with all risks properly included. During a debate or a war game, gaps become obvious. Also, a devil's advocate or war game can uncover misunderstandings in the way various members perceive a decision option. Once a misunderstanding is identified, clarify the point (Zsambok, et al, 1992).

Ultimately, the team leader is responsible for resolving value conflicts that a team cannot resolve by internal debate. This responsibility is a unique task of a leader. The leader, as a sole person sitting in judgment, can better subordinate one value to another, mindful of the team's mission and its goals (George, 1980).

9. Develop a Recommendation and Required Actions

Integrate policy decisions and tactics. In developing your recommendation, identify required tactical moves. If substantial political resistance exists, mold your recommen-dation by using an incremental approach to make a major policy change, thereby reducing the stakes in the near term. Craft a step-by-step approach in implementing your recommendation.

SECTION 3: A Standard Meeting Agenda

Start on time:

- Bring your team to order.
- Introduce yourself.
- State the purpose of the meeting.

Get to know each other:

- Conduct team member self-introductions.
- Review individual background and skills.
- Present personal expertise / interest on the issue.
- Establish member equity.

Set the stage:

- Restate the team's mission.

- Restate the executive sponsor's guidance.
- Foster a sense of shared mission.

Clarify team goals:

- Explain how the team's mission fits into the big picture.
- State major tasks to be accomplished and products.
- Provide a basis for determining team priorities.
- Make sure everyone understands the team goals.

Work out decision making issues.

- Establish a climate of consensus-style leadership.
- Discuss the need for consensus.
- Present the case for requiring everyone's input.
- Describe the role of reflective debate.

Confirm the meeting agenda:

- Review the meeting agenda.
- Suggest meeting timelines.
- Review the product desired.
- Get consensus on the meeting agenda.

Assign member roles and functions. Functional Experts, Sub-Group Leaders, etc.

Assign admin tasks: Spokesperson, Recorder, Timekeeper, etc.

Outline the team's conceptual framework and process plan:

- How should the team think about the issue?
- Framework for Grand Strategy?
- The Systems Approach?

Process:

- What is your plan to attack the problem?
- Tackle an easy issue first, then the hard ones.
- Get the history on the situation.
- Identify stakeholder interests.
- Assess the situation using member views or reframing.
- Brainstorm solutions.

- Build a consensus strawman, then argue, or start with the status quo and then tweak.
- Use the Delphi Technique.
- Assess the risks and alternative outcomes.
- Use consensus with qualifications.

Get Started: Go to the first step on your agenda.

Make Assignments: Issue task to team members. Require inputs within three to five days so things don't go cold.

Evaluate Team Processes:

- Allow ten minutes at the end for team self-evaluations.
- How did this meeting go? What didn't members like?
- Are we addressing the right issues?
- Are we spinning our wheels?
- What do we need to correct?
- Will this team succeed? Why or why not?

SECTION 4: Ground Rules for Team Members

1. Promptness: Team meetings are sacred. We start on time. Come prepared to participate and contribute to the team.
2. Team Goals: Understand the team's goals. When not clear, seek clarification at the outset, rather than waste time pursuing vague objectives. Do not begin working without good direction.
3. Member Roles: Understand your role and function on the team. Identify other team member roles and functions. Understand the interrelated nature of roles and functions. Integrate your work with that of others.
4. Member Contributions: Contribute to team success by participating actively in execution of assigned roles. Watch for disengaged members and try to bring them back into the team. Do not continue without attempting to improve the situation.
5. Teamwork: Work as a team. Step outside your role to help teammates. Understand it is not enough for you

just to help others—learn what caused the problem. There are several reasons for the need to help—an uneven distribution of workload, or an unwise employment of a member's expertise.

6. Debate the Issues: Everybody engages in reflective debate.
7. Personal Conduct: Adhere to norms for proper conduct in debate:
   - Use neutral language and ordinary, nontechnical terminology.
   - Discourage the use of "we-they" discourse.
   - Avoid old grievances about historical injustices.
   - Provide the team full access to information.
   - Keep communication channels open.
   - Focus on rationale rather than "positions."
8. Open Discussions: Speak your mind. But, do it in a way that does not jeopardize team unity. Avoid becoming emotional, and reverting to lingering rivalries.
9. Self -correct: Call "time out" to correct processes.
10. Team Evaluations: Take time to look at team processes. Be prepared to present your evaluation at the end of each session.

SECTION 5: Tactics for Dealing With Differences Among Team Members (Yates 1987)

1. Establish a sense of shared mission. An obvious, but critical task that provides a sense of self, fosters cooperation, controls fragmentation, and establishes member equity and contains defensiveness.
2. Create incentives to act. Deadlines, assigned responsibilities, and a structured process encourage all members to act and assume responsibility for team success. Time is money-produce something tangible and get it on the street.
3. Track evolution of problems and policy decisions. Tough problems trace a twisting course as they unfold. This

influences the team's intuition about how policy has taken shape, how the problem evolved to its present state, and how organizations have responded.

4. Understand the stakeholders. Understand both personality traits and bureaucratic interests of the stakeholders. Team leaders of joint/interagency team's need to get an accurate view of how various stakeholders will react to team activities.
5. Deal with extremes and the middle. There is a tendency for extreme, strident voices to dominate debate. Team leaders need to control strident voices and give the silent middle a secure opportunity to present their temperate views. Moderate views often reduce conflict.
6. Search for common ground and a shared vision of the future. Most teams have a set of common needs, or "common ground," that should be identified and expanded. The search relies on open discussion, discovery of common needs, and agreement on objectives.
7. Address winning issues first. Begin debate on issues that can be easily resolved. This forms a habit of successful conflict resolution within the team. It reemphasizes that team success means working together in forging consensus.
8. Take decisive action by using an incremental approach. When intense conflict and resistance exist, a practical approach is to employ a step-by-step strategy in solving the problem. Bold decisions, implemented incrementally, gain headway while reducing tension.
9. Build a few "strawman" proposals in concrete terms. To improve reflective debate and focus discussions on tangible issues, assign someone to build a few proposals. Teams work exceptionally well when they have strawman proposals to discuss, compare, and modify.
10. Attend to the needs of the implementers. Nothing gets done unless the supervisor makes it so. Pay attention to the problems your decisions pose for those who must implement higher-level directives.

SECTION 6: Tactics to Accelerate the Decision Making Process-Fast Teams

1. Track real time information. Fast teams track real time information on the environment and current operations to develop an intuitive and deep grasp of the strategic situation. Fast teams focus on today's critical concerns and current organizational operations to learn what's going on and what works.
2. Build multiple, simultaneous alternatives. During the decision process, fast teams immediately begin to build alternatives, using the team's understanding of the situation and diversity of experience. They include options that may not have widespread support, and rely on comparisons in debate to sharpen their preferences.
3. Rely on the advice of an experienced counselor. Fast teams seek outside advice of an experienced, usually older, counselor to act as a sounding board for ideas or to provide insight into a wide variety of issues. They are selective in choosing an advisor who is respected by his or her colleagues.
4. Try for consensus, but don't delay deciding. When it's time to decide, fast teams use a two-step procedure called "consensus with qualification." They debate the issue and attempt to forge a consensus. If a consensus does not emerge after everyone has had their say, the leader makes a choice, guided by input from the team. All may not agree with the decision, but everyone has a voice in the process.
5. Integrate policy decisions and tactics. Fast teams integrate their decisions with other policy decisions. In deliberations of strategic options, they briefly discuss required tactical moves in a "quick and dirty" fashion. Then, they refine options as necessary. Fast teams are able to better implement decisions because they prevent many of the headaches resulting from disconnected tactics.

GENERAL SUMMARY

The practice of decision making in teams, and the selection of a consensus process seems required by the environment where strategic leaders toil. First, the notion of VUCA suggests that it is virtually impossible for a single individual to be able to provide a best course of action; issues are simply too complex, the interest groups too varied, and the implications too hidden for traditional decision making. Secondly, teams are the fundamental building blocks that represent the decision making infrastructure in large, complex organizations characterized by: differences in values, ethics, morals, and culture; the globalization of the economy; and, for the military, the absence of a well-defined military threat. In such a fluid, information-laden, fast-paced environment, the varied team processes, systems, tactics, and techniques available are tools that a skillful strategic leader can use in the pursuit of critical decisions affecting national security.

In addition, systems such as GroupWare offer new ways of making decisions electronically by allowing brainstorming techniques to be applied on line in classrooms, office spaces, or labs. The leader is able to design an electronic meeting, and the participants are able to suggest ideas, rank them, vote on them, and reach consensus in an electronic environment that also permits discussion and human interaction. The conjunction of such systems, with video teleconferencing, can eliminate the need for costs and delays associated with travel.

10

STRATEGIC NEGOTIATIONS

The greatest misunderstanding about the negotiation process is that it is adversarial in nature. In actuality, it is not designed for those with a trial and debate mentality. It is a problem solving process in which each party may look across the table and regard its counterparts as [potential] advocates. —Colosi

Decision making-and the strategic leadership of decision making teams-is a process which moves an individual or a group toward common goals. However, people are not alike in their values and beliefs; there are huge differences among people within a single organization, and even greater differences between people in different organizations.

Strategic leaders must know how to operate across such boundaries that mark differences in expectations and perspectives, and competing values and goals. It is one thing to influence a group essentially in agreement; it is quite a different thing to influence a group with goals in conflict with those you want to pursue.

This sounds formidable, but we do it all the time. We call it negotiation.

WHAT IS NEGOTIATION?

Negotiation is a process whereby two persons or groups strive to reach agreement on issues or courses of action where there is some degree of difference in interest, goals, values or beliefs. The job of the negotiator is to build credibility with the "other side," find some *common ground* (shared interests), learn the opposing position, and share information that will persuade the "other side" to agree to an outcome.

One element of common ground advantageous to a negotiator is a common culture. Those belonging to a culture (team, family, military organization, race, nation, religion, etc.), have common values, beliefs and goals. We consider them to be on the "same sheet of music." Members of groups such as this have shared expectations that reduce conflict and facilitate collective effort. These cultural "norms" evolve from the storming and norming phases in the life of a group. Thus, the process used to arrive at these norms is a bargaining process-negotiation. Negotiation is different from arbitration and other forms of decision making. Unlike an arbitrator, a mediator or an adjudicator, the power to determine the facts, define the process and to make the decision in negotiations rests with the participants, not with a third party. In adjudication processes the objective is to create doubt in a third party's mind (judge, arbitrator) about the "facts" presented by the opposite side, with the goal of winning. In negotiations there is no third party; the party you must convince is your opponent.

Many failures in negotiations result from misunderstanding the basic fact that right and wrong are defined by the parties themselves, not by a third party; and decisions can be implemented and perpetuated in direct proportion to the relationship and reasoning of the participants:

Dinner, Anyone?

Spouse A: I didn't cook anything tonight. I thought we would go out.

Spouse B: I'm exhausted. We had a terrible day today, and I have to be in the office early tomorrow to continue this program review we are doing.

Spouse A: It's the same old story. Always exhausted. Always busy.

Spouse B: You're right. We need more fun. But tomorrow really is important. Just give me a break this one time, and we will go out Saturday, and do that more often; any Saturday you want.

Spouse A: That sounds like a deal.

A norm-forming negotiation led to agreement by Spouse A not to push to have dinner out on a particular night, in exchange for Spouse B's agreement to go out more often. In this case, we can assume the context is one of disagreement on specific expectations within a framework of shared objectives and trust, based on successful outcomes from previous negotiations. The initial needs are different; however, a shared interest is quickly found: the negotiation becomes a shared expectation-a norm. Norm-building is an essential aspect of cooperative and collegial effort. It is a kind of negotiation that depends on the trust that already exists in an established group, or partnership.

Negotiation in its purest sense is bargaining, a process in which two different sides attempt to resolve their differences by finding one set of goals or objectives that each accepts. When this happens, they have found common ground. Fisher and Ury, in their classic book, *Getting to Yes: Negotiating Agreement without Giving In*, contrast two different bargaining concepts, *positional negotiation* and *principled negotiation*. The following concepts are drawn from their writings and those of Colosi in *On and Off the Record*.

POSITIONAL NEGOTIATION

Positional negotiation is essentially adversarial. The negotiators see the process as "win-lose," in which any gains by the opponent are losses by the home team. A classic example of this type of negotiation is contract negotiations in the automobile industry. A union tactic in recent years has been to identify one of the "big three" manufacturers, one particularly vulnerable to the effects of a strike. This company is then targeted for hard negotiations around some key issue. When neither side yields on the issue, a strike ensues and persists until some agreement is reached or one side collapses under the cost of the strike. There are definite winners and losers in this type of negotiation.

Positional negotiation can be illustrated on a more personal basis by the bargaining that accompanies the purchase of a new car. The salesman has a sticker price to begin with. The customer has a desired purchase price. Each wants to come as close to his own figure as possible. The salesman's commission is based on the profit margin achieved, directly from the customer's pocket. The customer wants the lowest possible profit margin, directly from the salesman's commission. Each gains at the other's expense. It is true zero-sum and adversarial. These are examples of "hard" positional negotiation. The negotiators are demanding and unyielding. Positional negotiation can also be "soft." A "soft" bargainer is quite willing to make concessions to "keep the ball rolling." The two negotiators start at different positions in a bargaining range and compromise toward the middle. In "soft" bargaining, agreements are reached quickly. However, "soft" bargainers run a great risk if they happen to encounter a "hard" bargainer. Furthermore, "hard" and "soft" bargaining is zero-sum in nature. Both aim at splitting the pie in order to get what they want. In positional negotiation, each side stakes out its position, and simultaneously (a) attacks the other position and (b) defends its own.

The problem of positional negotiation is that an opponent may become an enemy by a demeaning personal attack. Fisher and Ury and Colosi consider this a big mistake. They think the goal of every effective negotiator is to get the opponent onto their turf-essentially onto their side of the bargaining table-so viewpoints will be similar. If the negotiation is successful, each negotiator will believe that the agreement is a good one. So, if you are a negotiator, your former opponent is going to be advocating a bit of your arguments to his/her boss, and you will be doing the same thing for him/her with your boss.

PRINCIPLED NEGOTIATION REQUIREMENTS

Principled negotiation has a great deal in common with the process of Consensus Team Decision Making. First of all there are four conditions which are essential if a principled negotiation is to have a successful outcome.

Principled Negotiations

Mutual trust.

A positive relationship.

Shared interests (goals or objectives).

Satisfactory zone of possible agreement.

Mutual trust comes from experience, either within the negotiation process or from previous contact. If it does not already exist, it must be built. A negotiator can be trusted when experience shows that person (a) is dependable and will do what he/she promises to do, and (b) does not create surprises. Surprises can take many forms: a sudden demand "out of the blue," a sudden opponent's threat, or an unexpected shift in position. In this sense, trust is a kind of conclusion about the credibility of the other side. Clearly, one of the objectives of a negotiator is to establish his/her credibility in the eyes of the other negotiator.

As a negotiator, your goal is to have more influence on the other side than they have on you. Your goals and objectives must be seen to gain merit while the goals and objectives of the other side lose merit. This means your presentation of "facts" and other evidence must be convincing. You must also create some doubt in the mind of the other negotiator about the validity of his/her position. In essence, you will be influencing that person's belief system, about both your position and his/hers. A positive relationship with the other negotiator is essential if you are to have this kind of influence. This sounds difficult, especially in view of the fact that negotiation has the potential for conflict. However, experienced negotiators emphasize that it is both possible and required.

A positive relationship makes possible the development of common ground; in principled negotiation the common ground can include similar goals and objectives. Instead of negotiating against each other, the negotiators form a team and negotiate "against" the problem. They now have shared interests.

Finally, a Zone of Possible Agreement (ZOPA) must exist. As a negotiator, you must know what your zone is. This may appear to apply more to positional than to principled bargaining because a ZOPA is the least favorable agreement you would accept, and the most favorable one you believe the other negotiator would accept. However, with a bigger pie, the ZOPA shifts for both in the positive direction. A negotiator must also have a Best Alternative To a Negotiated Agreement (BATNA). As part of the preparations prior to beginning negotiations, each negotiator must decide at what point it is best to cease negotiating and to be satisfied. Although the BATNA may change slightly as negotiations proceed, a negotiator will use the BATNA agreed upon by his team as a touchstone throughout the negotiation process. With a BATNA a negotiator never feels cornered or under pressure to yield to pressure from the other side— the predetermined goal has defined the point at which negotiations are no longer profitable and may be ended.

Negotiators rarely have the authority to make final decisions. They are sent as representatives of those who do have that authority, who are the "closers." As "closers," they have a significant advantage.

They are protected from the possibility that in a weak moment they will accept an impossibly poor agreement. In addition, if principled negotiation has not been possible, there may be times when the negotiator has no easy reply to a hard bargaining opponent. It may be useful to end a session with the need to go back and discuss options with your "closer." By the same token, a negotiator would never want to enter negotiations without detailed instructions from the "closer" as to what options are satisfactory and what options are not; i.e., the Zone of Possible Agreement and the Best Alternative to a Negotiated Agreement.

THE PRINCIPLED NEGOTIATION PROCESS

Once you have established the necessary conditions for negotiations, what is the advantage of principled negotiations? As with Consensus Team Decision Making, there is a process for principled negotiations. Each of these steps is discussed in detail below:

Principled Negotiation Requirements

People: Separate the people from the problem

Interests: Focus on interests, not positions

Options: Generate several before deciding what to do

SEPARATE THE PEOPLE FROM THE PROBLEM

A common failing when there is a difference of opinion or goals is to attack the opposing person while attacking the opposing position, especially if the attack is demeaning. It will unfailingly have negative outcomes in both decision making and bargaining. Experienced leaders and experienced negotiators separate the people from the problem. Some of the ways Fisher and Ury suggest are:

- Relationships. Bargaining, even principled bargaining, may involve strong comments about the substantive issues. It is only human nature that these, on occasion, are taken as personal attacks, generating emotions that block communication. A good relationship can be a vaccine against communication blockages. But the relationship needs to be built early in the game, just as a vaccine works best before exposure to the disease. Some negotiators do this by chatting in a friendly way during the breaks. On more consequential issues, negotiators may ask for and get a "book" on the other side, that includes background and interests, to facilitate building a good relationship.
- Perceptions. In the heat of battle, it is easy to view the opponent as a personal enemy, as opposed to someone who is just doing a job. Effective negotiators must get inside the heads of their opponents so they can see the issues as they do. From inside the opponent's frame of reference, many things become clear: why a given position is held so fiercely, where the vulnerabilities are, where there are doubts, and where there may be blind spots.

The primary goal of principled negotiation is to achieve rational outcomes in the best interest of both parties. However, sometimes this just doesn't work, and positional bargaining is the only option. Then it becomes imperative to know the issues well from your opponent's perspective while denying that advantage in turn. In that way, you can control your opponent's perceptions better than your opponent can control yours.

Perceptions come in many ways. Colosi makes a point of the importance of body language and tone as communications channels that give information, sometimes information of crucial value, to the other side. Fisher and Ury emphasize such things as acting inconsistently with expectations. For example, they believe an important part of the peace process between Israel and Egypt was that Sadat upset Israeli-and Arab- expectations by flying to Jerusalem in November 1977. "Holding the door" for your enemy is inconsistent with the perception of being an enemy; so do it.

- Emotion. The heat of battle is truly felt by all. And while a principled negotiator would not launch invective toward the other side, the other side might not be so principled. Experienced negotiators have long since learned how to manage their emotions. A part of this is understanding that there are going to be emotions. Skillful strategic leaders — and skillful negotiators — can turn anger on and can turn it off for effect, while at the same time avoiding the blow and counterblow that gets out of control. This is not always easy, especially when the other side is trying to destabilize your side by personal attack.

If under personal attack, promise — don't threaten: You might say, "These are personal attacks which are not relevant to the substantive issue, and for that reason they are unfair. If they continue, I am going to leave and return tomorrow. Perhaps we can make more substantive progress then." The essence of promise versus threat is that the statement takes the form of what the speaker will do as opposed to what will be done to the other party (Colosi).

- Communication. The essence of communication is the transmission of meaning. Fisher and Ury think much communication in positional bargaining fails because meaning is not clearly transmitted. Where the bargaining is positional, Colosi adds that one may want to be judicious about the direction of communication. If the bargaining is positional, the negotiator who gets "inside the other negotiator's head" has a competitive advantage.

> The mandate is for active listening, getting the other person to talk more- and thus reveal more. Listening with interest to what the other negotiator has to say pays dividends, you are getting valuable information about his/her position and intentions, without giving away your own.

These are only a few of the many ways to build a positive relationship. Your image as a negotiator must be that of someone who is credible, reliable, trustworthy, and principled. In many negotiations, this image can be used as a tool to move toward negotiating on the merits of the case, rather than on the relative hard-headedness of the negotiators.

INTERESTS

If a positive relationship can be established with the other negotiator, the only remaining ingredient for principled negotiation is finding shared interests that can serve as the common ground for generating creative options. (Remember that the defining characteristic of principled negotiation is making a bigger pie.) Interests are a key issue because interests are the factors underlying the decisions.

Fisher and Ury provide an example of how an understanding of the underlying interests may lead to a win-win solution, a bigger pie. In the Camp David negotiations between Israel and Egypt in 1978, the positions seemed to be non-negotiable. Israel occupied the Sinai and was not about to cede it back to Egypt. Egypt wanted it back and was not about to sign a peace agreement with Israel until that happened. Examination of the underlying interests, however, was revealing. Israel did not really want the Sinai; what it wanted was security. And Egypt did not really want to threaten Israel's security; what it wanted was the land back. So the solution to the problem (not the negotiated middle ground between two positions) was to return the Sinai to Egypt, on the condition that it be de-militarized. Once the interests were properly framed, the solution was relatively easy.

There is one final reason for an in-depth understanding of both sets of interests. Sometimes principled negotiation is not possible and harder positional bargaining must be used. When that is the case, it pays to know if there are divisions in the enemy camp. Colosi points out that there probably will be "stabilizers" who would bargain "soft," and "destabilizers" who would bargain very "hard" indeed, and might scuttle the negotiations if they could. A thorough understanding of the other side's case is essential for the exploitation of their differences.

OPTIONS

It is here that negotiators have the best opportunity to expand the pie. It is also here that principled negotiation begins to look a lot like Consensus Team Decision Making. There are three strong points of similarity. The first is that neither can go forward without common ground. In CTDM, it is shared goals and objectives; here it is mutual interests. The second is that a divergent, or creative, thinking phase is required. The third is that creativity can be squelched, and by much the same thing: premature evaluation and/or early closure. Fortunately, many of the tools that work for CTDM also work here.

The primary obstacle to expansion of the pie is that convergent thinking takes place too early in the process. For example, taking a narrow view of what is possible, or focusing upon obstacles rather than on possibilities. As in CTDM, these obstacles can be avoided by leadership that keeps options open and deliberately challenges tendencies toward closure. To make this happen, the negotiator must concentrate on actually leading the process, as opposed to being a participant in it. Here we see another similarity to the CTDM process, where one or more interested parties must monitor a process while they are also participating in it.

As long as options are kept open, many avenues for creative ideas may appear. One of the more interesting examples given by Fisher and Ury concerns dovetailed interests for mutual gain. These may result when the participants have different beliefs about possible outcomes and are willing to "bet" on their beliefs: An aging baseball player wants a salary increase and is confident he can perform well in the coming season. His manager does not agree. The player offers to bet on his belief. The manager agrees and a deal is struck. Each gets what he wants in the negotiation.

A Salary Negotiation

Buck: I'm sorry, Mr. Walden, but your salary offer just isn't good enough. I had a good year last year and I know that I can win at least 20 games this year.

Walden: Well, it is about the best we can do. After all, you are 38 years old and I don't think your arm is going to hold out for another season— not to win 20 games.

Buck: I am willing to bet it will. How would this be? I'll sign for what you are offering if you will give me a bonus for each game I win— one twentieth of the difference between what you are offering and what I want.

Walden: Why not?

MAINTAIN OBJECTIVITY

If there is one theme in principled negotiation, it is that the process should be rational and objective. Every effort must be made to de-personalize the process, to make it as far divorced from win-lose conflict as possible, and based on principles as firmly as possible.

In the CTDM process, explicit recognition is given the importance of monitoring and maintaining a high conceptual level. This is similar to *metacognitive* awareness in an individual which occurs when a person thinks about how he/she is thinking. In CTDM we monitor the process to provide feedback to the decision making team. In principled negotiation, a similar monitoring task is adopted to be sure the process does not drift off into conflict. The principled negotiator must avoid being drawn into a contest of wills, or into a subjective debate about whose view of an issue is better. If the process devolves into winning and losing, it becomes positional and contentious.

The vaccine against conflict is a continuous push for objectivity. If attacked on belief, ask where data might be found to check the accuracy of the belief. An excellent example given was based upon Law of the Sea negotiations about ocean bed mining. The United States wanted to pay no license fee for mineral rights to a parcel of sea bed. Some developing nations wanted a very hefty license fee imposed. Neither would budge. The deadlock was broken when an economic model was brought into play, which showed the probable profit from the mineral wealth in a parcel. It was evident that no company could afford the gamble that would be imposed by the fee the developing nations wanted. On the other hand, it was equally evident that some fee would be affordable. This model allowed a dispassionate examination of the problem and addressed the interests of both parties. The negotiators came to agreement on fees.

Pressure in negotiations can come from many sources: bribes ("... if you will just agree to this one point, we can get out of here..."); threats ("...if you don't agree to this, which is my bottom line, we will strike tomorrow ..."); manipulation ("... why can't you bring your boss; he would approve this deal even if you won't ..."); refusal to budge from a position ("... I won't go a cent lower."). The response is to look for an objective principle that can relieve the pressure.

TABLE MANNERS

Senior executives make a strong point about good manners in negotiations. Abusive behavior, and hitting back-giving them as good as you got-always backfires. The negotiator must constantly be in command of his or her behavior, particularly emotional responses to the behavior of the other side. Unprincipled negotiators may try to de-stabilize the opposition by any number of tricks and pressure tactics. The point is that it takes two to play. If the principled negotiator doesn't play, the unprincipled one is left huffing and puffing alone. It takes a great deal of patience, maturity and experience to refrain from responding in kind.

NEGOTIATIONS WITHIN NEGOTIATIONS

One aspect of negotiations seldom addressed is that of the negotiations which take place on each side of the table, in contrast to those which take place across the negotiating table.

In reality, the most difficult aspect of the negotiation process can be reaching consensus with your ratifier or your team members. Experienced negotiators prepare relentlessly and set aside time and energy for these "internal" negotiations. The effective management of your relationship with your organizational hierarchy may be the most important issue to ensure success.

WHEN PRINCIPLES WON'T WORK

Sometimes, even with the best of intentions and skill, a principled negotiator cannot bring the other side around. Sometimes, the other side simply won't play fair and use bullying, psychological warfare, or deliberate deception tactics. And, on occasion, there may be no evidence of dirty tricks but the issues are so monumental that trust is unthinkable. SALT negotiations is an example. There was ample evidence that both sides had a shared interest in negotiating a downsizing of the nuclear arsenal, both to lessen the global threat and to reduce its maintenance cost. But the potential consequences of possible deception in implementation made trust impossible. The talks could not bear fruit until both sides could agree on methods for inspection compliance.

The point is that trust doesn't exist in negotiation until it is established by credible actions. Even then agreements must be backed up by iron-clad ways of verifying compliance. Rose-colored glasses seem to be the favorite apparel of ex-negotiators who were taken to the cleaners by their previous opponents. Any negotiator must remember that he/she is entering a contest. There is a mandate for ethical behavior in this contest, and there are gains if it is principled. However, there are no judges or referees in this contest, and the assumption that an opponent will be playing by your ethical and principled rules is unwarranted. Trust may be a conclusion but trust may never be an assumption.

One of the essential elements of negotiation is knowing if there are viable alternatives. Again, this is like strategic leadership. When strategic goals are being nailed down, a good strategist envisions options and asks about the downside of each. Creative vision is necessary to identify the options, but it must be paired with analytic rigor in the evaluation phase.

What happens if they simply won't agree? With a BATNA (Best Alternative to a Negotiated Agreement), the question is already answered.

Without a BATNA, a negotiator doesn't know how important the negotiations are, and will be vulnerable to pressure from the other side — and that pressure will come. With a BATNA, the pressure switches to the other side, unless they also have prepared one. So the first element in preparation strategy is to develop the best BATNA possible. That doesn't mean just knowing that there is an alternative. It means searching for a good one, and even working hard to improve it. Negotiation may not be necessary if a good BATNA can be developed.

A Good BATNA

Joan smiled as she walked in her boss's office for her annual appraisal. The letter in her pocket felt good. It offered a starting salary in another firm 25 percent higher than his.

"Joan," said the boss, "you've done great work this year but we are really in a pinch on the raises we can give. I'm going to put you in for a 5% raise."

"Boss," said Joan, "I have two new patents that will make this company a bundle. I am worth more than that."

The boss asked, "How can you be so sure of that?"

Joan said, "I can be sure."

THE NEGOTIATION PROCESS

There can be no doubt that the process is a contest where each negotiator can take nothing for granted, and can never relax. Even if it is possible to establish mutual interests and move into the principled negotiation mode, prudence demands risk analysis and control. The more consequential the issue, the more important risk management is. The key to a successful negotiation process is preparation. Experienced negotiators say that you should prepare, prepare, prepare.

The Negotiation Process

Discover what the other side knows

Educate the other side on your position

Create doubt about the other side's position

Make the other side advocates for your position

Determine enforcement means

Enhance implementation through good relationship

Until the other side establishes trustworthiness by credible performance, you must learn as much about the other side's position as possible, while revealing as little as possible about one's own:

First, you should have completed preliminary work, to scope out what the other side's position and strategy will be, so you aren't hearing it in negotiations for the first time. Second, you should have selected your team with an eye toward enhancing your ability to figure out the other side — its strengths and its weaknesses. And your team should be highly disciplined in order to establish a good relationship. It should also be understood who talks for the team .

The second principle is to get the other side to lose confidence in its position while gaining confidence in yours. This is where "education" comes in- the process of selectively revealing information that strengthens your case while questioning that of the other side. It sounds like a breach of ethics to reveal information selectively to strengthen your case while weakening your opponent's. However, until trust is established, negotiation is a contest. You would not use your weak arm to arm-wrestle with a stranger. Ethics in negotiation has to do with being principled and fair, and neither demands complete disclosure.

The "decision" in negotiation is whatever the negotiators agree on, and can convince their ratifiers to accept. This, incidentally, is another reason for intense preparation prior to the actual negotiation. If you are not going to reveal weaknesses, you can be sure your opponent will not. You will need to discover them through meticulous spadework before the fact, with careful attention to body language, tone, and what your opponent does not say.

This leads to the third principle: creating doubt about the other side's position. As you educate the other side to see the advantages of your position, you want to undermine their confidence in their own position. These two principles, educating the other side on your position and creating doubt about their own position, are a cyclical process.

The fourth principle is to make the other side an advocate for your own position. Neither you nor they will have the power to decide. That power has been withheld by those who sent you to negotiate for them. They are your "ratifiers," your "closers." You are a better negotiator than they are, or you would not have been sent to do that job for them. So a part of your strategy is to manage the other side's access to your ratifiers. You don't want someone as good as you are to have access to your own decision makers.

The Ratifier

Customer: This dickering is getting on my nerves. I'll give you $15,599 for that car and not a penny more. That is my last offer.

Salesman: I don't know if we can do that, but I'll take it to my manager and see if he will approve it. (Later) I'm really sorry but my boss said we can't do that. We would lose money.

Customer: Well, if you don't know what kind of deal year boss will buy, I'm through negotiating with you. Bring him out and I will deal with him.

Salesman: I'm sorry. He was leaving just as I was talking to him. He won't be back until tomorrow.

Customer: Well, you know my position. Tell me what you think he will approve.

First, the customer and the salesman are doing positional bargaining. Given a "hard" position, the salesman takes the offer to his ratifier, thereby posturing as the customer's advocate, but protecting himself from having to say no. The ratifier, who may not even have been there, refused. The customer now demands to see the individual who has the authority to decide, but the salesman cannot afford to have his ratifier brought into the process. The customer then seeks to co-opt the salesman by asking him to frame something the ratifier will approve. This still may not work, but the salesman is now on the defensive, for at least a few moments. Negotiators must be very skillful in their use of psychological advantage. This remains true, though a less critical consideration, in principled negotiation.

The fifth principle is to enhance both enforcement and implementation by building in objectively verifiable means. Even with principled negotiation and trust, future doubt or suspicion can be avoided by including in the agreement some objective means for checking that the agreement is honored by both sides, and for enforcing compliance. Sales contracts, for example, have clauses that address the potential for default. A house loan is secured by a deed of trust. Equally, negotiated agreements should be written with some consideration of how non-compliance would be treated.

The sixth principle is that it is essential to maintain a good relationship with the other side. A good relationship enhances the operation of the preceding principles, and, indeed, may be essential to some of them. Further, if initial initiatives toward principled negotiation get no response from the other side, maintaining a good relationship "in spite of it all" may produce a change of heart with your opponent. Principled negotiation can emerge at almost any time, so long as one negotiator has been behaving in a principled manner all along. So the other side must be treated with courtesy and respect.

PREPARE, PREPARE, PREPARE

You may not have total discretion about the membership of your team. However, you are still responsible for the outcome. You also want to obtain basic understanding of the other side. If at all possible, you should include someone who has that understanding. That person will need to educate you before negotiations begin, and watch the other side as negotiations continue, interpreting the meaning of events you might miss. (Remember the process observer used in CTDM?) You also need experts on the substantive issues to be negotiated. Finally, you need a "second" who is an expert in human behavior and the negotiation process itself. This "second" will be your process observer, providing feedback on your behavior, how the other side is responding, and how your own team is reacting. Your "second" can also be a sounding board if a change in strategy seems necessary.

Your own team did a lot of debating on strategy and positions to be taken. Certainly, the other team also debated. A part of your team's charter is to look for evidence of that debate, to determine where the dissent is on the other side.

Your effort consists of using the full resources available to you to scope out the other team, their track records, their power structure, their ratifier, and whatever personal information you can discover to help you establish a positive relationship with your counterpart. Your might even include assigning responsibilities to your team members for developing counterpart relationships that would be supportive of those you will establish.

Your homework must include a detailed organization of your own team. All teams, yours and the opposition, will have "stabilizers" and "destabilizers." Stabilizers are members who make too many concessions in "soft" bargaining, and destabilizers are members who would make "hard" demands and even break off negotiations. Your task is to control your own team and exploit differences on the other team by identifying their stabilizers and destabilizers who can be managed to your own advantage. The organization of your own team should plan for contingencies, ensuring that you have an accurate and comprehensive record of what has transpired. At least one team member should be assigned the task of taking notes, and the negotiator should use these notes to get agreement from the other side as to what has transpired. If the other side can be induced to sign the notes, then you have gained an even greater degree of control.

A final note on team discipline added by Colosi is that information is contained in everything that happens. If a note is passed, the mere act of passing it may reveal that the current discussion has high relevance, and may also indicate a weakness or objective. Sudden whispering among team members is highly revealing. You, as an experienced negotiator, will have learned all this, but your team will not. Your preparation needs to include a "ground school" for your team on the tone and other psychological aspects of negotiation, and how to manage this facet of the negotiations.

Finally, you must establish a solid relationship with your ratifier. You need unambiguous understanding of his/her expectations, and ZOPA. You and the ratifier need a positive relationship because you are going to come back with something that is not exactly what was desired. You must build trust with your ratifier. A part of this will be keeping the ratifier informed as negotiations progress.

SUMMARY

This chapter has only begun to explore the intricacies of strategic negotiations, an extraordinarily important part of our professional leadership and personal lives.

With our negotiating skills, we protect our critical interests, make agreements that reduce conflict about expectations, encourage collective effort, and establish the foundations for long-lasting partnerships. Negotiation is not a war, nor is it a cause for antipathy. Properly principled, negotiation is a problem solving process in which initially opposing viewpoints can be brought into the fortunate circumstance of mutual gain-creating a bigger pie which then can be shared by all.

ORGANIZATIONAL PROCESSES AND LEADERSHIP REQUIREMENTS

The U.S. defense industry is a conglomerate of companies working in a global environment to supply the Defense Department with the vast range of materials and products, from shoe strings to stealth aircraft, needed for national security.

It is an organization of organizations, a system of systems, that under a single, fragile term gathers corporations and firms of all sizes and focuses them on the security interests of the U.S.

Great, far-reaching, exemplary, and revolutionary progress might begin in the minds of individuals, but accomplishment is often the result of the convergence of other resources, people and money best represented by the term organization.

Earlier chapters described the environment where public servants, or private entrepreneurs and managers, operate. Characterized as a context of "permanent white water," or as an environment that is volatile, uncertain, complex, and ambiguous, it levies special demands on strategic leaders who must operate successfully, and master tricky and precipitous currents.

The qualities most useful in transitioning from an operational stratum to one with higher challenges and demands are: the ability to function conceptually at a high level, to form and work with teams, and to lead in a process of consensus decision making.

These qualities are identified in the literature of Stratified Systems Theory, in the results of the Strategic Leader Development Inventory, in individual assessment feedback, in personal commitments to development, and in understanding consensus decision making. A strategic leader, committed to utilizing a high performing team as a way of successfully coming to grips with the policy and operational environment, is well on the way to advancing to more senior levels of responsibility.

WHAT ARE ORGANIZATIONS?

Organizations are fundamentally social structures where an individual in association with others has the potential to reach certain levels of fulfillment that might otherwise be unattainable. Organizations supply both a condition and a context for dealing with our various environments. Man is by nature gregarious, and seeks to join with others to achieve common purposes.

An individual with an interest in a military career as a soldier, becomes a member of an army. Organizations represent a culmination of a social order that links the individual to a collective body that in turn provides certain goods to the individual, while it simultaneously serves society.

A school is a learning organization; our community is a governing and service-providing organization; and the line of work we ultimately enter may be a business organization, a service organization, an industry or production organization, or a professional organization. In other words, "organizations are social inventions or tools developed by men to accomplish things otherwise not possible. They are social inventions that take a variety of people, knowledge, and usually, materials of some sort and give them structure and system to become an integrated whole" (Litterer 1973).

It is the character of organizations to gather the interests, needs, and desires of people into an entity that represents what it is that they want. Thus, a school gathers together the teachers and people of a society and transmits its culture and mores to the people. A hospital gathers together its physicians and other health care providers and its technology for the diagnosis and treatment of those who are ill. A government gathers together the range of citizen services-police and fire protection, economic development, the provision of roads, sewers, and other public works that also may be consistent with the basic needs of the governed-to express a certain quality of life for them.

Organizations wax and wane with the needs of a society. At times, a society might need to have the protection of large military forces, or of "big" government, or of directed education, or health care, or of specific voluntary societies and organizations that protect the wetlands, and certain threatened species. At other times, society might be able to dispense with some of those organizations, and allow more freedom, or simply the opportunity to organize in different ways. Thus, a conscript army might become voluntary; education, after a certain level of required schooling, might also become voluntary. Large medical centers might give way to decentralized clinics that are more accessible to people. In short, organizations have a kind of life that responds to the vagaries of the environment.

CHARACTERISTICS OF ORGANIZATIONS

STRUCTURAL FRAME. Virtually any text or treatment about organizations provide some taxonomy of attributes or qualities that can be derived from organizations. In *Reframing Organizations*, Bolman and Deal use the device of the "structural frame" to identify the parts and components of an organization, and of their relationship to each other, both internally and externally.

SIZE. An organization could also be characterized in terms of its size, and in some instances size alone will be a factor in the strategic environment. The Boeing Company, the world's leading commercial jetliner manufacturer, announced that it will buy McDonnell Douglas, the top builder of military aircraft. The new company will be the world's largest aerospace enterprise with assets of nearly $44 billion dollars, and a workforce of nearly 210,000 employees. This consolidation creates a firm that will have instant impact on domestic and international issues associated with the aircraft industry. Size matters! Similar organizations, the Department of Defense, The International Red Cross, Greenpeace, Nike, and Reebok reflect size as a factor.

INTERNAL PROPERTIES. But there are also internal properties. In *Reframing Organizations: Artistry, Choice, and Leadership*, Bolman and Deal cite four "properties" of organizations:

1. Organizations are complex, because of the work, the variety of people, internal divisions (e.g., offices, branches, directorates), and relations with other components outside the organization. This follows from the notion described by VUCA. It is the very mix of task and work, people, communication, problem solving and decision making, and their permutations and combinations that produce both causal and accidental effects in any given circumstance.
2. Organizations are surprising, in that any prediction of the impact of plans considered in reaching a decision are not fully reliable. The actions of a leader can be misinterpreted by others, or as sometime happens, interpreted to fit a particular model held by one of the participants. The Iran-Contra scandal seemed to be caused in part by the interpretations of some members

of the national security council staff as to the exact intentions of the President. Alexander George, writing in his book, *Presidential Decisionmaking*, discusses what he calls impediments to decision making in organizations, including tendencies to be narrow and parochial in identifying problems or in protecting the interests of one's own organization. Overstating the severity of problems, early dependence on proposed solutions, manipulation, and the use of procedural routines may be flaws and have negative effects on policies that are adopted.

3. Organizations are deceptive, in that structure, culture and practice frequently mask things that may really be occurring. The locker room of some professional or collegiate sports teams may be a better index of the true character of the team than the playing field itself. Ralph Nader exposed evidence that indicated that General Motors was producing a model of automobile that was "unsafe at any speed". Physicians, clergy, teachers, attorneys, jurists, and members of other respected professional organizations have sometimes concealed and withheld information from the public. Many organizations have hidden certain kinds of information that would be scandalous and harmful to the organization.
4. Organizations are ambiguous. Trying to figure out what really happens is complicated by such things as the quality and reliability of information, or the ability to properly identify the problem, or the size of the organization. It is not easy to know what might really be going on in an organization, and how the leader may be influencing its members.

OTHER WAYS TO CHARACTERIZE ORGANIZATIONS

MECHANICAL MODEL. There are still other ways to characterize organizations. One way is to see them in terms of a mechanical model which visualizes an organization in terms of inputs, processes, and outputs. In such a view, an organization is very much like a machine which might take a piece of metal or plastic, subject it to heat and pressure and other forces, and produce a component of an automobile. However, even in the mechanical view, and especially in terms of strategic decision making in government, the simple model becomes complex.

A simple input-output model describes inputs in terms of a set of information, options, and recommendations that are processed by the decision maker, and describes outputs as a complementary set of decisions, or actions for implementation. The process, comparable to a series of computerized machines on the factory floor, consists of a series of stages that inputs and outputs pass through. These stages are characterized by a cadre of people—gatekeepers, special assistants, counselors, secretaries, and confidants—whose perceived task is to help the decision maker understand the environment, and the sets of problems that emerge from it. A danger is that the problem may be so influenced by ministers and counselors that the decision maker may not see pure inputs; similarly, an executive decision might be distorted or even not acted upon by the bureaucracy or organization. In fact, at times, some agent acting on behalf of an executive might short circuit the process (Alexander George).

BIOLOGICAL MODEL. So, even in the mechanical model, rational and logical in its problem solving, there is the influence of living beings in organizations. That leads to still another view of an organization as a biological model; in this view, an organization passes through stages of birth, growth, maturity, aging, and death. In reality, most organizations could be viewed in that frame.

An organization is born out of a need; it grows and reaches a level of survivability; it exists for a period of time in a stable, maturing, and developing condition—profits are up, students are graduating, people are healing from surgeries, détente and peace is achieved; it ages gracefully, or not, perhaps evolving, changing form-consolidating, downsizing, expanding-and ultimately reaching a stage where its product, or its service, or its role is no longer necessary or relevant.

For example, emergency management in the last half century in the United States has moved from a concentration on protection of citizens from nuclear attack to protection from hurricanes, earthquakes, and floods; from an office in the White House to disaggregated offices in several federal agencies to re-organization as an independent agency. Its programs have often been declared irrelevant, and the Congress has seemed to announce its death more than once without shedding a tear. Yet, it survives. Businesses come and go. CEOs move from one corporation to another, often with a mandate to "heal" a sick patient on some form of life support system. Organizations grow and change in reaction to the stimulus of the environment and what it demands at any point in time.

Each of these models, the mechanical and the biological, might be used as analogies, or frames when attempting to analyze the condition of an organization. But, despite the notion of a frame, many organizations do not seem to have boundaries. They are made up of multiple constituencies, their resources are drawn from disparate sectors of the economy, government, or the private sector, and the impact they have is experienced in widely separate quarters. A company that mines coal, for example, is connected to commercial power companies, to regulators of the federal Department of Energy, to other regulators in the Environmental Protection Agency, to OSHA, to unions, lobbyists, investors, utilities, local and state jurisdictions, the media, and other energy sources.

CONCLUSION

People affiliate with organizations to pursue some purposeful activity of benefit to them at a particular time. Organizations can arise from a variety of sources-economic, recreational, educational, artistic-and can be either mechanistic, or biologic; in the latter case, organizations sometimes seem to take on a life of their own and a specific life-cycle can be discerned. However an organization is structured, it holds great potential to enable its members to achieve a level of success they might not otherwise attain. On the other hand, an organization can become self-serving, and ignore or otherwise limit opportunities for its members. Most strategic leaders carry out their role in an organization, however it is cast and molded. The Chief of Naval Operations, the Speaker of the House of Representatives, the Secretary of the Department of Transportation, and the CEO of IBM are all strategic leaders in different environments, all volatile, uncertain, complex, and ambiguous. Even those who seem to set off on a singular quest (one thinks of Ralph Nader) and burn with the zeal of reform, often end up having to establish, and/or work with organizations whose influence, assets, and other resources can be leveraged against formidable, stable, and powerful organizations.

ORGANIZATIONS AS SYSTEMS

Organizations represent a complex mix of the following: vision, goals, objectives, and purposes; routines and practices; people; machines; and both an internal (culture, values, ethics) and external relationship (other organizations, interest groups, and the environment). Knowing an organization's purpose, what it does, and how it does it seldom tells a leader all that needs to be known: the more complex parts of an organization are its vision, values, power, and how these elements affect the people in the organization.

Some of the complexities and interrelationships between and among the CEO and different levels of employees, and a concern for the environment, are seen in the following excerpt describing a corporate organization:

In the second story of a wooden lodge overlooking a meadow and pond veiled by mist, Tom Chappell, the CEO and co-founder of Tom's of Maine, exhorts his 75 employees to contemplate nature. Normally these workers would be churning out fennel toothpaste, calendula deodorant, honeysuckle shampoo and other aromatic aids to personal hygienics. But on this overcast Tuesday morning, the company' executives, salesmen, toothpaste mixers and warehouse workers are gathered at an off-site location to discuss the company's commitment to the environment as articulated in its "mission statement." Attendance at the meeting is mandatory; Chappell has shut down the company's plant, at a cost of more than

$100,000 to insure that everyone is present. Chappell kicks off the morning program with a brief homily that traces his own environmentalism back to a childhood spent among idyllic river valleys and mountain ranges near Pittsfield, Mass., and on the coastal islands of Maine. . . he suggests that everyone turn to their neighbor and briefly describe their own relationship to nature, which they all proceed, self-consciously, to do.

Next, the employees participate in a 90-minute game that uses a computer model to simulate a local fishing industry. Competing in teams for imaginary ships, cash and troves of fish, they plunder and inevitably destroy the fragile ecosystem. In the aftermath of their collective remorse, they are asked to discuss, in small groups, ways to improve their environmental stewardship, then to present their ideas...to the entire gathering. The morning concludes with a poem. As the meeting adjourns, everyone strolls outside for a company picnic, set beside a hillock of evergreens beneath a luminous gray sky (Barasch 1997).

Four areas in this chapter, elaborated on in following chapters, are vision; values and ethics; culture; and power. All organizations implicitly have these "areas", though their strength and influence is not always recognized nor easily acknowledged.

VISION

GM Vision Statement...

World Leader in transportation products and related services. We will earn our customer's enthusiasm through continuous improvement, driven by the integrity, teamwork, and innovation of GM people.

For a strategic leader, the first priority may be the conception and articulation of what it is that the organization can do and be, and the way to get there. In their book, *Leaders*, Warren Bennis and Burt Nanus say: "Leaders articulate and define what has previously remained implicit or unsaid; then they invent images, metaphors, and models that provide a focus for new attention. By so doing, they consolidate or challenge prevailing wisdom." This task, conceptual at first, but communicative at a later time, seems to be central to finding an appropriate niche for an organization, one that is differentiated enough to attract members and focused enough to bring together their power and influence on some critical task.

Typically we expect a leader to be several things. The President of the United States is simultaneously the head of state, the commander-in-chief of the Armed Forces, the head of the executive branch of the government, the principal ambassador for foreign policy. The CEO of a major cooperation is expected to have similarly broad roles, including an economic one, in leading his or her corporation. Annually at the State of the Union address to the nation, or at the stockholder meeting, the leader expresses his or her vision of what the organization is about and what it brings to its citizens or shareholders. "One of the things about leadership is that you cannot be a moderate, balanced, thoughtful, careful articulator of policy. You"ve got to be on the lunatic fringe." GE's Jack Welch sees the role of a strategic leader as someone who takes time to see beyond the stars.

Beyond the techniques and processes of developing and articulating a vision, a strategic leader needs to do two things. First, there is the notion of gathering information about the total environment, both internal and external. If broadly conceived as an ongoing process, a leader can gather information from clients, constituents, competitors, allies, friends and foes; in short, from a range of people with interests in issues germane to the organization. Second, if this gathering stage is followed by continuous processing and analysis of the information, the leader, in concert with others, can begin to "make sense" of the environment, and can begin to shape and communicate the vision that would provide the focus for the organization.

This two-step process seems to be a necessary part of strategic leadership, and seems to emerge directly from the attributes of strategic leaders described in the SLDI (conceptual flexibility, consensus decision making, and team development). While a vision may be derived in a rational way, we can also recall that in classical terms, in the Bible or in epics like the

Odyssey, the heroes were mindful of dreams and other non-rational inspiration to help them visualize situations and deliver the people from an enemy, or solve some other threatening problem. A strategic leader has to be tuned to both the rational and the irrational, the linear and the circular, the scientific and the artistic.

Many organizations are led through implicit visions of members of the organization. That may be sufficient during early stages of the life of the organization where the momentum and enthusiasm of its members propel it to a position of initial stability. But, at other times, when the organization is enmeshed in a fight for institutional survival (the downsizing of components of the Army, for example, or an airline going out of business), leaders can gather information and begin to reformulate the vision of that particular organization so that it emerges from the crisis better focused on its possible futures.

The role of the strategic leader is to move the organization forward toward some objective; it can be as diverse as implementing some program of government, or directing the stewardship of a nation's religious beliefs. The articulation of a vision is part of the complex role for a strategic leader.

VALUES AND ETHICS

An organization must have a set of values from which ethical practices logically flow; organizations might also use the term philosophy. NASA's vision (ad astra per aspera) creates an image of an organization whose values revolve around rigorous science and engineering and the indomitable spirit of man. The Coast Guard describes its core values as honor, respect, and devotion to duty. The values of organizations like the Boy Scouts are set out in oath and motto. Private corporations and businesses also express their values with slogans.

That organizations would have a set of core values should not be so surprising. Members influence the organization, and an organization often draws people with common interests, values and ethical codes; the organization then simply externalizes the private values of its individual members. A church, for example, espouses a set of values in itself; in turn, the congregation solidifies the values of the organization while privately practicing those beliefs. An environmental organization attracts people interested in preserving natural aspects of things; these values are subscribed to by its members who promote those precepts as members of the organization. This symbiotic relationship between the organization and its members is critical to organizational survival.

Beyond the question of personal integrity that suggests a set of commonly held moral beliefs and practices, a strategic leader must espouse a set of values for the organization. A strategic leader must serve as an exemplar to other members of the organization in a responsible way, by faithfully serving the interests of the organization. Such a view calls for strategic leaders not to abuse their roles and positions of power.

The larger task for the strategic leader is to engender in the organization a sense of responsibility for both the internal and external environments. For a public official, that means following democratic authority, participating in public policy determination, and considering fully the impacts of such decisions on the whole of society. Exercise of a public office carries with it the obligation to object to policies that might be harmful or discriminatory to certain segments of society. For a private sector official, it may mean appropriate responsiveness to a board of directors, and to consideration of the impacts of a strategic decision on the environment. The role of the strategic leader is to foster and maintain a climate of values and ethical practice within the organization through which it can fulfill its public and private responsibilities.

CULTURE

An organization that adopts an ethical and value-oriented environment has taken the first step toward establishing a culture that promotes the aims of the institution. The subject of culture itself will be treated more fully later in this text. Our interest here is in the role of the strategic leader in understanding and shaping the culture of an organization.

Every organization, and every block or component within any organization has a way of doing things. Some of them are trivial, though they would include: how long you take for lunch; whether you pay attention to the boss; if not, who really does count; what reports are important; and whom to have coffee with. At a more important level, culture includes an ethical climate, a sense of stewardship for the resources of the organization and for its members, and a sense of civic and public responsibility. Organizations, for example, might adopt a school and serve as mentors for children there; or support environmental issues, or advocate equal opportunity.

To some extent culture can be developed and implemented in much the same way that other changes are introduced in the organization. Such an initiative might well lead to a breath of fresh air in the organization. Pope John XXIII allowed many changes to flow from a world-wide meeting of the bishops of the Catholic Church in the early 1960s; a cultural shift in certain practices in the church. Discontinuing the use of Latin for ceremonies was a significant change.

In most instances, culture develops unnoticed. A leader can become aware quite suddenly and dramatically, as is the case with unwanted news, that there is a "cancer in the White House", or there is "malaise" in the nation, or that something is rotten in Denmark. Culture expresses itself in featured news stories about Texaco and gender discrimination, about Aberdeen and sexual harassment, about Tailhook, and other pernicious events. In those instances, the culture of particular organizations obscured any sense of otherwise ethical behavior.

Culture also is often expressed positively in non-verbal terms, by symbols, representations, colors, logos, songs and anthems. It is the nature of symbols to express what is often difficult to express verbally. The President of the United States is by virtue of his office a symbol. Images of the President standing at attention at Dover Air Force Base; or, signing a bill; or, delivering the State of the Union address, are rooted in our culture of respect for the office of the President.

The task of the strategic leader is to notice what is really happening in the organization beyond the wiring diagram, beneath the glossy reports, and behind what he hears. The same diligence that the leader might use in discerning and gathering information prior to establishing a vision for an organization might well serve in determining its culture.

POWER

We've mentioned previously that it is part of the nature of an organization to gather and consolidate power. It is through power, and its surrogate politics, that an organization accomplishes its purposes and fulfills its mandates whether it comes from legislation, or the policies of a board of directors, or from the inherent and critical nature of the organization. Such power not only defines the essential purposes of the organization, but also provides the means to achieve its objectives.

And it is precisely in its consolidation of power that an organization can dare to be great and can gain those goals that fulfill the aspirations of its members. Thus, a firm that makes automobiles and that seeks to be a world class manufacturer in that industrial segment will use its economic, technical, and artistic power to design, engineer, manufacture, and sell enough vehicles to gain a sizable market share.

The role of the strategic leader is to use the power inherent in the organization to leverage that power through alliances, both formal and informal, with the power in other organizations. The strategic leader also needs to be conscious of the corruption that sometimes lies with the exercise of power.

PEOPLE

Project Focus: Hope*

Recognizing the dignity and beauty of every person, we pledge intelligent and practical action to overcome racism, poverty and injustice.

And to build a metropolitan community where all people may live in freedom, harmony, trust and affection.

Black and white, yellow, brown and red from Detroit and its suburbs of every economic status, national origin and religious persuasion we join in this covenant. Ideally, organizations provide opportunities for individuals to reach the highest levels of achievement. Individuals join an organization to pursue a career, to earn a living, to engage in professional activity, and to associate with others who may have the same goals. An organization offers the fulfillment of dreams or aspirations.

If the fit between the individual and the organization is sound, the association between them might last a lifetime. People join a particular religion and never leave it; others become lifelong employees of a corporation. In those instances, the organization meets the needs of the individual, and the individual contributes to the good of the institution. Each gets a level of satisfaction that is sufficient for continued association.

Conversely, if the fit between the individual and the organization is unsound, the association might be temporary, and disappointing. A recruit may enter one of the military services, and find the discipline and rigor do not provide the satisfaction necessary for continued membership. A student may enter a college and find that the requirements and other aspects of academic life are not satisfying.

One of the phenomena associated with large organizations is a certain impersonality. Even after working "together" in the same place for years, some people realize that they don't really know a particular person. And the larger, more diverse and geographically dispersed an organization may be, the more complex is the communication about things critical and essential to the organization. The "front" office becomes impersonalized as "them", usually in a pejorative way. In turn, the front office sees its employees as lacking the attitudes and skills that are critical for continued success. Thus, an uneasy climate of suspicion and tamped-down hostility may begin to affect an organization. People begin to feel unimportant, uninvolved, even unloved.

One of the critical tasks of the strategic leader is to recognize and provide for the needs of the members of the organization. Many organizations, recognizing the value and importance of employees have begun to take significant actions to improve the conditions that would allow employees to satisfy their human needs, and thus contribute more substantially to the good of the organization. In other words, they have begun to examine the characteristics of human resources and provide a better fit between the individual and the organization.

Conditions where employees were largely regimented, perceived to be replaceable parts in a large enterprise, such as an assembly line, or working in a bureaucracy, or as a member of the armed forces, have changed to accommodate more of the human resource dimensions. Flexibility has replaced rigidity. Hours of work have been adjusted in some cases, and telecommuting, flex time and other accommodations have been introduced to keep pace with the larger environment. The work force itself reflects a diversity in gender, ethnicity race, age, interests, and skills. Jobs are rotated so that people do not become bored. Recognition of a commonality of interests is leading to more win-win solutions.

The radical idea of sharing power with more and more members of organizations seems to fall under the broad category of empowering. The proverbial suggestion box has given way to allowing workers to suggest changes without recourse to someone's approval. Based on the premise that people want to contribute and can do so in a meaningful way, the strategic leader will find the balance between the "inmates running the asylum" and responsible contributions; in the end, it may simply be an application of the maxim offered by management consultant, Tom Peters: "Involve everyone all the time" (Peters, 1987).

A strategic leader can enhance the culture of an organization through the approaches that he or she takes toward people; how they are recruited, trained, and brought into the organization; how they are rewarded and counseled while they are in the organization; the opportunity they have to contribute to the organization; the measure of independence and trust as part of self-managing teams; in short, the extent to which the culture of the organization provides for their recreational, social, and professional development.

CONCLUSION

The task of strategic leadership in VUCA environments is critical. Organizations—nations, large elements of government, multi-national corporations, and national associations carry within their cultures, values, vision, political aspects, and the lives of people. It is a complexity that corporate and other strategic leaders might recognize in this series of statements posed by McCaskey:

We are not sure what the problem is.

We are not sure what is really happening.

We are not sure what we want.

We do not have the resources that we need.

We are not sure who is supposed to do what.

We are not sure how to get what we want.

We are not sure how to determine if we have succeeded.

In spite of these uncertainties, strategic leaders still must be effective decision makers. Understanding more about subtle qualities in organizations-vision, values and ethics, culture, and power-about the relationship of people who are members of the organization, and about managing and leading during transitional periods-may make you a better leader, able to act with increased wisdom, purpose, and prudence.

11

VALUES AND ETHICS

INTRODUCTION

Values and ethics are central to any organization; those operating in the national security arena are no exception. What exactly do we mean by values and ethics? Both are extremely broad terms, and we need to focus in on the aspects most relevant for strategic leaders and decision makers. What we will first discuss is the distinctive nature of ethics for public officials; second, the forces which influence the ethical behavior of individuals in organizations; and third, explore the actions strategic leaders can take to build ethical climates in their organizations.

THE CHARACTER OF VALUES AND ETHICS

Values can be defined as those things that are important to or valued by someone. That someone can be an individual or, collectively, an organization. One place where values are important is in relation to vision. One of the imperatives for organizational vision is that it must be based on and consistent with the organization's core values. In one example of a vision statement we'll look at later, the organization's core values - in this case, integrity, professionalism, caring, teamwork, and stewardship- were deemed important enough to be included with the statement of the organization's vision. Dr. John Johns, in an article entitled "The Ethical Dimensions of National Security," mentions honesty and loyalty as values that are the ingredients of integrity. When values are shared by all members of an organization, they are extraordinarily important tools for making judgments, assessing probable outcomes of contemplated actions, and choosing among alternatives. Perhaps more important, they put all members "on the same sheet of music" with regard to what all members as a body consider important.

The Army, in 1986, had as the theme for the year "values," and listed four organizational *values*-loyalty, duty, selfless service, and integrity-and four individual *values*- commitment, competence, candor, and courage. A Department of the Army pamphlet entitled *Values: The Bedrock of Our Profession* spent some time talking about the importance of *values*, and included this definition:

Values are what we, as a profession, judge to be right. They are more than words-they are the moral, ethical, and professional attributes of character . . . there are certain core values that must be instilled in members of the U.S. Army-civilian and uniformed soldier alike. These are not the only values that should determine our character, but they are ones that are central to our profession and should guide our lives as we serve our Nation.

Values are the embodiment of what an organization stands for, and should be the basis for the behavior of its members. However, what if members of the organization do not share and have not internalized the organization's values? Obviously, a disconnect between *individual and organizational values* will be dysfunctional. Additionally, an organization may publish one set of values, perhaps in an effort to push forward a positive image, while the values that really guide organizational behavior are very different. When there is a disconnect between *stated and operating values*, it may be difficult to determine what is "acceptable." For example, two of the Army's organizational values include candor and courage. One might infer that officers are encouraged to "have the courage of their convictions" and speak their disagreements openly. In some cases, this does work; in others it does not.

The same thing works at the level of the society. The principles by which the society functions do not necessarily conform to the principles stated. Those in power may covertly allow the use of force to suppress debate in order to remain in power. ("death squads" are an example.) In some organizations, dissent may be rewarded by termination-the organizational equivalent of "death squad" action. In others, a group member may be ostracized or expelled.

Group members quickly learn the *operating values*, or they don't survive for long. To the extent they differ from *stated values*, the organization will not only suffer from doing things less effectively, but also from the cynicism of its members, who have yet another reason for mistrusting the leadership, or doubting its wisdom.

VALUES PROVIDE THE BASIS FOR JUDGMENTS ABOUT WHAT IS IMPORTANT FOR THE ORGANIZATION TO SUCCEED IN ITS CORE BUSINESS.

So, there are some disconnects, and these disconnects create problems. However, the central purpose of *values* remains. They state either an actual or an idealized set of criteria for evaluating options and deciding what is appropriate, based on long experience. The relevance of the Army's *values*, for example, is apparent. When soldiers may be called upon to expose themselves to mortal danger in the performance of their duty, they must be absolutely able to trust their fellow soldiers (to do their fair share and to help in the event of need) and their leaders (to guard them from unnecessary risk). So the Army's *values* prescribe conditions that facilitate trust, a necessary element in willingness to face danger. Without trust, risk tolerance will be low, as will combat effectiveness.

TO BEHAVE ETHICALLY IS TO BEHAVE IN A MANNER THAT IS CONSISTENT WITH WHAT IS GENERALLY CONSIDERED TO BE RIGHT OR MORAL. ETHICAL BEHAVIOR IS THE BEDROCK OF MUTUAL TRUST.

So how do values relate to *ethics*, and what do we mean by ethics? One of the keys is in the phrase we quoted above from the DA pamphlet: "Values are what we, as a profession, judge to be right." Individually or organizationally, values determine what is right and what is wrong, and doing what is right or wrong is what we mean by ethics. To behave ethically is to behave in a manner consistent with what is right or moral.

What does "generally considered to be right" mean? That is a critical question, and part of the difficulty in deciding whether or not behavior is ethical is in determining *what* is right or wrong.

Perhaps the first place to look in determining what is right or wrong is society. Virtually every society makes some determination of morally correct behavior. In Islamic countries, a determination of what is right or moral is tied to religious strictures.

In societies more secular, the influence of religious beliefs may be less obvious, but still a key factor. In the United States much of what is believed to be right or wrong is based in Judeo-Christian heritage. The Ten Commandments, for many people, define what is morally right or wrong. Societies not only regulate the behavior of their members, but also define their societal core values. "Life, liberty, and the pursuit of happiness" represent core American values.

Experience often has led societies to develop beliefs about what is of value for the common good. (Note that societies differ from one another in the specifics, but not in the general principles.) One example is the notion of reciprocity. ("One good deed deserves another.") Another is the notion of good intent. ("A gentleman's word is his bond.") Yet, a third is the notion of appreciation of merit in others regardless of personal feelings. ("Give the Devil his due.")

These all contain implied "shoulds" about how people interact and behave toward one another in groups, organizations, and societies. These "shoulds" define collective effort because they are fundamental to trust and to team relationships that entail risk. The greater the potential risk, the more important ethical practices become.

Organizations, to some extent, define what is right or wrong for the members of the organization. Ethical codes, such as West Point's "A cadet will not lie, cheat, or steal, or tolerate those who do," make clear what the organization considers to be right or wrong. To quote again from the DA Pamphlet, "Values: The Bedrock of Our Profession," statements such as:

Loyalty to the Nation, to the Army, and to the unit is essential.

Selfless service puts the welfare of the Nation and the accomplishment of the assigned mission before individual welfare. All who serve the Nation must resist the temptation to pursue self-gain, personal advantage, and self-interest ahead of the collective good.

[Integrity] is the basis for trust and confidence that must exist between the leaders and the led. Furthermore, integrity is demonstrated by propriety in one's personal life.

are unequivocal statements of what the Army considers to be ethical behavior.

What does "generally considered to be right" mean? All one needs to do is to look at the positive values of society and the organizations one belongs to, and what is right or wrong should be evident. There is another aspect to be considered, however, and that is the influence of societal or organizational norms. Norms are the unstated rules, usually informally reached by the members of a group, which govern the behavior of the group's members. Norms often have a greater effect on what is and isn't done by the members of a group than formal rules and regulations.

The reason norms are important for a discussion of ethics and values is that norms may allow or even encourage certain behavior as "OK" that is not in keeping with society's or an organization's stated values. When there is a disconnect between stated and operating values, it may be difficult to determine what is "right." An example might be a company that has among its stated values to treat everyone with dignity and respect, but whose norms have permitted and perhaps even encouraged a pattern of sexual harassment over a number of years. Do those in the organization know that the behavior is wrong, but condone it nevertheless? Is it clear to the Bosnian Serbs that ethnic cleansing is unethical and wrong, or would it fall under the mantle of behavior that is considered to be acceptable in that society? Listen to the arguments in support of ethnic cleansing that have been made, and you will find that many of the perpetrators argued that they did nothing wrong, and were only righting previous wrongs done to them.

THE PUBLIC TRUST

If ethics and morality are important for groups and organizations, they should also be important for public officials, and for very much the same reasons. York Willbern, in an article entitled "Types and Levels of Public Morality," argues for six types or levels of morality (or ethics) for public officials. By public officials, he means those who are in policy making positions in public institutions; in other words, strategic decision makers in the government, including the national security arena. The six levels he differentiates are: basic honesty and conformity to law; conflicts of interest; service orientation and procedural fairness; the ethic of democratic responsibility; the ethic of public policy determination; and the ethic of compromise and social integration.

WILLBERN'S LEVEL OF PUBLIC MORALITY

- ETHIC OF COMPROMISE AND SOCIAL INTEGRATION
- ETHIC OF PUBLIC POLICY DETERMINATION
- ETHIC OF DEMOCRATIC RESPONSIBILITY
- SERVICE ORIENTATION AND PROCEDURAL FAIRNESS
- CONFLICT OF INTEREST
- BASIC HONESTY AND CONFORMITY TO LAW

BASIC HONESTY AND CONFORMITY TO LAW. "The public servant is morally bound, just as are other persons, to tell the truth, to keep promises, to respect the person and the property of others, and to abide by the requirements of the law" (Willbern). In many ways, this level only describes the basic adherence to moral codes that is expected of all members of a group or society. There are some basics of behavior that are expected of all if a society is to function for the collective good. For public officials, there is an additional reason why it is important to adhere to these basic moral codes and laws: they have more power than the average member of the society, and hence more opportunity for violation of those codes or laws. There also is the negative example that misconduct by public officials provides.

CONFLICT OF INTEREST. This relates to public officials, because it deals with the conflict between advancing the public interest, which a public official is charged to do, and advancing one's self-interest. The duty here is to ensure that the public interest comes first, and that one does not advance his own personal interest at the expense of the public.

Willbern uses embezzlement of public funds, bribery, and contract kickbacks as examples of pursuing personal interests at the expense of those of the public. The requirements for public officials to divest themselves of investments that might be influenced by the performance of their duties (or put them in trust) and to recuse themselves in situations where they have a personal interest are designed to help public officials avoid conflicts of interest. Ultimately, it still comes down to the individual making an ethical decision.

Avoidance of conflict of interest is often difficult because it is often hard to separate personal and public interests, and because individuals as private citizens are encouraged to pursue private interests through any legal means. One of the areas where there is the greatest potential for conflicts of interest is where public officials deal with private organizations which are pursuing their private interests, and where any decision by a public official on allocation of resources will favor some private interest. The fields of government contracting and acquisition are two areas where the possibility of conflicts of interest is high.

SERVICE ORIENTATION AND PROCEDURAL FAIRNESS. This level relates closely to the last, and deals with the responsibility of public officials to ensure their actions serve the public, and that the power they wield is used only for that purpose. It is easy to abuse the power that comes with public office. Procedural safeguards are designed to prevent that abuse. The moral obligation of public servants is to follow established procedures, and not to use their power to circumvent those procedures for their own convenience or benefit. Power must be used fairly and for the benefit of the public. One can again think of examples of public officials who have violated this moral charge by using their influence and power for their own benefit or for the benefit of special interest groups, or who have circumvented established procedures for their own benefit or convenience. One frequent example is the use of government vehicles or aircraft for nonofficial business.

These first three levels of public morality share one important characteristic: they all relate to the behavior or conduct of public officials. These three levels are the areas that get most of the attention in discussions of ethics, this is where public officials are most likely to get in trouble. However, there are three additional levels of public morality equally important. These deal with the content of what public officials do, "the moral choices involved in deciding *what* to do, in pursuing the purposes of the state and the society" (Willbern).

THE ETHIC OF DEMOCRATIC RESPONSIBILITY. Given that public officials are operating within a democratic system, they either are elected by the people or appointed by an elected official. This confers upon them the obligation to carry out the will of the people. However, public officials also have the responsibility to make moral choices consistent with their own values, and that may be in conflict with what they perceive to be the will of the people.

Willbern contends that the public official acts according to his or her own judgment, rationalizing that it would be the will of the people if they were well enough informed on the issue. To give one example of this level of public morality, consider whether or not the representative in Congress is morally bound to support policies and legislation which his constituents overwhelmingly support but he personally opposes.

THE ETHIC OF PUBLIC POLICY DETERMINATION. This level involves the most difficult ethical choices, because it concerns making moral judgments about public policies. The responsibility is to make moral policies; the difficulty is in determining how moral a policy is. Public policies almost always deal with very complex issues, where ethical choices are rarely clear, and it is often difficult to determine if a policy is right or wrong. For example, many public policies deal with the distribution of limited resources. Is it right or wrong to slash funding for one program, or to increase funding for another? In almost any decision, there will be winners and losers, and there will be some benefit for some and cost to others. "Right" and "wrong" may not apply. Equity and fairness are important considerations, but not always easy to discern. The determination of how much funding to provide for national security, and which social programs to fund, involves ethical choices of the most difficult type. What is the difference between equality and equity? Consider the controversy around affirmative action programs: are they examples of moral public policies?

THE ETHIC OF COMPROMISE AND SOCIAL INTEGRATION. This final level deals with an area not as salient as some of the others. It deals with the necessity for compromise in a society. A society with irreconcilable differences on fundamental issues will be torn apart. Hence, it becomes a moral obligation of public officials to engage in give and take, working toward compromise in the policies they develop. One often sees legislators in our political system establishing positions where they may not get all they want from particular legislation, but will settle for some of what they want. Willbern contends that compromise, rather than standing on principle, is moral, because without compromise there will be discord and conflict, and disintegration rather than integration of the society.

Public officials are given the trust of the public to develop and carry out policies that are in the public's best interest. Living up to this trust has a significant impact on the national will; public confidence is essential to the exercise of national power. Public officials have a moral duty to act in a trustworthy manner.

Why, then, do individuals behave unethically? One reason is the complexity of the issues leaders deal with, and the difficulty in many instances of determining which is the most ethical alternative. There are several systemic factors. One is the competition for scarce resources. It is easy to slip into unethical acts to gain a competitive advantage in the race for position or power. A second is conflicting loyalties, which Johns labels "the most troublesome ethical dilemma facing public officials." The Iran Contra affair is a case of unethical behavior on the part of North, Poindexter, Secord, and McFarlane because of misplaced loyalty to the executive chain of command.

Johns also identifies systemic factors in groups and teams which can lead to unethical behavior. One is *groupthink*, which can occur in a homogeneous group with a strong leader. A second is the presence of idealogues: individuals who view their own extreme positions as "right" and any opposing positions as "wrong." A third is the organization's response to dissent. There are few incentives for "whistleblowers" or those who try to expose unethical behavior in organizations. Organizational norms encourage "going along" and discourage questioning the unethical actions of others. This can quickly compromise ethical standards in any organization.

CAUSES OF UNETHICAL BEHAVIOR

INDIVIDUAL

- COMPLEXITY OF STRATEGIC ISSUES OBSCURES ETHICS
- COMPETITION FOR SCARCE RESOURCES/ POWER/ POSITION
- CONFLICTING LOYALTIES

GROUP

- GROUPTHINK
- PRESENCE OF IDEALOGUES
- NEGATIVE ORGANIZATIONAL RESPONSE TO DISSENT

ETHICS IN PRACTICE

Kenneth R. Andrews, in "Ethics in Practice," contends that there are three aspects to ethical behavior in organizations: the development of the individual as an ethical person, the effect of the organization as an ethical or unethical environment, and the actions or procedures developed by the organization to encourage ethical behavior and discourage unethical behavior.

INFLUENCES ON ETHICAL BEHAVIOR

- PRIOR DEVELOPMENT OF INDIVIDUAL AS ETHICAL PERSON.
- THE ORGANIZATION AS AN ETHICAL ENVIRONMENT.
- PROCEDURES THAT ENCOURAGE ETHICAL BEHAVIOR.

Most of an individual's ethical development occurs before entering an organization. The influence of family, church, community, and school will determine individual values. The organization, to a large extent, is dealing with individuals whose value base has been established. This might imply that ethical organizations are those fortunate enough to bring in ethical individuals, while unethical organizations brought in unethical people. But it is not that simple. While the internalized values of individuals are important, the organization has a major impact on the behavior of its members, and can have a positive or negative influence on their values. One example of the development of ethical individuals is the service academies. In their admissions processes, the academies attempt to get individuals of good character with the values integral to the military profession. However, the academies also recognize that their core values may be different than those prevalent in society, and they devote considerable effort to the development and internalization of their core values. As is evident from periodic breaches of integrity at the academies, e.g., cheating scandals, these attempts to instill core values do not always succeed.

There are three qualities individuals must possess to make ethical decisions. The first is the ability to recognize ethical issues and to reason through the ethical consequences of decisions. The ability to see second and third order effects, one of the elements of strategic thinking, is very important. The second is the ability to look at alternative points of view, deciding what is right in a particular set of circumstances. This is similar to the ability to reframe. And the third is the ability to deal with ambiguity and uncertainty; making a decision on the best information available.

ATTRIBUTES FOR ETHICAL DECISIONS

- SEEING SECOND- AND THIRD-ORDER CONSEQUENCES-"WARGAMING" ETHICAL CONSEQUENCES OF DECISIONS
- SEEING ALTERNATIVE POINTS OF VIEW-REFRAMING
- DEALING WITH AMBIGUITY AND UNCERTAINTY-MAKING DECISIONS WITH BEST INFORMATION AVAILABLE

As important as these individual characteristics are, the influence of the organization is equally important. The ethical standards that one observes in the organization will have a significant effect on individual behavior. "People will do what they are rewarded for doing" (Andrews). The organization has its greatest impact in the standards it establishes for ethical and unethical conduct in its formal reward systems. Informal norms also have a strong influence on individuals' behavior as do the actions of the leaders of the organization. Strategic leaders must understand that their actions, more than words alone, will determine the operating values in the organization.

The influence of the organizational context is underscored in "Why Be Honest If Honesty Doesn't Pay?" In this article, Bhide and Stevenson note that there often are no economic or other incentives to encourage ethical behavior and discourage unethical behavior. They contend that it most often is the dishonest individual who gets ahead, and that cases where unethical behavior was punished are far outweighed by those in which there either were no consequences or unethical behavior was rewarded. The Gordon Ghekkos of the world (the unethical corporate executive played by Michael Douglas in the movie "Wall Street") often get ahead, because they rarely are held to account for their actions.

While these observations might lead one to a cynical view of ethics in organizations, Bhide and Stevenson come to a different conclusion. They see room for optimism despite the lack of financial gain for ethical behavior, or the absence of negative consequences for unethical behavior. Their reasoning is based in the fact that so many people *do* behave ethically, in spite of the apparent lack of gain. Ethical behavior must be intrinsically rewarding; and most people behave ethically because it's the right thing to do. People are guided by their personal value systems. They often "choose the harder right instead of the easier wrong" specifically because of their intrinsic values of what is right.

Bhide and Stevenson make this caveat:

We should remember, however, that this...works only as long as most of us live by an honorable moral compass. Since our trust isn't grounded in self-interest, it is fragile. And, indeed, we all know of organizations, industries, and even whole societies in which trust has given way either to a destructive free-for-all or to inflexible rules and bureaucracy. Only our individual wills, our determination to do what is right, whether or not it is profitable, save us from choosing between chaos and stagnation.

ETHICAL RESPONSES

Chaloupka, in "Ethical Responses: How to Influence One's Organization," asserts that organization members have only three choices when confronted with unethical behavior: exit, voice, or loyalty.

Exit is the most direct response: if you can't live with behavior that does not meet your own ethical standards, leave. However, exit is not only a direct response, it is a final one, so the personal and organizational consequences must be considered. The most important personal consequences are the costs. Where do you go from there? What other options are available? How marketable are you? Can you afford the financial loss?

There are specific organizational consequences as well. Will the ethics of the organization's leaders change? Will they do business with someone else who doesn't have the high standards you do? In leaving, one gives up the ability to influence the organization directly. When considering exit, one must ask, "Could I have had more of an impact by remaining in the organization and trying to change it from within?"

Voice. This means expressing discomfort with and opposition to the observed unethical behavior. To whom do you voice your objections? The obvious choice is your supervisor. But what if your supervisor condones the unethical behavior, or worse, is its source? You may be jeopardizing your position, and maybe your membership in the organization. A second choice is to go to senior management. This also has potential risk. The senior leadership may be condoning or even directing the unethical behavior. This action may bring your loyalty into question. If so, your objections may be covered up or ignored, and you may end up being forced out of the organization.

On the other hand, it may be that the senior leadership is unaware of the unethical behavior, and you may have initiated an organizational response eliminating unethical behavior and restoring ethical standards. A third option is to go public, to engage in "whistleblowing." This is also risky, because it can lead to reprisals with negative consequences. The level of risk depends on the commitment of the organization to high ethical standards and on its willingness to encourage whistleblowing in its own best interests. Many organizations have shown commitment to ferreting out unethical individuals and maintaining high ethical standards by establishing procedures for anonymous reporting of ethical breaches and safeguards to protect whistleblowers.

Exit and voice may be combined. An individual resigns in protest and goes public with his or her reasons for leaving. This leaves the individual vulnerable to the label of an employee who quit before being fired, but it also can lead to increased credibility as someone acting on conviction in spite of personal cost. Exit combined with voice is most effective if taken by someone at the upper levels of the organization. An organization can more easily ignore the "exit + voice" of a lower level employee than it can the resignation of a strategic leader, followed immediately by a press conference. The widely publicized resignation of former President Bush from the National Rifle Association over what he viewed as extreme actions is an example of exit combined with voice. It undoubtedly had a much greater effect on the NRA than the resignation of someone less well known and respected. The resignation of James Webb as Secretary of the Navy is another example of effective exit combined with voice.

Loyalty. The final response to unethical behavior in an organization is loyalty. This is the alternative to exit. Instead of leaving, the individual remains and tries to change the organization from within. Loyalty thus discourages or delays exit. Loyalty also may discourage public voice, since being loyal to the organization means trying to solve problems from within without causing public embarrassment or damage. Loyalty can also encourage unethical behavior, particularly in organizations which promote loyalty above all. These organizations discourage exit and voice, and basically want their members to "go along" with organizational practices. An interesting question is, "Can an individual be loyal to an organization by engaging in exit or voice as a response to unethical behavior?"

Chaloupka maintains that both exit and voice must exist for continued organizational effectiveness. Additionally, an organization cannot maintain high ethical standards without mechanisms for eliminating unethical behavior. Also, loyalty is not always a virtue. Loyalty should be predicated on the organization's ethical demonstration that it is worthy of loyalty. If the organization condones unethical behavior, it relieves the individual of any responsibility to be loyal.

BUILDING AN ETHICAL CLIMATE

How can the strategic leaders of an organization build an ethical climate? Andrews suggests a number of steps that foster corporate ethics. First are the actions of the strategic leadership and the way they deal with ethical issues. The pattern of top leaders' behavior determines organizational values. A second step is to make explicit ethics policies. Ethical codes are one common example. The next step is to increase awareness of how to apply those ethical codes. Training on how to deal with situations with an ethical dimension, and how to anticipate situations that involve ethical choices, can go a long way toward ethical institutional practices. Another step to increase the salience of ethics is to expand the information system to focus on areas where ethics may come into play. Knowing what actually is going on in the organization is essential to understanding the ethical principles which govern behavior. The information system should also support ethical behavior, and allow the strategic leader to know when or where there are potential ethical breaches so that corrective action can be taken. The real danger is that when unethical behavior is unnoticed, or not punished, members will assume it is condoned by the organization's leadership.

CONCLUSION

Establishing moral principles means determining the core values which should guide the organization. O'Brien suggests four for consideration: localness, merit, openness, and leanness. By localness, he means adopting a philosophy of pushing power down to the lowest level possible, and encouraging initiative and autonomy. By merit, he means directing actions toward the overall goals of the organization, and what is best for all. By openness, he means being forthright and honest in all dealings. And by leanness, he means efficient use of resources and economies when possible.

ULTIMATELY, THE QUEST FOR ORGANIZATIONAL TRANSFORMATION MUST BEGIN WITH A PERSONAL COMMITMENT WITHIN EACH INDIVIDUAL TO PURSUE MORAL EXCELLENCE.

O'BRIEN

Encouraging leaders to pursue their own moral development is critical at higher levels because strategic leaders set the moral climate for the organization. O'Brien believes that moral development is even more important than professional development. "Creating a culture based on moral excellence requires a commitment among managers to embody and develop two qualities in their leadership: virtue and wisdom." However, creating an organization characterized by moral excellence is a lengthy process. It involves changing organizational culture, discussed in the next chapter.

12

ORGANIZATIONAL CULTURE

One of the primary responsibilities of strategic leaders is to create and maintain the organizational characteristics that reward and encourage collective effort. Perhaps the most fundamental of these is organizational culture. But what do we really mean by organizational culture? What influence does it have on an organization? How does one go about building, influencing or changing an organization's culture?

THE IMPACT OF CULTURE

Why is culture so important to an organization? Edgar Schein, an MIT Professor of Management and author of *Organizational Culture and Leadership: A Dynamic View*, suggests that an organization's culture develops to help it cope with its environment. Today, organizational leaders are confronted with many complex issues during their attempts to generate organizational achievement in VUCA environments. A leader's success will depend, to a great extent, upon understanding organizational culture.

Schein contends that many of the problems confronting leaders can be traced to their inability to analyze and evaluate organizational cultures. Many leaders, when trying to implement new strategies or a strategic plan leading to a new vision, will discover that their strategies will fail if they are inconsistent with the organization's culture. A CEO, SES, political appointee, or flag officer who comes into an organization prepared to "shake the place up" and institute sweeping changes, often experiences resistance to changes and failure. Difficulties with organizational transformations arise from failures to analyze an organization's existing culture.

WHAT IS ORGANIZATIONAL CULTURE?

There is no single definition for organizational culture. The topic has been studied from a variety of perspectives ranging from disciplines such as anthropology and sociology, to the applied disciplines of organizational behavior, management science, and organizational communication. Some of the definitions are listed below:

A set of common understandings around which action is organized, . . . finding expression in language whose nuances are peculiar to the group (Becker and Geer 1960).

A set of understandings or meanings shared by a group of people that are largely tacit among members and are clearly relevant and distinctive to the particular group which are also passed on to new members (Louis 1980).

A system of knowledge, of standards for perceiving, believing, evaluating and acting . . . that serve to relate human communities to their environmental settings (Allaire and Firsirotu 1984).

The deeper level of basic assumptions and beliefs that are: learned responses to the group's problems of survival in its external environment and its problems of internal integration; are shared by members of an organization; that operate unconsciously; and that define in a basic "taken -for-granted" fashion in an organization's view of itself and its environment (Schein 1988).

Any social system arising from a network of shared ideologies consisting of two components: substance-the networks of meaning associated with ideologies, norms, and values; and forms-the practices whereby the meanings are expressed, affirmed, and communicated to members (Trice and Beyer 1984).

This sampling of definitions represents the two major camps that exist in the study of organizational culture and its "application strategies." The first camp views culture as implicit in social life. Culture is what naturally emerges as individuals transform themselves into social groups as tribes, communities, and ultimately, nations. The second camp represents the view that culture is an explicit social product arising from social interaction either as an intentional or unintentional consequence of behavior.

In other words, culture is comprised of distinct observable forms (e.g., language, use of symbols, ceremonies, customs, methods of problem solving, use of tools or technology, and design of work settings) that groups of people create through social interaction and use to confront the broader social environment. (Wuthnow and Witten 1988). This second view of culture is most relevant to the analysis and evaluation of organizational culture and to cultural change strategies that leaders can employ to improve organizational performance.

BEHAVIOR AND ARTIFACTS

We can also characterize culture as consisting of *three levels* (Schein 1988). The most visible level is behavior and artifacts. This is the observable level of culture, and consists of behavior patterns and outward manifestations of culture: perquisites provided to executives, dress codes, level of technology utilized (and where it is utilized), and the physical layout of work spaces.

All may be visible indicators of culture, but difficult to interpret. Artifacts and behavior also may tell us what a group is doing, but not why. One cartoon which captures this aspect shows two executives sitting at their desks in an office. Both have large billed black and white checked hats. One is saying to the other, "I don't know how it started, either. All I know is that it's part of our corporate culture."

VALUES

At the next level of culture are values. Values underlie and to a large extent determine behavior, but they are not directly observable, as behaviors are. There may be a difference between stated and operating values. People will attribute their behavior to stated values:

ASSUMPTIONS AND BELIEFS

To really understand culture, we have to get to the deepest level, the level of assumptions and beliefs. Schein contends that underlying assumptions grow out of values, until they become taken for granted and drop out of awareness. As the definition above states, and as the cartoon illustrates, people may be unaware of or unable to articulate the beliefs and assumptions forming their deepest level of culture.

To understand culture, we must understand *all three levels*, a difficult task. One additional aspect complicates the study of culture: the group or cultural unit which "owns" the culture. An organization may have many different cultures or subcultures, or even no discernible dominant culture at the organizational level. Recognizing the cultural unit is essential to identifying and understanding the culture.

Organizational cultures are created, maintained, or transformed by people. An organization's culture is, in part, also created and maintained by the organization's leadership. Leaders at the executive level are the principle source for the generation and re-infusion of an organization's ideology, articulation of core values and specification of norms. Organizational values express preferences for certain behaviors or certain outcomes. Organizational norms express behaviors accepted by others. They are culturally acceptable ways of pursuing goals. Leaders also establish the parameters for formal lines of communication and message content-the formal interaction rules for the organization. Values and norms, once transmitted through the organization, establish the permanence of the organization's culture.

WHAT RELEVANCE DOES ORGANIZATIONAL CULTURE HAVE TO LEADERS IN FEDERAL AGENCIES?

One of the most perplexing issues facing leaders within the Department of Defense and other agencies of the federal government can be classified under one rubric-change. Government organizations' responses to events such as the "re-invention of government", downsizing and defense conversion, shrinking operating budgets, acquisition reform, and the military's expanded role in operations other than war are requiring leaders to make course corrections. Leaders in these organizations are being challenged to think differently, to:

- Reconceptualize the role their organization plays in government
- Reconceptualize, the goals of their organization, and
- Reconceptualize how people in their organizations will work together to achieve these goals.

The term reconceptualize is emphasized here because the 21st century challenges for strategic leaders in this country involve interpreting what appears to be the same world in radically different ways. For example, not only must the Department of Defense work to make "jointness" achieve its potential, it must also reconceptualize how it can effectively operate with domestic and foreign civilian agencies in activities other than war. So DOD's goals of providing global deterrence and warfighting capability must be reconceptualized into simultaneously providing the capability for coalition building, peacekeeping, and humanitarian operations.

Strategic leaders have an additional set of challenges. They have to create the means and the opportunities to infuse their employees with new ways of looking at themselves and their capabilities. Leaders' new ideologies and values need to be communicated effectively, internalized by employees, and then translated into productive methods of thinking and working. The useful techniques for overcoming these challenges fall within the domains of evaluating and transforming organizational cultures.

ORGANIZATIONAL CULTURE IS ALSO A SYNTHESIS OF SUBCULTURES

Sociologists Gary Fine and Sherryl Kleinman discuss how distinct societies are composites of interacting subcultures rather than a single overarching culture. Organizations consist of subgroups that have specific characteristics and a sense of identification. Within organizations, people can easily classify themselves and others into various social categories or groups based on identification with their primary work group, occupational or professional skills, union membership, or age cohort. (Ouchi 1980, and Ashforth and Mael 1989). Subgroups in organizations can and do create subcultures that comprise specific networks of meaning; yet, at the same time, they remain associated with the ideologies and values of the organization's leadership. For example, at a macro level the culture that is attributed to the Department of Defense comprises the distinct cultures of the different military services and the corps of civil servants assigned to each service agency (Builder 1989). A closer examination of each service culture reveals still greater cultural differentiation among occupational specialties, specific units within the service, and between line and staff personnel. Yet all of these subcultures adhere to the core ideologies, values and norms of the DOD.

Numerous studies of organizational culture have highlighted that the formation and maintenance of culture requires interpersonal interaction within subgroups. For example, research led by Meryl Louis (Louis, Posner, and Powell 1983) demonstrated the benefits of subgroup interaction to newcomers "learning the ropes" of the jobs. Survey respondents in their first job experience reported that the three most important socialization aids were:

- Interaction with peers
- Interaction with their supervisor
- Interaction with senior co-workers.

Interaction with peers on the job was viewed as most important in helping newcomers becoming effective employees. Interaction is important for the acculturation of newcomers. However, to get a grasp on how cultures are formed and promulgated we need to ask: "what is the content of interpersonal interaction in work settings?"

Research conducted by John VanMaanan and Steven Barley (1984) provides some insight to this question. They discovered that the content of the interaction is behavioral and cognitive in nature. During initial interactions with newcomers, the established occupational community transmits to new members those shared occupational practices (including norms and roles), values, vocabularies and identities-all examples of the explicit social products that are indicative of culture in organizations. These findings were reinforced by Sonja Sackmann's research on subcultures in a medium sized conglomerate in the United States. She found that subcultures were found to form on the basis of functional domains; principally in their biased knowledge of events in the organization, in their biased explanations of cause and effect relationships, and in their patterns of behavior. The conglomerate's production division consisted of three subcultures: electronics production, shop floor production, and product inspection. Sackmann reported:

Each subgroup was influenced by the nature of its particular work. This "local" orientation also differentiated each group from the others. All three groupings clearly distinguished between "we" and "them". This distinction was supported by my observations of them. They dressed differently, and they worked in distinctly different work spaces that were furnished differently. They took separate breaks during the day, and the tone in which they interacted varied it its degree of roughness. The electronics group talked about "job security," "a small company," and "health and dental insurance." The shop floor production group talked about "more work," "upgrade of assembly," and "being in control of the job." [Discussion] themes in the shop floor production group were oriented toward people, growth in the division/company, and strategy. The inspection group mentioned an "expanded inspection department," "improvements in quality control," the "quality control system," or "partnership." Some [other discussion] themes in the group were growth of the division/company and orientation toward people (Sackmann 1992).

Organizations do not, however, always have homogeneous subcultures. The explicit social products produced by subcultures within organizations can be widely diverse and even result in countercultures. Such was the case of the Army Air Forces as its early proponents, such as Brig. General Billy Mitchell, tried to assert the value of airpower against the resistance of the traditional warfighting cultures of the Army and the Navy. The culmination of the airpower counter culture's assertiveness, both through word and deed resulted in the formation of the Air Force as a separate service in 1947. Similar examples of military counter cultures also exist in the Navy (e.g., Admiral Rickover's nuclear submarine counterculture) and the Army (e.g., General Hutton's skunkworks that created the armed helicopter)(Zald and Berger 1978).

In a more contemporary example, researchers Joanne Martin and Caren Siehl from Stanford University (1983) conducted an analysis of the events and stories related to John Delorean's tenure as division head at General Motors. They concluded that Delorean created a subculture counter to the corporate GM culture based in the core values of loyalty, hierarchy, and conformity. Executives were expected to show deferential respect for authority and accept deferential treatment from subordinates; openly express loyalty to the corporation; and to be conservative in their choices of wardrobe and office decoration.

Delorean took steps to create a counter culture that would try to force innovations when he could not get his ideas accepted by his superiors. Capitalizing on the support of his followers, Delorean and his people expressed a new culture with an alternative set of core values, preferring productivity to deference, objective measures of performance to subjective measures of conformity, and independence to blind loyalty. They dressed in contemporary styles, redecorated their offices in bright bold colors and modern furniture, and discarded GM's bureaucratic procedures for streamlined decision making processes. Delorean also refused to participate in the ceremonies and rituals of deference that were widely practiced in the corporation. As an ultimate rejection of GM's core values, Delorean attacked a GM icon, the Corvair (before Ralph Nader) for faulty construction, its unsafe performance and persistent maintenance problems. For a while, Delorean was able to maintain a delicate balance within the dominant culture's latitude of tolerance, but eventually met with disfavor; he was asked to leave the company and the counter culture disintegrated.

These examples illustrate that countercultures can have both productive and unproductive outcomes. Perhaps the key to a counterculture's success (i.e., the promulgation of its ideology, values and norms) is the group's ability to demonstrate how its idiosyncrasies are consonant with the core ideologies, values and norms of the dominant culture. The counter cultures in the military services still possessed the ethos of warfighters, albeit through different forms of warfighting technology. Overtime, the strategic bomber, the nuclear submarine, and the attack helicopter were embraced by their respective service cultures. The Delorean analysis illustrates how counter cultures can be dysfunctional and ultimately extinguished when they advocate a complete rejection of the dominant culture's ideology, values, and norms.

THE SYMBIOSIS BETWEEN THE ORGANIZATION'S OVERALL CULTURE AND ITS SUBCULTURES

Some people may debate which comes first in an organization: the organizational culture or the organization's subcultures. The question that is relevant to this chapter is how do the ideologies, values, and norms of subcultures compliment the organizational culture advocated by leadership? Explaining this relationship requires an understanding that cultures provide members with a reliable means to interpret a highly ambiguous environment. It is the leader's responsibility to specify the features of the environment that are relevant to the organization and then provide the supporting assumptions and rationale for its operating strategies.

The leader's cultural messages should address ambiguities that are beyond the scope of any organizational subculture to explain to employees. Returning to Sonja Sackmann's research with a U.S. conglomerate, she found that the top management team "defined and framed the slice of reality in which organizational members behaved in their role as employees." Top management consistently made highly visible business and personnel decisions that reinforced the business' ideologies, values and norms for success. Her interviews throughout the organization revealed that the functional subcultures shared the top manager's conceptualizations of how tasks were accomplished in the organization; how employees could advance; the ways employees related to each other; the ways adaptation and change were accomplished; and how new knowledge was acquired and perpetuated. The bottom line is that distinct subcultures in the organization were united in their understanding of how they had to perform to produce successful organizational outcomes.

Sackmann's findings provide important insight for leaders who are trying to influence organizational culture in light of the potential influence of organizational subcultures. Leaders should recognize that their cultural messages should specifically address cultural ambiguities associated with subculture practices within the organization, and limit their attempts to eliminate distinctions that are important to subculture's identities. In other words, leaders have a better chance of creating or transforming an organizational culture if they accept and foster productive organizational subcultures and consistently communicate how employees must perform in order for the organization to achieve its objectives.

Cultural change then relies on leaders' communication techniques that cross subcultural boundaries and carry messages about ideologies, values and norms that can be internalized by all employees. Memos and vision statements cannot achieve all of these objectives. Leaders, however, have a variety of sophisticated cultural communication techniques at their disposal to link subcultures to overarching cultural objectives of their organizations.

CULTURAL FORMS AS LINKING MECHANISMS

Cultural forms function as the linking mechanism by which networks of understanding develop among employees. (Trice, 1988) The cultural forms shown in the table on pages 293-94 act as a medium for communicating ideologies, values, and norms. Cultural forms enable leaders to transmit messages about desirable culture to influence thinking and ways of behaving. Cultural forms also address the emotional aspects of organizations that are commonly referred to as cohesion or camaraderie. Organizational scholars Janice Beyer and Harrison Trice elaborate on this point: Cultural forms not only aid sensemaking through the meanings they convey; they also aid the sensemaking process through the emotional reassurances they provide that help people persist in their coping efforts. Forms provide a concrete anchoring point, even if the meaning they carry are vague and only imperfectly transmitted....Also many cultural forms involve the expression of emotion and, by this venting of emotions, help people to cope with stress.

Federal agencies are replete with cultural forms that serve these purposes. However the challenges facing strategic leaders of these agencies involve creating and orchestrating cultural forms that can foster change and have longevity beyond their tenure. Cultural forms that have longevity by their nature such as rites and ceremonies reaffirm the organization's core ideologies, values and norms.

HOW CAN LEADERS DETECT DESIRABLE AND UNDESIRABLE CHARACTERISTICS OF ORGANIZATIONAL CULTURE?

Productive cultural change will occur if leaders correctly analyze the organization's existing culture, and evaluate it against the cultural attributes needed to achieve strategic objectives. Consequently, leaders must first possess a clear understanding of the strategic objectives for their organization and identify the actions needed to reach those objectives. These two tasks by themselves are difficult, particularly for the federal agencies that are experiencing volatile rates of change and reorientation. Nevertheless, without these specifications, any cultural transformation is a blind exercise.

Next conduct an analysis of the organizations existing ideologies, values and norms. Two critical questions that leaders should ask are: (1) Are existing explanations of cause and effect relationships, and acceptable beliefs and behaviors applicable to the organization's achievement of strategic objectives? (2) Are organizational members facing ambiguities about the external environment and internal work processes that can only be clarified by organizational leadership?

A List of Definitions that Distinguish : Frequently Studied Cultural Forms

Rite: Relatively elaborate, dramatic, planned sets of activities that consolidates various forms of cultural expressions into one event, which is carried out through social interactions, usually for the benefit of an audience.

Ceremonial: A system of several rites connected with a single occasion or event.

Ritual: A standardized, detailed set of techniques and behaviors that manage anxieties, but seldom produce intended, technical consequences of practical importance.

Myth: A dramatic narrative of imagined events, usually used to explain origins of transformations of something . Also, an unquestioned belief about the practical benefits of certain techniques and behaviors that is not supported by demonstrated facts.

Saga: An historical narrative describing the unique accomplishments of a group and its leaders-usually in heroic terms.

Legend: A handed-down narrative of some wonderful event that is based in history but has been embellished with fictional details.

Story: A narrative based on true events-often a combination of truth and fiction

Folktale: A completely fictional narrative.

Symbol: Any object, act, event, quality, or relation that serves as a vehicle for conveying meaning, usually by representing another thing.

Language: A particular form or manner in which members of a group use vocal sounds and written signs to convey meanings to each other.

Gesture: Movements of parts of the body used to express meanings.

Physical: Those things than surround people physically setting and provide them with immediate sensory stimuli as they carry out culturally expressive activities.

Artifact: Material objects manufactured by people to facilitate culturally expressive activities.

Adapted from Trice, 1984.

FORMULATING STRATEGIES FOR TRANSFORMING CULTURES IN ORGANIZATIONS

Strategic leadership needs to be transformational if it is to serve the organization. Transformational leaders must operate from a foundation of high morality and ethical practices and have a fundamental understanding of the highly complex factors that support and make possible collective effort in an organization. They must personally act in accord with productive values and beliefs, and they must teach others to do the same. They must promulgate the culture. The key method strategy leaders should follow to transform cultures is to teach symbolically. This type of strategy involves the artful crafting of new stories, new symbols, new traditions, and even new humor so that the ambiguities surrounding organizational life can be productively managed by all members of the organization. Without collective understanding-shared networks of revised meaning- the new ways of acting and thinking cannot be internalized by organizational members.

Culture is deep seated and difficult to change, but leaders can influence or manage an organization's culture. It isn't easy, and it cannot be done rapidly, but leaders can have an effect on culture. Schein outlines some specific steps leaders can employ:

- What leaders pay attention to, measure and control. Something as simple as what is emphasized or measured, over time, can have an effect on an organization's culture. One example of this is an emphasis on form over substance. If leaders pay more attention to form, an organizational culture can develop where people start to believe that the substance of a recommendation is less important than the way it is presented. One can recall when more attention was paid to the format of viewgraphs used in a briefing than what was said; what we characterize as "eyewash."

- Where do you think people will focus their effort once it becomes accepted that a slick presentation is what the leaders are looking for? How could you go about changing that aspect of the organization's culture? Consider cultural assumptions and beliefs underlying a "zero defects" organizational mentality. "You must always be perfect; mistakes aren't allowed." If this assumption reflects a dysfunctional aspect of an organization's culture, how would you go about changing that perception?
- Leader reactions to critical incidents and organizational crises. The way leaders react to crises says a lot about the organization's values, norms and culture. Crises, by their nature, bring out the organization's underlying core values. Often, this is where rhetoric becomes apparent. Reactions to crises are normally highly visible, because everyone's attention is focused on the incident or situation. Disconnects between actions and words will usually be apparent, and actions always speak louder than words. Additionally, a crisis not only brings a great deal of attention, it also generates a great deal of emotional involvement on the part of those associated with the organization, particularly if the crisis threatens the organization's survival. This increases the potential for either reinforcing the existing culture, or leading to a change in the culture. Such a crisis can provide an opportunity for a leader to influence the organization's culture in either a positive or a negative way.
- Deliberate role modeling, teaching, and coaching. Nothing can take the place of leaders "walking their talk." The personal example of a strategic leader can send a powerful message to the members of an organization, particularly if it is ethical and consistent. Reinforcing that example with teaching and coaching will help others to internalize the desired values.
- Criteria for allocation of rewards and status. The consequences of behavior-what behavior is rewarded and what is punished-can significantly influence culture.

If the organization reacts to new ideas by ridiculing the ideas and those who propose them, it won't take long before people believe that new ideas are not welcomed or desired. One belief of perceived organizational culture is reflected in the statement: "Don't raise questions or suggest improvements, because nothing will come of it and you will just get in trouble." If you were in an organization's strategic leader, what steps could you take to alter the reward system to change this aspect of the culture?

- Criteria for recruitment, selection, promotion, retirement and excommunication. One of the powerful ways of changing an organization's culture is through the type of people brought into, retained, and advanced in the organization. You should be able to establish a desired culture base in an organization by bringing in and advancing individuals with the values you want, and eliminating those with undesired value bases.

That is what organizations are attempting when they propose tightening up admissions standards to screen out undesirables. This strategy is consistent with the belief that the problems experienced by the organization result from a few "bad apples" and do not reflect systemic problems. However, if a strong culture bias exists, it may be too strong to be changed by selection alone.

The military academies are organizations which change over one fourth of their membership every year, which should provide an opportunity for changes to the organizational culture as new members are brought in. The catch, however, is that the socialization of those new members rests in the hands of those who are already part of the existing culture. How could the military academies make systemic culture changes not negated by the socialization process new members go through?

- Organizational design and structure. As we mentioned earlier, modifying the organization's basic structure may be a way of changing the existing norms, and hence the culture. For example, a culture of mistrust between the leaders and the members of an organization may be exacerbated by a "line" structure that discourages vertical communication.

- Organizational systems and procedures. The simplest definition of culture is "that's the way we do things around here." Routines or procedures can become so embedded that they become part of the culture, and changing the culture necessitates changing those routines. We can all think of organizations where a weekly or monthly meeting takes on a life of its own, becomes more formalized, lengthy, and elaborate, and becomes the only way information moves within the organization. Changing the culture to improve communication may only be possible by changing the meeting procedures or eliminating the meetings altogether.
- Design of physical space, facades, and buildings. The impact of the design of buildings on culture can easily be illustrated by considering the executive perks in an organization. Which organization do you think will have a more open and participative culture, one where top executives have reserved parking spaces, top floor offices, a special elevator and an executive dining room, or one where the executive offices are not separated from the rest of the company and executives park and eat in the same place as their employees?
- Stories about important events and people. This is a way that culture is perpetuated in an organization, in that it helps define and solidify the organization's identity. By what events and stories they emphasize, leaders influence that identity.
- Formal statements of organizational philosophy, creeds, and charts. This is the way leaders most often try and influence their organizations, and encompasses the vision or mission statement and statements of the organization's (or the leader's) values and philosophy. By themselves, however, formal statements will have little effect on the organization's culture. They must be linked to actions to affect culture.

Schein has five guidelines for the leader:

1. Don't oversimplify culture or confuse it with climate, values, or corporate philosophy. Culture *underlies* and largely *determines* these other variables. Trying to change values or climate without getting at the underlying culture will be a futile effort.
2. Don't label culture as solely a human resources (read "touchy-feely") aspect of an organization, affecting only its human side. The impact of culture goes far beyond the human side of the organization to affect and influence its basic mission and goals.
3. Don't assume that the leader can manipulate culture as he or she can control many other aspects of the organization. Culture, because it is largely determined and controlled by the members of the organization, not the leaders, is different. Culture may end up controlling the leader rather than being controlled by him or her.
4. Don't assume that there is a "correct" culture, or that a strong culture is better than a weak one. It should be apparent that different cultures may fit different organizations and their environments, and that the desirability of a strong culture depends on how well it supports the organization's strategic goals and objectives.
5. Don't assume that all the aspects of an organization's culture are important, or will have a major impact on the functioning of the organization. Some elements of an organization's culture may have little impact on its functioning, and the leader must distinguish which elements are important, and focus on those.

CONCLUDING THOUGHT

An understanding of culture, and how to transform it, is a crucial skill for leaders trying to achieve strategic outcomes. Strategic leaders have the best perspective, because of their position in the organization, to see the dynamics of the culture, what should remain, and what needs transformation. This is the essence of strategic success.

13

STRATEGIC VISION

A specialist was hired to develop and present a series of half-day training seminars on empowerment and teamwork for the managers of a large international oil company. Fifteen minutes into the first presentation, he took a headlong plunge into the trap of assumption. With great intent, he laid the groundwork for what he considered the heart of empowerment-team-building, family, and community. He praised the need for energy, commitment, and passion for production. At what he thought was the appropriate time, he asked the group of 40 managers the simple question on which he was to ground his entire talk: "What is the vision of your company?" No one raised a hand. The speaker thought they might be shy, so he gently encouraged them. The room grew deadly silent. Everyone was looking at everyone else, and he had a sinking sensation in his stomach. "Your company does have a vision, doesn't it?" he asked. A few people shrugged, and a few shook their heads. He was dumbfounded. How could any group or individual strive toward greatness and mastery without a vision? That's exactly the point. They can't. They can maintain, they can survive; but they can't expect to achieve greatness. —Mapes (1991)

SKY Magazine

Vision is a widely used term, but not well understood. Perhaps leaders don't understand what vision is, or why it is important. One strategic leader is quoted as saying, "I've come to believe that we need a vision to guide us, but I can't seem to get my hands on what 'vision' is. I've heard lots of terms like mission, purpose, values, and strategic intent, but no-one has given me a satisfactory way of looking at vision that will help me sort out this morass of words. It's really frustrating!" (Collins and Porras 1991). To understand vision, clarify what the term means.

DEFINING VISION

One definition of vision comes from Burt Nanus, a well-known expert on the subject. Nanus defines a vision as a realistic, credible, attractive future for [an] organization. Let's disect this definition:

- Realistic: A vision must be based in reality to be meaningful for an organization. For example, if you're developing a vision for a computer software company that has carved out a small niche in the market developing instructional software and has a 1.5 percent share of the computer software market, a vision to overtake Microsoft and dominate the software market is not realistic!
- Credible: A vision must be believable to be relevant. To whom must a vision be credible? Most importantly, to the employees or members of the organization. If the members of the organization do not find the vision credible, it will not be meaningful or serve a useful purpose. One of the purposes of a vision is to inspire those in the organization to achieve a level of excellence, and to provide purpose and direction for the work of those employees. A vision which is not credible will accomplish neither of these ends.
- Attractive: If a vision is going to inspire and motivate those in the organization, it must be attractive. People must want to be part of this future that's envisioned for the organization.
- Future: A vision is not in the present, it is in the future. In this respect, the image of the leader gazing off into the distance to formulate a vision may not be a bad one.

A vision is not where you are now, it's where you want to be in the future. (If you reach or attain a vision, and it's no longer in the future, but in the present, is it still a vision?)

Nanus goes on to say that the right vision for an organization, one that is a *realistic, credible, attractive future for that organization*, can accomplish a number of things for the organization:

- It attracts commitment and energizes people. This is one of the primary reasons for having a vision for an organization: its motivational effect. When people can see that the organization is committed to a vision-and that entails more than just having a vision statement-it generates enthusiasm about the course the organization intends to follow, and increases the commitment of people to work toward achieving that vision.
- It creates meaning in workers' lives. A vision allows people to feel like they are part of a greater whole, and hence provides meaning for their work. The right vision will mean something to everyone in the organization if they can see how what they do contributes to that vision. Consider the difference between the hotel service worker who can only say, "I make beds and clean bathrooms," to the one who can also say, "I'm part of a team committed to becoming the worldwide leader in providing quality service to our hotel guests." The work is the same, but the context and meaning of the work is different.
- It establishes a standard of excellence. A vision serves a very important function in establishing a standard of excellence. In fact, a good vision is all about excellence. Tom Peters, the author of *In Search of Excellence*, talks about going into an organization where a number of problems existed. When he attempted to get the organization's leadership to address the problems, he got the defensive response, "But we're no worse than anyone else!" Peters cites this sarcastically as a great

vision for an organization: "Acme Widgets: We're No Worse Than Anyone Else!" A vision so characterized by lack of a striving for excellence would not motivate or excite anyone about that organization. The standard of excellence also can serve as a continuing goal and stimulate quality improvement programs, as well as providing a measure of the worth of the organization.

- It bridges the present and the future. The right vision takes the organization out of the present, and focuses it on the future. It's easy to get caught up in the crises of the day, and to lose sight of where you were heading. A good vision can orient you on the future, and provide positive direction. The vision alone isn't enough to move you from the present to the future, however. That's where a strategic plan, discussed later in the chapter, comes in. A vision is the desired future state for the organization; the strategic plan is how to get from where you are now to where you want to be in the future.

Another definition of vision comes from Oren Harari: "Vision should describe a set of ideals and priorities, a picture of the future, a sense of what makes the company special and unique, a core set of principles that the company stands for, and a broad set of compelling criteria that will help define organizational success." Are there any differences between Nanus's and Harari's definitions of vision? What are the similarities? Do these definitions help clarify the concept of vision and bring it into focus?

An additional framework for examining vision is put forward by Collins and Porras. They conceptualize vision as having two major components: a Guiding Philosophy, and a Tangible Image. They define the guiding philosophy as "a system of fundamental motivating assumptions, principles, values and tenets." The guiding philosophy stems from the organization's core beliefs and values and its purpose.

CORE BELIEFS AND VALUES

Just as they underlie organizational culture, beliefs and values are a critical part of guiding philosophy and therefore vision. One CEO expressed the importance of core values and beliefs this way: I firmly believe that any organization, in order to survive and achieve success, must have a sound set of beliefs on whichit premises all its policies and actions. Next, I believe that the most important single factor in corporate success is faithful adherence to those beliefs. And, finally, I believe [the organization] must be willing to change everything about itself except those beliefs as it moves through corporate life. (Collins and Porras 1991)

Core values and beliefs can relate to different constituents such as customers, employees, and shareholders, to the organization's goals, to ethical conduct, or to the organization's management and leadership philosophy. Baxter Healthcare Corporation has articulated three *Shared Values: Respect for their Employees, Responsiveness to their Customers, and Results for their Shareholders*, skillfully linking their core values to their key constituencies and also saying something about what is important to the organization. The key, however, is whether these are not only stated but also operating values.

Collins and Porras have provided examples of core values and beliefs from a survey of industry they conducted, and cite the following examples, among others:

- About People

  Marriott: "See the good in people, and try to develop those qualities."

- About Customers

  L.L. Bean: "Sell good merchandise at a reasonable price; treat your customers like you would your friends, and the business will take care of itself."

- About Products

  Sony: "We should always be the pioneers with our products—out front leading the market. We believe in leading the public with new products rather than asking them what kind of products they want."

- About Management and Business

  Motorola: "Everything will turn out alright if we just keep in motion, forever moving forward."

PURPOSE

The second part of guiding philosophy is purpose-why the organization exists, what needs it fills. Collins and Porras believe a good purpose statement should be "broad, fundamental, inspirational, and enduring." Consider this purpose statement: "The purpose of the United States Naval Academy at Annapolis, MD, is to prepare midshipmen to become professional officers in the naval service." Or this purpose statement from Apple Computer: "To make a contribution to the world by making tools for the mind that advance humankind." How do these statements of purpose stack up?

Whether individual, team, organization or nation, a sense of purpose and direction is essential to commitment. A shared sense of purpose is the glue that binds people together in common cause, often linking each individual's goals with the organization's goals. Properly formulated, a shared sense of purpose provides understanding of the need for coordinated collective effort — for subordinating individual interest to the larger objective that can be achieved only by the collective effort. When it is long range in nature, it is the basis for detailed planning for the allocation of resources. When it is noble and inspiring, it gives dignity and respect to those participating in the effort. And, when it promises a better future, it gives hope to all who seek it.

The second major component of vision is tangible image. This is composed of a mission and a vivid description. Mission is "a clear and compelling goal that serves to unify an organization's effort. An effective mission must stretch and challenge the organization, yet be achievable" (Collins and Porras). There are four ways of approaching developing a mission statement: targeting, common enemy, role model, and transformation. Targeting means developing your mission statement around a clear, definable goal. An example is the mission Merck Pharmaceuticals set in 1979: To establish Merck as the preeminent drug-maker worldwide in the 1980s. The common enemy approach is to focus the mission on overtaking or dominating a rival. Athletic shoe, automobile, and telecommuncations companies are all examples of areas where competition with rivals dominates company missions. Role model missions take an exemplar in another industry, and benchmark off that exemplar. For example, a mission "To be the Microsoft of retail sales companies" employs the role modeling technique. Finally, the internal transformation approach mission tends to focus on the internal remaking, restructuring, or rebirth of an organization. One example of a transformational mission might be the Army's recent efforts to transform itself into a newer, leaner Army positioned for the 21st century.

This may be a good point to address the confusion over the use of the terms purpose, mission and vision. Collins and Porras view purpose and mission as components of vision. Others, such as Nanus, differentiate between mission and vision. Nanus states, "A vision is not a mission. To state that an organization has a mission is to state its purpose, not its direction." Further complicating the semantics, different organizations may have mission statements, vision statements, purpose statements, or all three. To take one example, Quorum Health Group, Inc. a hospital management company, differentiates between its mission and vision this way:

MISSION STATEMENT

Quorum Health Group, Inc., is a hospital company committed to meeting the needs of clients as an owner, manager, consultant or partner through innovative services that enhance the delivery of quality healthcare.

VISION STATEMENT

Quorum Health Group, Inc., will be valued for its expertise in hospital management and its ability to positively impact the delivery of quality healthcare.

What are the differences between these two statements? Note that the mission is oriented in the present ("QHG is a company . . ."), while the vision is oriented in the future ("QHG will be valued . . ."). The mission states what QHG does in relatively concrete terms (meet the needs of clients by providing services that enhance the delivery of quality healthcare), while the vision states what it wants to do in more idealistic terms (be valued for its expertise and its ability to positively impact the delivery of quality healthcare).

One final example may illustrate how confused mission and vision can become. The Coca-Cola Company in 1994 published a booklet entitled "Our Mission and Our Commitment." In that booklet, the company defines their mission as follows:

We exist to *create value for our share owners* on a long term basis by building a business that enhances The Coca-Cola Company's trademarks. This also is our ultimate *commitment*. As the world's largest beverage company, we refresh that world. We do this by developing superior soft drinks, both carbonated and non-carbonated, and profitable non-alcoholic beverage systems that create value for our Company, our bottling partners, and our customers.

Does this sound like a mission, a vision, or a combination of both?

In Collins and Porras's framework for vision, their last element is a vivid description or picture of the end state that completion of the mission represents. They view this as essential to bringing the mission to life.

A vivid description gives the mission the ability to inspire and motivate. Look back at the Coca-Cola Company mission shown above. Does it paint a vivid description of completion of the mission, or would The Coca-Cola Company have to amplify the mission statement?

To put this all together, Collins and Porras present the following framework:

core beliefs and values + purpose = guiding philosophy

mission + vivid description = tangible image

guiding philosophy + tangible image = vision

Note that, as opposed to Nanus, Collins and Porras do not focus on a vision statement, but on a vision as consisting of elements shown above. It's worth exploring the properties of a good vision. Nanus has several guidelines for creating a realistic, credible, attractive future for an organization:

PROPERTIES OF A GOOD VISION

- A good vision is a mental model of a future state. It involves thinking about the future, and modeling possible future states. A vision doesn't exist in the present, and it may or may not be reached in the future. Nanus describes it like this: "A vision portrays a fictitious world that cannot be observed or verified in advance and that, in fact, *may never become reality*" (emphasis added). However, if it is a good mental model, it shows the way to identify goals and how to plan to achieve them.
- A good vision is idealistic. How can a vision be realistic and idealistic at the same time? One way of reconciling these apparently contradictory properties of a vision is that the vision is realistic enough so that people believe it is achievable, but idealistic enough so that it cannot be achieved without stretching. If it is too easily achievable, it will not set a standard of excellence, nor will it motivate people to want to work toward it. On the other hand, if it is too idealistic, it may be perceived as beyond the reach of those in the organization, and discourage motivation. A realistic vision for that software company might be to maintain their current market share and produce instructional software that meets quality standards. Realistic, yes; but inspiring? No. A realistic yet also idealistic vision might be: *To become the industry leader in the development of state-of-the-art instructional software products, known for the quality and the innovativeness of their design.*
- A good vision is appropriate for the organization and for the times. A vision must be consistent with the organization's values and culture, and its place in its environment. It must also be realistic. For example, in a time of downsizing and consolidation in an industry, a very ambitious, expansionistic vision would not be appropriate. An organization with a history of being conservative, and a culture encouraging conformity rather than risk taking, would not find an innovative vision appropriate. The computer software company

mentioned above, with a history of producing high quality instructional software, would not find a vision to become the industry leader in video games or virtual reality software an appropriate one.

- A good vision sets standards of excellence and reflects high ideals. Generally, the vision proposed above for the software company does reflect measurable standards of excellence and a high level of aspiration. The actual measure could be the external reputation of the company, as assessed by having users evaluate the company and its products.
- A good vision clarifies purpose and direction. In defining that "realistic, credible, attractive future for an organization," a vision provides the rationale for both the mission and the goals the organization should pursue. This creates meaning in workers' lives by clarifying purpose, and making clear what the organization wants to achieve. For people in the organization, a good vision should answer the question, "Why do I go to work?" With a good vision, the answer to that question should not only be, "To earn a paycheck," but also, "To help build that attractive future for the organization and achieve a higher standard of excellence."
- A good vision inspires enthusiasm and encourages commitment. An inspiring vision can help people in an organization get excited about what they're doing, and increase their commitment to the organization. The computer industry is an excellent example of one characterized by organizations with good visions. A recent article reported that it is not unusual for people to work 80 hour weeks, and for people to be at work at any hour of the day or night. Some firms had to find ways to make employees go home, not ways to make them come to work! What accounts for this incredible work ethic? It is having a sense of working organizations that are building the future in a rapidly evolving and unconstrained field, where an individual's work makes a difference, and where everyone shares a vision for the future.

- A good vision is well articulated and easily understood. In order to motivate individuals, and clearly point toward the future, a vision must be articulated so people understand it. Most often, this will be in the form of a vision statement. There are dangers in being too terse, or too long-winded. A vision must be more than a slogan or a "bumper sticker." Slogans such as Ford Motor Company's "Quality Is Job One" are good marketing tools, but the slogan doesn't capture all the essential elements of a vision. On the other hand, a long document that expounds an organization's philosophy and lays out its strategic plan is too complex to be a vision statement. The key is to strike a balance.
- A good vision reflects the uniqueness of the organization, its distinctive competence, what it stands for, and what it is able to achieve. This is where the leaders of an organization need to ask themselves, "What is the one thing we do better than anyone else? What is it that sets us apart from others in our area of business?" A good example of a visioning process refocusing a company on its core competencies is Sears. A few years ago, Sears had expanded into areas far afield from its original business as a retailer. Among other things, Sears began offering financial services at their stores. Poor performance led Sears to realize that they could not compete with financial services companies whose core business was in that area, so they dropped that service and eliminated other aspects of their business not related to retailing. Interestingly, Sears' primary competitor is Wal-Mart, an organization with a very clear and compelling vision. Sam Walton found a niche in providing one stop shopping for people in rural areas, and overwhelmed "Mom and Pop" stores with volume buying and discounting. Wal-Mart is very clear about their vision, and has focused on specific areas where they can be the industry leader. The key is finding what it is that your organization does best. Focus your vision there.
- A good vision is ambitious. It must not be commonplace. It must be truly extraordinary. This property gets back

to the idea of a vision that causes people and the organization to stretch. A good vision pushes the organization to a higher standard of excellence, challenging its members to try and achieve a level of performance they haven't achieved before. Inspiring, motivating, compelling visions are not about maintaining the status quo.

DEVELOPING A VISION

At this point you should know what a good vision consists of, and recognize a vision statement when you see one. But how does a strategic leader go about developing a vision for an organization? Nanus also offers a few words of advice to someone formulating a vision for an organization:

- Learn everything you can about the organization. There is no substitute for a thorough understanding of the organization as a foundation for your vision.
- Bring the organization's major constituencies into the visioning process. This is one of Nanus's imperatives: don't try to do it alone. If you're going to get others to buy into your vision, if it's going to be a wholly shared vision, involvement of at least the key people in the organization is essential. "Constituencies," refer to people both inside and outside the organization who can have a major impact on the organization, or who can be impacted by it. Another term to refer to constituencies is "stakeholders"- those who have a stake in the organization.
- Keep an open mind as you explore the options for a new vision. Don't be constrained in your thinking by the organization's current direction - it may be right, but it may not.
- Encourage input from your colleagues and subordinates. Another injunction about not trying to do it alone: those down in the organization often know it best and have a wealth of untapped ideas. Talk with them!
- Understand and appreciate the existing vision. Provide continuity if possible, and don't throw out good ideas

because you didn't originate them. In his book about visionary leadership, Nanus describes a seven-step process for formulating a vision:

1. Understand the organization. To formulate a vision for an organization, you first must understand it. Essential questions to be answered include what its mission and purpose are, what value it provides to society, what the character of the industry is, what institutional framework the organization operates in, what the organization's position is within that framework, what it takes for the organization to succeed, who the critical stakeholders are, both inside and outside the organization, and what their interests and expectations are.
2. Conduct a vision audit. This step involves assessing the current direction and momentum of the organization. Key questions to be answered include: Does the organization have a clearly stated vision? What is the organization's current direction? Do the key leaders of the organization know where the organization is headed and agree on the direction? Do the organization's structures, processes, personnel, incentives, and information systems support the current direction?
3. Target the vision. This step involves starting to narrow in on a vision. Key questions: What are the boundaries or constraints to the vision? What must the vision accomplish? What critical issues must be addressed in the vision?
4. Set the vision context. This is where you look to the future, and where the process of formulating a vision gets difficult. Your vision is a desirable future for the organization. To craft that vision you first must think about what the organization's future environment might look like. This doesn't mean you need to predict the future, only to make some informed estimates about what future environments might look like. First, categorize future developments

in the environment which might affect your vision. Second, list your expectations for the future in each category. Third, determine which of these expectations is most likely to occur. And fourth, assign a probability of occurrence to each expectation.

5. Develop future scenarios. This step follows directly from the fourth step. Having determined, as best you can, those expectations most likely to occur, and those with the most impact on your vision, combine those expectations into a few brief scenarios to include the range of possible futures you anticipate. The scenarios should represent, in the aggregate, the alternative "futures" the organization is likely to operate within.
6. Generate alternative visions. Just as there are several alternative futures for the environment, there are several directions the organization might take in the future. The purpose of this step is to generate visions reflecting those different directions. Do not evaluate your possible visions at this point, but use a relatively unconstrained approach.
7. Choose the final vision. Here's the decision point where you select the best possible vision for your organization. To do this, first look at the properties of a good vision, and what it takes for a vision to succeed, including consistency with the organization's culture and values. Next, compare the visions you've generated with the alternative scenarios, and determine which of the possible visions will apply to the broadest range of scenarios. The final vision should be the one which best meets the criteria of a good vision, is compatible with the organization's culture and values, and applies to a broad range of alternative scenarios (possible futures).

IMPLEMENTING THE VISION

Now that you have a vision statement for your organization, are you done? Formulating the vision is only the first step;

implementing the vision is much harder, but must follow if the vision is going to have any effect on the organization. The three critical tasks of the strategic leader are formulating the vision, communicating it, and implementing it. Some organizations think that developing the vision is all that is necessary. If they have not planned for implementing that vision, development of the vision has been wasted effort. Even worse, a stated vision which is not implemented may have adverse effects within the organization because it initially creates expectations that lead to cynicism when those expectations are not met. Before implementing the vision, the leader needs to communicate the vision to all the organization's stakeholders, particularly those inside the organization. The vision needs to be well articulated so that it can be easily understood. And, if the vision is to inspire enthusiasm and encourage commitment, it must be communicated to all the members of the organization.

How do you communicate a vision to a large and diverse organization? The key is to communicate the vision through multiple means. Some techniques used by organizations to communicate the vision include disseminating the vision in written form; preparing audiovisual shows outlining and explaining the vision; and presenting an explanation of the vision in speeches, interviews or press releases by the organization's leaders. An organization's leaders also may publicly "sign up" for the vision. You've got to "walk your talk." For the vision to have credibility, leaders must not only say they believe in the vision; they must demonstrate that they do through their decisions and their actions.

Once you've communicated your vision, how do you go about implementing it? This is where strategic planning comes in. To describe the relationship between strategic visioning and strategic planning in very simple terms, visioning can be considered as establishing where you want the organization to be in the future; strategic planning determines how to get there from where you are now. Strategic planning links the present to the future, and shows how you intend to move toward your vision. One process of strategic planning is to first develop goals to help you achieve your vision, then develop actions that will enable the organization to reach these goals.

CONCLUSION

An organization must and can develop a strategic plan that includes specific and measurable goals to implement a vision. A comprehensive plan will recognize where the organization is today, and cover all the areas where action is needed to move toward the vision. In addition to being specific and measurable, actions should clearly state who is responsible for their completion. Actions should have milestones tied to them so progress toward the goals can be measured.

Implementing the vision does not stop with the formulation of a strategic plan - the organization that stops at this point is not much better off than one that stops when the vision is formulated. Real implementation of a vision is in the execution of the strategic plan throughout the organization, in the continual monitoring of progress toward the vision, and in the continual revision of the strategic plan as changes in the organization or its environment necessitate. The bottom line is that visioning is not a discrete event, but rather an ongoing process.

A FORMULA FOR VISIONARY LEADERSHIP

Burt Nanus sums up his concepts with two simple formulas (slightly modified):

STRATEGIC VISION X COMMUNICATION = *SHARED PURPOSE*

SHARED PURPOSE X EMPOWERED PEOPLE X

APPROPRIATE ORGANIZATIONAL CHANGES X STRATEGIC THINKING =

SUCCESSFUL VISIONARY LEADERSHIP

Each one of the terms places unique and special demands on the strategic leader. If you can put these elements together in an organization, and you have a good vision to start with, you should be well on the way to achieving excellence. Collins and Porras affirm: "The function of a leader-the one universal requirement of effective leadership-is to catalyze a clear and shared vision of the organization and to secure commitment to and vigorous pursuit of that vision."

14

VISION AND THE MANAGEMENT OF CHANGE

WHY CHANGE?

Change is pervasive in our society and a fact of life in organizations (Goodfellow 1985). Where does the impetus for change come from? The simple answer is that the impetus to change comes from the environment. Effective strategic leaders understand that change in the strategic environment is a continuous process.

By environment, we can mean the internal organizational environment, but more often, we are talking about the external environment. Organizations are awash in the external environment, and a sea change in the environment (e.g., the rifled musket, steam-driven warships, the jet engine, the Age of Information) can cause an unresponsive organization to founder. A part of strategic leadership is understanding when environmental change implies a need for organizational change and when it does not. Making internal changes to accommodate external change is reactive, and strategic leadership should be proactive. This is where a well-crafted, wel- managed strategic vision can help balance reactive and proactive changes.

Change is about survival. Change is especially necessary in organizations that wish to prosper in a volatile, uncertain, complex, and ambiguous environment. If changes rocking the external environment were *temporary*, the slow and uncertain pace at which organizations change would matter less. But, the reverse is true. Powerful forces in the environment are pressuring public and private organizations to alter *permanently* existing structures, policies, and practices (Bolman & Deal, 1991).

Globalization is one example of pressure to change. With globalization comes greater competition, especially for workforce quality. Wider differences in the skills, attitudes, and needs of the workforce are coupled to increases in communications problems. Geographic dispersion creates conflict between regional offices (e.g., unified commands) and the central headquarters as well as conflict among regional offices. Globalization creates the challenge of building cohesion and common purpose in the face of cultural and organizational differences. All of this is complex because many of the variables in the equation are not under the control of the leaders who are creating the vision for change.

Peace is another example of pressure to change. Peace necessitates, at least in the minds of some people, the need for reduction in the size of military forces. With smaller military forces comes the need for increased capabilities because the number and diversity of missions has increased. Also, reduced budgets create friction among the CINCs and among the services.

Another example of environmental pressure for change is information technology. Information technology facilitates structural decentralization and downsizing. People must develop new skills. Power often shifts from centralized functions to operating units.

Demographic changes in the population are creating enormous pressure for change in organization. Structural responses to demographic diversity include policies and programs like equal opportunity and affirmative action. The changing workforce has varied needs (e.g., religious and language) and often creates new training requirements. Friction and conflict develops between demographic groups.

In the private sector, deregulation has created major structural changes in some industries (e.g., the break-up of Ma Bell, the proliferation of airline companies, and the merging of major defense contractors). People in the workforce can sense that they can be cut loose without warning. Deregulation can bring major shifts in power (e.g., from the government to the consumer). And, deregulation results in the need for the redefinition of organizational mission and culture.

Change is absolutely necessary for the survival of individuals and organizations. The question isn't whether or not to implement change. Over the long run, you have no choice unless you are willing to become irrelevant. The strategic environment, over which you have little or no control, is in a state of constant change and it's your job to sense when changes in the organization are going to be necessary.

Therefore, the first real question is what role are you going to assume? Domain defender? Reluctant reactor? Anxious analyzer? Or, enthusiastic prospector? If you choose to play only one role and that in a fixed manner over time, then you and your organization will survive for as long as the environment tolerates that role. A successful strategic leader knows which role to play at what time, and he/she knows when to change roles. Once the role is sorted out, you can ask the other really important questions: What changes are necessary and desirable? How do you go about managing change?

STRATEGIC LEADER ROLES IN RESPONSE TO THE ENVIRONMENT*

- DOMAIN DEFENDER
- PERCEIVE LITTLE OR NO UNCERTAINTY IN THE ENVIRONMENT.
- MAKE MINOR ADJUSTMENTS IN ORGANIZATIONAL STRUCTURE AND PROCESSES.
- LIKELY CANDIDATE FOR DERAILMENT AND EXTINCTION.
- RELUCTANT REACTOR
- PERCEIVE SOME CHANGE AND UNCERTAINTY.
- NOT LIKELY TO MAKE SUBSTANTIAL ADJUSTMENTS UNTIL FORCED TO DO SO.
- MAY SURVIVE, BUT AT THE MARGINS.

- ANXIOUS ANALYZER
- PERCEIVE A GOOD DEAL OF CHANGE AND UNCERTAINTY.
- WAIT UNTIL COMPETITORS DEVELOP A RESPONSE AND THEN ADOPT IT.
- LIKELY TO SURVIVE, IF NOT FIRST OVERRUN.
- ENTHUSIASTIC PROSPECTOR
- PERCEIVE CONTINUALLY CHANGE AND LOTS OF UNCERTAINTY.
- REGULARLY EXPERIMENTS WITH POTENTIAL RESPONSES TO TRENDS.
- SURVIVES AND PROSPERS OVER THE LONG RUN.

* Adapted from Goffee and Jones, 1996.

WHAT IS CHANGE?

Organizational change is about making alterations to the organization's purpose, culture, structure, and processes in response to seen or anticipated changes in the environment. Strategic management of change is all about identifying and embedding in the organization those changes that will ensure the long-term survival of the organization. How do we think about change?

CHANGE

- CONDITION AND PROCESS
- PLANNED OR UNPLANNED?
- TACTICAL OR STRATEGIC?
- EVOLUTIONARY OR REVOLUTIONARY?

CONDITION AND PROCESS. Change can be thought of as a condition and a process. Change as a condition describes what is happening in the environment; it is part of the reality we must accept. Change as a condition may profoundly influence our organization, but it takes place externally and we have little control over it.

Change as a process is what we foster internally in response to changes in the environment. It is the leadership and management actions we take to change the organization. Therefore, unlike changes in the environment, change as a process is ours to influence (Sullivan & Harper, 1996).

PLANNED OR UNPLANNED? Change can be planned or unplanned. Both can be good, both can be bad. Unplanned change just happens in reaction to unseen or unanticipated influences. Often, it is difficult to tell where the change came from and how it was initiated. Paradoxically, planned change is all about maintaining the organization's relevancy in the face of environmental pressures.

TACTICAL OR STRATEGIC? Tactical change occurs in the short-term and, more often than not, is short-lived. "Fad-surfing" is a sure symptom of tactical change. In the face of changes in the environment, many leaders often reach out and grasp the "fad du jour" [e.g., one-minute manager, management by objective (MBO), TQM, TQL]. Then the next day, they grasp at the next "fad du jour," whip-sawing the organization with inconsistent messages and inconsequential behavior. This attempt to manage change is a sure sign that the leaders do not understand the environment, the organization, or both.

	UNPLANNED CHANGE	PLANNED CHANGE
TACTICAL	KNEE-JERK REACTION	ROUTINE ADJUSTMENTS
STRATEGIC	SPONTANEOUS OPPORTUNITY	BUILDING ROBUSTNESS

Strategic change is about leveraging vision to get at fundamental aspects of the organization, including the organization's direction and its culture. Strategic change is about forging organizational robustness in the face of environmental pressures. Hence, an accurate and insightful view of the current reality is as important as a clear vision (Senge 1990). Robustness is the timely capacity to anticipate and adapt to environmental change in order to maintain competitive advantage. Improving and maintaining robustness takes three interdependent forms. First, it is a function of comprehensive environmental scanning, accurate articulation of values, beliefs, and assumptions, the freedom to question values, beliefs and assumptions, creativity to formulate new options, and tolerance of risk in the pursuit of a new course. Second, robustness is about resource self-sufficiency. Often, the capital investment/reinvestment required to implement change is huge. Third, robustness is about maintaining contact and managing credibility with strategic constituencies.

ROBUSTNESS

- THE CAPACITY TO ADAPT AND MAINTAIN COMPETITIVE ADVANTAGE
- OPENNESS: THE FREEDOM TO QUESTION ONE'S OWN BELIEFS AND ASSUMPTIONS
- RESOURCE SELF-SUFFICIENCY: THE MEANS NEEDED TO PUT PLANS INTO ACTION
- CONSTITUENCY SUPPORT: MAINTAINING CONTACT, CREDIBILITY, AND COMMITMENT

EVOLUTIONARY OR REVOLUTIONARY? Change can be evolutionary or revolutionary. It can take place gradually within an existing paradigm, or it can be a dramatic shift to an entirely new paradigm. In addition to being gradual, evolutionary change usually is linear, and sequential. The downside of evolutionary change is that it is predictable. Competitors can figure out what your organization is doing and where it is going.

Revolutionary change is about transforming the organization. The revolution can be small or it can be sweeping. The path of transformational change, while not linear and sequential, can be made predictable to people inside the organization through proper planning and communication.

Both evolutionary and revolutionary change can be legitimate strategic choices under the right environmental conditions. Environmental conditions can be defined by velocity, mass, and complexity. The velocity of change is the rate change takes place. The mass of the change is how widespread it is. And, the complexity of change means that change never occurs in isolation. Each change affects other changes in often unseen, unanticipated, or misunderstood ways that lead to unintended second- and third-order effects (Sullivan & Harper 1996).

GENERALIZED EFFECTS OF CHANGE

Can we anticipate the generalized effects of change on people? Within the domain of human behavior, the answer is yes. Four main effects are salient: self-confidence, confusion, loss, and conflict.

Change can cause people to feel incompetent, needy, and powerless, in short, to lose self-confidence. It is essential for the people in the organization to be involved in planning and executing change, to have opportunities to develop new skills required by the change, and to depend on psychological support mechanisms put in place before, during, and after the change is implemented.

Change can create confusion throughout the organization. Change alters the clarity and stability of roles and relationships, often creating chaos. This requires realigning and renegotiating formal patterns of relationships and policies.

By definition, change creates loss and therefore generates interpersonal conflict. Change can create loss of meaning and purpose. People form attachments to symbols and in symbolic activity. When the attachments are severed, people experience difficulty in letting go of old attachments. Avoiding or smoothing over these issues drives *conflict* underground, where it can fester and boil over. The psychological wounds that come with change require the creation of arenas where issues can be dealt with that may require symbolic healing (Bolman & Deal 1991).

CHANGE CAN:

- CAUSE PEOPLE TO FEEL BAD ABOUT THEMSELVES.
- CREATE CONFUSION AND UNPREDICTABILITY.
- CREATE LOSS.
- GENERATE INTERPERSONAL CONFLICT.

Implementing Change

How does a major change take hold and become infused throughout the organization? The answer comes from being broad-minded rather than narrowly focused. A strategic leader must develop sensing networks, expand the target audience, gather and broaden the power base, alert the organization that change is coming, actively manage the planning and execution processes by linking every day-to-day action to the vision for change, continually communicate the vision for change to key internal and external constituencies, know about and plan for overcoming resistance, and be prepared for unexpected but necessary mid-course corrections (Goodfellow 1985).

A KEY INDICATOR OF A SUCCESSFUL CHANGE AGENT IS THE NUMBER OF INTERNAL AND EXTERNAL SENSING NETWORKS HE/SHE DEVELOPS, MAINTAINS, AND USES.

DEVELOP SENSING NETWORKS. Most strategic leaders consciously develop and maintain a variety of information and power networks. These networks may be the sources of information that change is necessary. In addition to serving as sources of information, these networks also serve as sounding boards for new ideas. The people in these networks must be trusted by the leader, and familiar with the leader's thought processes.

SELECT THE TYPE OF CHANGE. What type of change is needed? The answer depends on the nature of changes in the environment, how well strategic leaders have scanned the environment and anticipated the need for change, and the nature of the organization itself. Two forms of interest here are revolutionary change and evolutionary change.

CHANGE

- PLANNED OR UNPLANNED?
- TACTICAL OR STRATEGIC?
- EVOLUTIONARY OR REVOLUTIONARY?

Research shows that organizations can get so immersed in inertia that they require revolutionary changes to adapt successfully to the changing environment. In other words, some organizations may not be able to change in spite of warnings from the environment. General Motors and IBM are two examples of organizations that almost became irrelevant because they persisted with their unimaginative products despite the risks imposed by Japanese car manufacturers and the rise of the personal computer. They could not visualize another way of doing things. Can you think of examples within the defense establishment where change mistakenly was avoided, or the wrong kind of change was selected?

In "stuck" organizations, quantum changes seem to occur only after a significant decline in organizational performance; often a leader is recruited from outside the organization. This is because leaders from outside the organization bring a new way of seeing the world; they are not trapped by the cultural norms and conventions that created the inertia. Revolutionary change is the way to save an organization that has lost its competitive advantage and slipped perilously close to the abyss of irrelevancy. The downside to revolutionary change is that it tends to accentuate the negative generalized effects discussed earlier. The alternative approach argues that successful change does not come from tumultuous and radical change, but from gradual and incremental change. Gradual and incremental change is easier to plan for, easier to implement than revolutionary change, and tends to be less bloody. Arguably, gradual change is the preferred method; however, the choice between evolutionary change and revolutionary change will be driven by the pace of change in the environment and how well strategic leaders have kept up with those environmental changes.

SELECT THE RIGHT METAPHOR. The underlying issue with selecting a metaphor is the connections or mutual influences among words, mind-sets, and behaviors. There are five

LANGUAGE IS THE VEHICLE FOR THE EXPRESSION OF MIND-SETS. things that strategic leaders should consider when selecting the metaphor for change:

- First, avoid "fad-surfing." At best, this results in the illusion of change.
- Second, listen closely to how the change is being talked about-the words and metaphors used. This allows you to test the clarity of intent and understanding of the

change. Inconsistencies in language and metaphor can lead to unnecessary fear and unwarranted confusion about the nature and scope of the change.

- Third, help people shape language and metaphor so that the message is consistent. Helping people find appropriate words and symbols will make it possible for them to move in the same direction.
- Fourth, examine the efficacy of metaphors that may be expressions of your own mind-set. When attempting to replace an old system with a new one, a poor choice of metaphor may imply that the old system is being left in place, or being merely upgraded. Terms such as "problem-solver," "trouble-shooter," and "change agent" may be more limiting than useful.
- Fifth, explore imaginative ways of talking about change that may excite people. Try to avoid slogans, jargon, and euphemisms such as " no more Task Force Smiths," "right-sizing," and "total quality management." Choose a metaphor that will make your people feel connected to what you are trying to achieve (Goldberg 1997).

CREATE THE VISION. Successful change is hinged on a picture of a desirable future. Vision can provide both a corporate sense of being and a sense of enduring purpose. Without a sensible vision, change efforts can dissolve into a list of confusing projects that take the organization in the wrong direction. It is important that the vision be easy to communicate (Kotter 1995).

VISION IS ABOUT ACTION. VISION CAN EMPOWER BOTH LEADERS AND FOLLOWERS TO IMPLEMENT CHANGE.

EXPAND THE TARGET AUDIENCE. As the need for change begins to crystallize, the strategic leader can begin to expand discussions to a broader cross-section of organizational members, paying careful attention to their reactions, suggestions, and alternatives. This actually is a search for allies within the organization and with strategic constituencies outside the organization.

STRATEGIC CHANGE IS BROAD-BASED, NOT NARROW. INCLUSION IS BETTER THAN EXCLUSION.

Expanding the discussion is a way to gain greater clarity around the issues, to get key people to begin to talk about the issues, and to build support. Gradually, people in the organization will become aware that change is imminent. Their expectations will begin to build that problems are going to be solved, things are going to get better, and procedures are going to change. But, at this point, there will be few if any specifics to complete the picture (Goodfellow 1985).

GATHER AND BROADEN THE POWER BASE. As the strategic leader develops greater clarity around the need for change, he/she will begin to pay attention to power figures in the organization, and may commission studies of alternatives. Study groups, part of participatory decision making, require personnel involvement and build pockets of support in the organization. By setting the agenda of study groups, timing the sequence of studies, and selecting the leaders and members of each study group, the strategic leader maintains influence over the process.

IT IS IMPORTANT TO AVOID SENDING THE MESSAGE THAT THE OLD WAY IS WRONG. A BETTER TACT IS TO HELP PEOPLE REALIZE THAT TIMES HAVE CHANGED AND THE ORGANIZATION MUST CHANGE.

Study groups can serve the purpose of educating, generating cohesion and support, coopting power figures, and building momentum for change. (Yes, giving the issue of change to a study group also can be a way to impede or retard change.) Individual and collective discussions surrounding the recommendations of various study groups generate give-and-take exchanges regarding specific proposals until a broad consensus is reached about the need for and direction of change.

If study groups come up with recommendations opposed by the strategic leader, the leader usually can establish hurdles and blocks to such ideas without openly opposing them. Additionally, the strategic leader can use information networks to disseminate throughout the organization those ideas which he/she supports (Goodfellow, 1985).

ALERT THE ORGANIZATION. As consensus within the organization is reached, the strategic leader begins to describe an emerging vision, often in very specific terms, for the organization as a whole. For the first time, the leader may affix a stamp of approval to new thrusts or new initiatives (Goodfellow, 1985).

At some point, after studying the issues and building support for change both inside and outside the organization, the strategic leader will make a formal announcement of the change. Announcing change should be carefully planned and well-timed for maximum effect. The announcement can, and should, take many forms, from speeches to the board of directors, to distributing pamphlets, to dinner or lunch presentations, and to informal discussions.

UNDERSTAND THAT, ULTIMATELY, YOU CANNOT KEEP CHANGE A SECRET. DON'T EVEN THINK ABOUT IT.

COMMUNICATE THE VISION. Getting the word out is key. Change is not possible unless people are willing to help. Speeches and newsletters help communicate the vision, but the most powerful medium is the behavior of the strategic leaders in the organization. Very visible executive-level leaders must behave in ways that are consistent with the vision. Strategic leaders, those who communicate the vision well, must incorporate messages about the vision into their hour-to-hour activities and use every communication channel to get the word out (Kotter, 1995).

A CLASSIC ERROR IN CHANGE MANAGEMENT IS TO UNDER COMMUNICATE THE VISION BY A FACTOR OF TEN.

CREATE A SENSE OF URGENCY. If people think that the organization is doing fine, there will be little motivation for change. Successful change starts when the people in the organization take a hard look at the organization's competitive situation, market position, technological advances, and performance. A frank and open discussion of the potentially unpleasant facts about new competition, shrinking budgets, flat performance, lack of growth, and other

DO NOT FALL INTO THE TRAP OF BECOMING PARALYZED BY THE DOWNSIDE POSSIBILITIES OF CHANGE.

indices of declining competitive position can create in the minds of people the need for change. A strategic leader can create that sense of urgency by painting the facts and by presenting the undesirable outcomes that may result from maintaining the status quo.

MANAGE THE PLANNING AND EXECUTION PROCESSES. The strategic leader's public announcement of a vision for change usually includes the unveiling of an accompanying plan (or the need to develop such a plan) and the appointment of a key member of the organization charged with turning the vision into a reality.

The first key to turning a strategic vision into reality comes in linking actions, accountability, and time-lines to the vision for change, and then working the plan. Changes and revisions to the strategic plan will be necessary, but if the strategic leader doesn't insure that the vision for change evolves into a plan for specific action, the vision will devolve into feathers and smoke.

The second key in turning a strategic vision into reality is to designate a person charged with the everyday orchestration of the change. The strategic leader should avoid getting into the weeds of change management, and remain at the strategic level, scanning the environment, servicing strategic constituencies, and communicating the vision. The champion or change agent must be a credible member of the organization who has the trust and respect of key power figures and constituencies inside and outside the organization. This person must be committed to the change, must have the power and resources to make things happen, and must clearly support the change through everyday behaviors, communication, and execution management.

A STRATEGIC PLAN FOR CHANGE

- VISION FOR CHANGE (WHY)
- STRATEGY FOR CHANGE (HOW)

- BROAD GOALS (WHAT)
- NARROWER OBJECTIVES (WHAT)
- SPECIFIC ACTIONS (WHAT)
- ACCOUNTABILITY (WHO)
- TIME-LINES (WHEN)
- A MONITORING SYSTEM (INTEGRATION)
- FEEDBACK LOOPS (ADJUSTMENTS)

EMPOWER OTHERS TO ACT ON THE VISION. Too often, people in the organization understand the vision and want to help transform the organization. But they can't. The strategic leader must remove blocks to change, call for new behaviors consistent with the vision, and, most importantly, visibly reward the new behaviors.

CHANGE REQUIRES THE REMOVAL OF OBSTACLES. THIS IS THE STRATEGIC LEADER'S JOB.

PLAN FOR AND CREATE SHORT-TERM WINS. Success breeds success. Most people won't go on a long journey unless they can see tangible short-term payoffs. Strategic leaders look for ways to obtain clear gains in performance, however small, and reward people who are involved through personal recognition, promotions, and bonuses. While short-term wins are important for building momentum, a wise strategic leader will not become focused on short-term performance. Nevertheless, commitments to short-term wins can help keep the urgency level up and force analytical thinking that can clarify and revise the vision, if necessary.

YOU CAN'T EAT AN ELEPHANT IN ONE BITE.

PLAN TO OVERCOME RESISTANCE. Anyone who has ever been in an organization (and that's just about everyone) knows that even small amounts of expected change lead to decreased organizational effectiveness, if just in the short-term. Change suggests letting go of old habits, roles, processes, procedures, and structure. There is uncertainty about new requirements and excessive concern about the future. All of this results in anxiety, stress, conflict, and resistance. Failure by the strategic leader to understand the causes for and results of resistance often leads to delays and even failure in implementation.

RESISTANCE TO CHANGE:

- IS A NORMAL HUMAN TRAIT.
- IS A FUNCTION OF PERSONALITY.
- DEPENDS ON PERCEIVED EFFECTS.
- DEPENDS ON WHETHER OR NOT IT IS IMPOSED FROM THE OUTSIDE.

What is it that impedes or derails the implementation of change? The answer is complex. Part of the answer may lie in the style and behavior of the organization's leaders. The greater the size and complexity of the organizations, the less inclined senior executives are to sit down with their subordinates and participate in a formal, step-by-step process to develop long-term plans for the future.

Controlling the rumor mill is another way to decrease resistance to change. This is difficult in a large, complex organization because hierarchies tend to resist providing information downward until every detail of the plan is complete. This is a mistake. Smart leaders keep the organization informed about what needs to change and why, what isn't going to change, and how the actual change is going to be implemented. Periodic information briefings about the status of the change should figure prominently in the plan for change. This serves to slow down the grinding of the rumor mill.

One way to decrease resistance is to plan for and allow people to participate in decisions which affect them. Participation in decision making gives people a sense of involvement and increases the probability of commitment to change. Scheduling change is another way to overcome resistance. If people know when they are no longer required to do things one way and are expected to move to a new way of doing things, they tend to waste less effort, experience less frustration and stress, and tend to be less resistant. Another critical factor to overcoming resistance is support from the top. It is important that the strategic leaders in the organization demonstrate their commitment to change by being spokes-persons for the change, by providing incentives for change, and by embodying the change. One way to guarantee resistance is to announce an immediate and unexpected change. This provides a shock wave in the thinking of people who are part of the organization. In the minds of those people, the shock wave often takes the form of "They're trying to keep something from us" or "They don't have a clue about what they're doing." This leads to embarrassment and loss of face on the part of the leader and the followers. This takes us beyond resistance to the question of why change often fails (Goodfellow 1985). This is discussed in detail alter in this chapter.

CONSOLIDATE IMPROVEMENTS. Occasionally, it will be time to pause and review what has gone on and what is going on. Perhaps the vision needs revision, perhaps not. Perhaps it is time to move from small wins to big wins. Past successes can

SHORT-TERM WINS ARE IMPORTANT, BUT DON'T DECLARE VICTORY TOO SOON.

become spring boards to even greater wins if the leader takes time to consolidate improvements by recognizing the people who made the improvements possible.

INSTITUTIONALIZE CHANGE. In the final analysis, change sticks when it becomes part of the organizational culture- it becomes part of "the way we do things around here." There are two techniques for institutionalizing change. First, show people how the change has helped improve performance and competitive advantage. Helping people make the connections between their efforts and improvements requires communication. Second, the strategic leader makes sure that the next generation of top leaders personify the vision. If requirements for promotion and advancement do not change in a manner consistent with the vision, the change rarely lasts. Bad succession decisions can undermine years of hard work (Kotter 1995).

MAKE SURE YOU ANCHOR CHANGE IN THE ORGANIZATION'S CULTURE. THE KEY HERE IS SUCCESSION PLANNING.

A CHANGE IN STYLE

Unfortunately, change does not happen as easily as described above. Very few leaders can introduce major changes required to cope with environmental pressures. Due to their prior training and experience, they are simply unable to develop the vision needed to transform the organization. They are caught in a web of pre-existing structures, organizational politics, and comfortable traditions. This is the bureaucratic mentality (Conger 1989). Because bureaucracies, especially large ones, consist of pools of specialized managers and leaders, people have precise roles where their duties and regulations are narrowly prescribed. In bureaucracies, a constricted understanding of one's role is emphasized. As a person moves up through the organizational hierarchy, he/she is rewarded for being effective within a narrow scope of responsibility. There often is no encouragement on the part of the bureaucracy to develop a wide perspective on the organization and its purpose.

As a result, leaders often arrive at the top of their organization with a myopic sense of the world and their organization's place in it. These rigid mind-sets often play themselves out as the leader tries to fit an inappropriate paradigm to a situation that either does not call for change or calls for more creative change. Yet, to be sensitive to the environment and strategic opportunities, a strategic leader needs an unfrozen mind-set, a broad perspective, and a vision (Conger 1989). Too often, inexperienced or insensitive strategic leaders who have risen through the bureaucracy assume that when the they say "do it," everyone responds. We can see (since change efforts fail) that this simply isn't true. In large, complex organizations, the ability of one person, even the leader, to influence an entire organization through a "telling" style of leadership becomes increasingly remote (Goodfellow, 1985).

THE "TELLING" STYLE OF LEADERSHIP

- THIS IS WHAT YOU DO.
- THIS IS WHEN YOU DO IT.
- THIS IS HOW YOU DO IT.
- GET OVER IT!

BIBLIOGRAPHY

Ahmad, Imtiaz: *State and Foreign Policy: India's Role in South Asia*, New Delhi, Vikas, 1993.

Ajit, K: *A History of Indian Economic Thought. Routledge History of Economic Thought Series*, London, Routledge, 1993.

Ashok, Vasant: *Indian Economy in the World Setting*, Bombay, Himalaya, 1988.

Behari, Madhuri: *Indian Economy since Independence: Chronology of Events*, Delhi, D.K. Publications, 1983.

Bhagwati, Jagdish: *India in Transition: Freeing the Economy*, Oxford, Clarendon Press, 1993.

Bhuleshkar, Vasant: *Indian Economy in the World Setting*, Bombay, Himalaya, 1988.

Byres, J.: *The State and Development Planning in India*, Delhi, Oxford University Press, 1994.

Calman, J.: *Toward Empowerment: Women and Politics in India*, Colorado, Westview Press, 1992.

Dahiya, L.N.: *Dynamics of Economic Life in Rural India*, Delhi, Gian, 1991.

Das, Kishore: *Economic History of Mughal India: An Annotated Bibliography, 1526-1875*, Calcutta, Santiniketan, 1991.

Desai, Vasant: *A Study of Rural Economics: A Systems Approach*, Bombay, Himalaya, 1983.

Dhingra, C.: *The Indian Economy: Resources, Planning, Development, and Problems*, Delhi, Sultan Chand, 1983.

Diwakar, D.M.: *Agriculture and Industry: Dynamics of Imbalances in India*, New Delhi, Manak, 1991.

Goldsmith, W.: *The Financial Development of India, 1860-1977*, New Haven, Yale University Press, 1983.

Guhan, S.: *The World Bank's Lending in South Asia*, Washington, Brookings Institution, 1995.

Gupta, B.: *Black Income in India*, New Delhi, Sage, 1992.

Ishwar, C.: *The Indian Economy: Resources, Planning, Development, and Problems*, Delhi, Sultan Chand, 1983.

Jha, P.R.: *Agriculture and Economic Development*, New Delhi, Ashish, 1988.

Joshi, Vijay: *India: Macroeconomics and Political Economy, 1964-1991*, Washington, World Bank, 1994.

Kashyap, C.: *National Policy Studies*, New Delhi, Tata McGraw-Hill for the Lok Sabha Secretariat, 1990.

Kishore, K.: *Economic History of Mughal India: An Annotated Bibliography, 1526-1875*, Calcutta, Santiniketan, 1991.

Kohli, Rajan: *Structural Change in Indian Industries*, New Delhi, Capital Foundation Society, 1994.

Leslie, J.: *Toward Empowerment: Women and Politics in India*, Colorado, Westview Press, 1992.

Little, I.M.D.: *India: Macroeconomics and Political Economy, 1964-1991*, Washington, World Bank, 1994.

Maheshwari, Shriram: *Rural Development in India: A Public Policy Approach*, New Delhi, Sage, 1995.

Mongia, J.N.: *India's Economic Development Strategies, 1951-2000 A.D.*. New Delhi, Allied, 1986.

Mukerji, S.K.: *Science in India: A Changing Profile*, New Delhi, Indian National Science Academy, 1984.

Pranab, K.: *The Political Economy of Development in India*, Delhi, Oxford University Press, 1984.

Ray, S.K.: *Indian Economy*, New Delhi, Prentice-Hall, 1987.

Rothermund, Dietmar: *An Economic History of India from Pre-colonial Times to 1986*, London, Croom Helm, 1988.

Sinha, R.K.: *Economic Development since Independence*, New Delhi, Deep and Deep, 1988.

Subbarayappa, B.V.: *Science in India: A Changing Profile*, New Delhi, Indian National Science Academy, 1984.

Suraj, B.: *Black Income in India*, New Delhi, Sage, 1992.

Terence, J.: *The State and Development Planning in India*, Delhi, Oxford University Press, 1994.

INDEX

◆◆◆